HOUSE NO. 5

PARADISE ON PAROS

a memoir

© 2018 Sandra St. John

Published by Spica Press, LLC

Spica

Printed in the United States of America

All rights reserved. No part of this publication may be used or reproduced in any manner whatsoever without written permission of the publisher. The only exception is brief quotations in printed reviews.

Cover design by Damonza Design

Photographs by Sandra St. John & Bob St. John

BOB ST. JOHN

HOUSE NO. 5

PARADISE ON PAROS

a memoir

Guided by The Fates, an artist and a writer find an island of inspiration on the other side of the world.

Author of *Landry: The Legend and The Legacy; South Padre: The Island and Its People; On Down The Road: The World of The Rodeo Cowboy* & many other respected volumes.

These lessons and others learned on Paros, a small, beautiful island in the Cyclades:

DON'T DRIVE ON THE WALKWAYS.
NEVER PUT THE SWEATER NEXT TO THE CHICKEN.
AT AN ART CENTER, LEARN ABOUT YOURSELF.
&
ALWAYS ENJOY THE LOVE YOU FIND!

Dedication

This book, lovingly written about heroes and paradise, is dedicated to my inspiration: Sandy, my guiding light, my dance partner and wife – she leads me to laughter and joy.

Because of her, the heroic nature of the people of Paros – born there or moved there – finds a spotlight that illuminates the wonderful nature of friendship and the joy of learning about people and places.

Together, Sandy and I demonstrate that Greece's famed Fates have a global reach. We found our paradise; we hope you are finding yours.

Appreciation

Thanks to the many people who live on Paros, especially our dear friends. Because of the friendship of the great Kostas Akalestos and his family, the many people who answered questions patiently and, especially the tranquility of an entire Greek island, we found paradise in House No. 5.

Additionally, this book would not have been possible without Larry Powell, without whose editorial skills it might still be languishing in Word docs.

Keep the music going; we always want one more dance.

And, thank you, dear readers, for sharing our adventure of a lifetime.

Sincerely,

Bob St. John
A Texan With Paros In His Heart

Contents

DEDICATION ix
APPRECIATION xi
BOOK ONE - THE PLACE & THE PEOPLE 1
PRELUDE - THE BEAUTIFUL ISLAND. 3
CHAPTER 1 - TRAVELING WITH THE FATES. 7
CHAPTER 2 - THE GOAL IS PLACE, NOT PLACES 13
CHAPTER 3 - DO THE FATES WORK IN REAL ESTATE? 25
CHAPTER 4 - KOSTAS & THE MAGIC OF HOUSE NO. 5 41
CHAPTER 5 - A NEW WORLD & THE LAUNDRY. 53
CHAPTER 6 - A MAN WHO KNOWS HIS WORLD 61
CHAPTER 7 - NO JET LAG: THE VATICAN, PRELUDE TO EASTER, A SOARING ZAPATO & SURGERY, ALL ON THE WAY TO PAROS 73
CHAPTER 8 - OUR SPECIAL EASTER 87
CHAPTER 9 - BEFORE THE STORM 99
CHAPTER 10 - THE PAROS FERRY: HEROES AND HELL 111
BOOK II - AMONG THE MONUMENTS: AMERICAN HISTORY ON PAROS
. . . . 137
CHAPTER 11 - THE FATES' LONE STAR INFLUENCE 139
CHAPTER 12 - A POET, ART & ISLAND IMAGES. 151
CHAPTER 13 - A MYSTERIOUS FIGURE, AN ANCIENT QUARRY & THE FATES AGAIN. 161
CHAPTER 14 - THE AEGEAN CENTER'S ENDURING LEGACY 173
CHAPTER 15 - 'OXI!' — THE WORD OF LEGEND 189
CHAPTER 16 - A NEW AND BETTER REALITY: BUILDING MODERN PAROS. 197
CHAPTER 17 - TRYING TO REACH PAROS AFTER 9/11 203
CHAPTER 18 - AFTER 9/11 ON PAROS. 219
BOOK III - WHAT THE FATES GAVE US 225
CHAPTER 19 - ONE MAGIC MOMENT IN A BOOK STORE 227
CHAPTER 20 - VISITING THE NEIGHBORS 235
CHAPTER 21 - FOREVER YOUNG: THE ONE AND ONLY
 GRANETTA. 247
CHAPTER 22 - SNAPSHOTS IN THE PARK 263

CHAPTER 23 - THEO, THE APOLLON GARDEN AND THE WORLD
.... 271
CHAPTER 24 - SANDY, THE FRENCHMAN & THE FRESCOES 285
CHAPTER 25 - FRANK AND GAIL, THE SUNSETS AND CHANGES 295
CHAPTER 26 - MR. PATELIS' *KAPELOS,* BINKOS & BASKETBALL .. 305
CHAPTER 27 - ANIMAL HOUSE & THE PLUM SWEATER 315
CHAPTER 28 - PAROS – A PLACE FOR HEARTS 333
A FINAL NOTE ABOUT THIS BOOK......................... 341

BOOK ONE
THE PLACE & THE PEOPLE

Prelude
THE BEAUTIFUL ISLAND

Once again, I was sitting peacefully on the stone porch of the pristine white concrete and marble house with deep blue shutters and doors, the traditional motif of this wonderful island, Paros.

In the reality of a crushingly-paced, 24-hour, offline and online modern world, it would seem impossible to actually discover that special, calm place where dreams of unpressured tranquility become enjoyable reality.

But we had. Yes, we'd found it – on the other side of the world from our busy lives.

House No. 5 is our "dream home," exquisitely situated on a rocky point on the slightly southwestern side of the island. This perfect place overlooks an inlet of the deep blue Aegean Sea that surrounds Paros in the archipelago of the Cyclades, the central Greek islands. It is a place for reflection, adventure and appreciation of life and each other.

Near dusk, the *vorias*, the prevailing northern wind, was high and powering the waves that rushed to land maybe a hundred yards below my vantage point. The sea arrived with force and in swooshing and rhythmic sounds that filled the air as it crashed against the rocks, transforming the energy into fascinating sprays of white foam.

On this late, late afternoon, under a clear October sky, my artist wife, the beautiful Sandy, joined me to watch the arrival of a magnificent sunset that seemed both surreal and, yet, orchestrated just for us. The sun's descent turned Paros's mountains dark gray in the fading light. West of our upland vantage point, across the sea, on distant Sifnos, the disappearing sun lit the crests of that island's terrain in a farewell crimson if only for a few minutes.

The moon, appearing nearly translucent in the light of space, had begun to take shape before dusk and was framed by the archway entrance of our island home while suspended over the steps of the bamboo-roofed, stone veranda. It would intensify and glow as it moved across the darkening sky to brighten the night and cast nocturnal shadows about us.

From our elevated veranda, across a mile of sea, we watched the nightly routine of the neighboring island Antiparos as it became silently illuminated with tiny points of light appearing as sparkling diamonds. Closer to us, just south of House No. 5, we could see a small, old ferry eerily creeping away from the dock at Pounta on its 15-minute commute to Antiparos.

Above us? A beautiful display of the heavens. I cannot recall such a multitude of stars glowing as brightly as they do on the clear nights so prevalent on Paros.

What wonderful "optics," to use 21st century phrasing. And we were privileged to see this magnificence from our beloved House No. 5.

It is a fantasy, a dream of so many, to come to a Greek island and find a place of quiet joy on the rich blue Aegean. And our willing partners in these fantasies, the Cyclades, do appear to be out of a fairy tale.

Fittingly, Greece is a land of myths, mystery, magic and fantasy. Sometimes, on the island of Paros, from the combination of all that and the dreaming, there comes a marvelous reality.

I had found a wonderful kind of calm and serenity on our initial trip to Paros in 1992 and the island has been our refuge from stress and pressure ever since.

The first time there, I did not know exactly what I was looking for other than another vacation from work and an escape from the fast pace in a life where happily-taken photographs end up stored in misplaced albums that silently await the touch of a once-familiar hand.

Paros and our dream house and experiences are never misplaced. They are forever pleasantly, wondrously, enjoyably lingering. House No. 5, a home that echoes with our laughter, is there and, also, importantly, are the people of Paros – heroes living among history, philosophers and artists, and, so wonderfully, our friends.

CHAPTER 1

TRAVELING WITH THE FATES

The first time Sandy and I saw Paros was near dusk on an April day in 1992. We stood happily, excitedly next to each other on the second deck of a creaky, weathered ferry. Two "kids" on an adventure with a sensation of "This is gonna be great!"

This craft, a veteran of countless voyages, had carried us on a five-hour trip from the busy, ancient port of Piraeus on the southern side of Greece, just southwest of the modern, busy sprawl of Athens to this (hopefully) special destination.

The contrast between the mainland and the serenely elegant island was immediately evident.

We'd arrived by traveling southeast on a tranquil sea from Piraeus toward an open horizon and the magical Greek islands of the Cyclades. The ferry had made stops at a couple of other islands, their glistening white houses and buildings and windmills and chapels scattered on rocky hills and mountainsides of green and brown. These islands were surrounded by an Aegean Sea that seemed too blue to be real. The bright afternoon sun made the islands even more visible to landlocked North Texan eyes.

At dusk, though, as we approached Paros Harbor, the ferry encountered two huge rock formations. The route between them gave them their name, the Portes, i.e., the Doors. They are statuesque and impressive and serve as a marker on the final approach by sea to Paros.

The Portes had always been thought of as a beneficial welcoming formation until, eight years after we first saw them, there would be a terrible tragedy on a stormy night that would forever change locals' and travelers' perception of the Portes.

***

AUTHOR'S NOTE: *Many heroes emerged from that night, including a man you will meet who is our dear friend and who has played a key role in helping us explore the joy of life on Paros.*

***

On this first journey, as our ferry neared Paros's capital Paroikia, the town looked like something out of a dream. There is no better way to describe it from the eyes of a Texan accustomed to pre-fab homes, dusty prairie and East Texas forest.

Paroikia's white chapels and houses, vivid in the sun, were beginning to dim from their daytime glowing whites in the approaching evening. The town's lights, looking as if they were lanterns set aflame along the shore, sent streaks of yellow dancing atop the suddenly dark water.

In spite of our catnapping, Sandy and I were terribly tired of traveling. We'd combined our long flight from Dallas to London to Athens – 14 or 15 or more hours in a plane, but who was counting? – with the five-hour ferry ride to Paros. That fatigue quickly subsided in the adrenaline rush of actually seeing Paros.

The island was a destination that had found us as much as we had found it. Finding Paros? Paros finding us? There had been such an incredible influence of fate and happenstance – experiences that can't be explained other than there's just more "out there" than we know. Paros had not even been on the charts of our vacation plans but once we chose it as our destination and arrived, it was like being given key roles in a theatre-in-the-real. We were, somehow, following a script and hadn't needed a rehearsal.

Before we returned home from that initial visit, and in spite of bungling around like newcomers, it was as if we were in place – in the *right* place. There were feelings of belonging, which certainly transcended time and culture and language barriers. I am of Scotch-Irish ancestry and I am dramatically language-challenged when it comes to Greek. I can find no connection to Greece in my family background, but after we settled in on Paros, I kept having these mysterious feelings that I'd been there before. Maybe they were just wishes coming true.

MAKING PLANS: BULLS OR WHAT?

Our original plans were to take periodic trips to various countries such as Italy, France and Spain. Sandy, in her career as a ventriloquist/singer entertaining on cruise ships, had seen those places and many more in her travels around the world.

She also told me that she had learned one key lesson: You cannot really get to know a place or its people in a single morning or afternoon or while enduring an all-day excursion punctuated by a rush back to the ship to depart for another port.

As Sandy says, "You get a lot of pictures of a lot of places you really don't know anything about."

We both wanted to go somewhere and stay. We wanted to know the place and its people. I'm a writer, she's an artist – time is our benefactor, our partner in understanding. I was leaning toward Spain or Italy or France, no doubt influenced by my lifelong preoccupation with Ernest Hemingway and his writing.

Maybe, I suggested, we could go to Pamplona and I could run with the bulls!

"It wouldn't surprise me if you did," Sandy replied. She's witnessed many of my crazy adventures that occurred even though I was supposedly at a mature age.

Italy and France also sounded interesting. I had taken French in college, making only a "C" in the initial course. That was a ridiculous grade so I took the same course again to improve my grade point average. I made a "C" again, exposing something about my linguistic shortcomings that I would rather not have known.

Ah, but Greece. *There* was a culture. *There* was a nation. *There* was ancient history with modern people. And surely there'd be someone to help me with the language.

Being intrigued by scenes of the Greek islands in the 1982 John Cassavetes film *The Tempest* led to watching Greek-themed movies such as *Summer Lovers* and *Shirley Valentine* and then, once again, viewing the 1965 Anthony Quinn classic, *Zorba the Greek*.

So somewhere within us there was an awakening of the fantasy shared by so many: visiting a romantic Greek island. Sandy had been to Athens but not the Cyclades, though other shipboard entertainers had told her about them in glowing terms.

I have had a number of Greek friends such as Tito Nicholas, who left a journalism career to start a labeling business, and Louie Canelakes, popular Dallas barkeeper and his *yaya* (grandmother) and Chris Semos, a respected and adored Dallas politician and civic leader. Visit Greece, they always advised.

And I don't know if this was coincidence or if it was a suggestion by the famous Greek Fates. I'd known Tula Johnapelus, a retired secretary for the world-famous Dallas Cowboys for years. Her family, I'd only recently discovered, came from a small village in the Sparta region of southern Greece.

The name of the village is St. John. Prophesy or The Fates at work? The signs were there. So, led by The Fates, we were on our journey.

CHAPTER 2

THE GOAL IS PLACE, NOT PLACES

How we found Paros was a combination of research and desire. Sandy, who once bought a key used book we'll get to later, was interested in ancient Greek history. I was more interested in finding a special place to relax. So, we began planning a trip to a yet-to-be determined Greek island where, without a doubt, we would discover a villa overlooking the sea.

A villa overlooking the sea? A person can dream, right?

Of course, we'd want to spend time in Athens on the way back home. We wanted to see the Acropolis, the Parthenon and museums and the ruins of the Temple of Apollo in Delphi. We wanted to cram all we could into my two-week vacation because we'd probably never come back and because we also wanted to go to France, Spain and Italy and – you get the drift: Move quickly, pause, move quickly. Optimistic at the time, but, in retrospect, foolish.

Our research uncovered what seemed to be endless groups of Greek islands, but as we looked at a map we were drawn to the Cyclades, consistently described in travel books as "the quintessential Greek Islands." In the digital age, which hadn't quite arrived when we began looking for "The Island," the description of "quintessential" had survived because the island's charm had survived.

There are more than 200 islands in the Southern Aegean. They are mostly uninhabited and believed to be mountainous remains of a mass of land that once connected Greece with Asia Minor. Unless you buy into the Greek myths. Then you get a different interpretation.

The name "Cyclades" is derived from the Greek word for circle, *kyklos*, and the islands indeed form an elongated circle around Delos, the mythical birthplace of the twin Greek gods, Artemis and her brother Apollo, children of Greek gods Zeus and Leto.

Myths exist side by side with history in Greece. One myth has it that the islands got their name after Poseidon exiled nymphs to the area and turned them into small rocky islands. These nymphs were called "Cyclades."

When you encounter the historic facts of the Cyclades and Mother Greece, that is when you begin to feel for certain that the "New World" you come from is exactly that: a *new* world. Archaeological discoveries reveal the Cycladic culture was thriving at least as early as 4500 B.C., long before "Columbus sailed the ocean blue" in 1492 A.D.

As we looked through travel guides to learn about the islands, we discovered that the Cyclades were coveted by artists because of the clean, clear light.

It was as if we were being guided by a fantastic Ouija board when we pointed to an island neither of us had ever heard of: Paros.

We skimmed travel guidebooks and found that Paros is an island of 920 square kilometers (or 120 square miles in "Texan") with a population at that time of some 8,000 people and famous for its fabulously white and translucent Parian marble, which was used in works such as the Venus de Milo and the Temple of Apollo. Paros's major city of Paroikia, with a population of around 3,000 people, was built on the site of an ancient city and has one of the earliest

Byzantine churches, *Panagia Ekatontapyliani*, known as "The Church of 100 Doors."

There are many other interesting and intriguing attractions on Paros. But guidebooks cannot capture the sensation of actually being in a place and embracing its people.

As we planned our first trip, a key consideration for us was that Paros wasn't an excessively popular tourist island, such as other Cyclades sites, i.e., Santorini and Mykonos. We didn't want to be among thundering hordes of tourists trampling a small island. Paros, after all, is small with a 118-kilometer (about 73 miles) shoreline, meaning you could see the Aegean from almost anywhere on Paros.

Also, Paros was the hub of the ferry network, making it easy for us to take day or overnight trips to see other islands.

But what we really wanted was something magic: that private villa by the sea.

CHASE SCENES IN A MOVIE

As we plotted and planned, watched the calendar and, finally, set out, it seemed as if we would never get to Paros to find that special villa – the island is small but the journey from Dallas, Texas, was absolutely BIG.

We had been traveling for almost two days, most of it in planes from Dallas to London to Athens, but then there was that three-hour layover at Gatwick and an adventurous taxi ride from the Athens airport to the port city Piraeus where we had one all-too-brief overnight reprieve at the Savoy Hotel, a convenient hotel which had been recommended by the widow of football great Bobby Lane.

Our first important discovery? Welcome to the world of Greek taxi drivers.

Some of the drivers we've had over the years in Athens have been friendly, informative and more cautious than others. These "others," however, are a wild bunch whose skills reminded me of my taxi rides in Mexico City. Ah, but those Greek cabbies: You felt as if you were an actor filming a chase scene in a spy movie set in Athens!

Our driver that first year took us on a race, dodging in and out of traffic from the airport through Athens to Piraeus, barely missing people on motorbikes, women riding bicycles, pedestrians on sidewalks and anyone who mistakenly ventured a step or two into the streets.

That's in addition to close calls with other drivers in cars of all sizes and buses and fellow cabbies honking and yelling and making the same maneuvers and… What a brush-with-death sensation!

But he was polite and nice, welcoming us and pointing out places of interest along the way that were rendered in and out of focus due to speed and sudden maneuvers.

Finally – or maybe not a moment too soon – we were at the Savoy Hotel in Piraeus, a few blocks up a steep street from the harbor where ferries continually arrive and leave at all hours. We snacked in the hotel's dining area and then crashed for the night in our room and got up early the next morning for the final leg of our first trip.

THE GREEKS HAVE A WORD FOR IT, BUT I'M NEVER SURE WHAT IT IS

Another less terrifying taxi took us to the port, although it would have been easily within walking distance from the Savoy had it not been for our luggage. We also hoped we'd be taken directly to the Paros-bound ferry. Hope – we live with hope on the road.

Alas, there was some confusion, so the driver let us out near a ticket booth that wasn't all that close to our ferry. I asked the guy in the booth for tickets to Paros. While I tried my best to use a Greek accent, he thought I said "Poros."

"Paaaaros." I repeated. "*Oxi Pooros* (No Pooros). *Ne* Paaaaros"

(Yes Paros.)." In the hope that my Greek would translate, I smiled and added, "Si… uh, *ne* Paaros." I always had problems with yes and no in Greek. To my resolutely Texas ears "*Ne*" sounds like "nay" but actually means "yes" while "*oxi*" means "no." I'd created an international challenge at the ticket booth.

Sandy and I have this game with a simple scoring system: We award points for positive moves and take them away for negative ones. It would have taken me the rest of my life to catch up on points had we ended up on Poros, much closer to the mainland in the Saronic Gulf Islands by the Northern Peloponnese, i.e., nowhere near Paros.

Drachma, the Greek currency in use before the *Euro*, was especially a problem for me on that first trip. There were nine bills ranging in worth from 10,000 to 10 *drachmas* and five different coins. Unorganized and getting somewhat rattled, I had bills and coins in four different pockets and tried the patience of not only the ticket seller but people behind me in line, although I did apologize by saying *"Efharisto* (thank you)," while meaning to say "*Signomi* (excuse me)."

I handed over a clutch of money to the clerk and crammed what I hoped was the correct change into one of my pockets and we were off in a hurry to locate the ferry.

I am not alone in being challenged by Greek. Stories abound. Many foreigners especially have problems with the language. Famous traveler Robert Pierce once wrote about the confusion. He focused on the challenge of something as simple as wishing somebody a good day, "*Kalimera.*" *Kali* means good and *mera* means day. Instead he was greeting people with "*Kalimeros.*" *Meros* translates into "toilet."

At least on that first trip I wasn't wishing everybody a "good toilet."

Sometimes, even if you know the phrase, it translates differently in Greek. If you want to say, "He put me under pressure," I'm led to believe that it translates in Greek as *"Muvale ta dhio podhia"* meaning,

"He put both my feet in one shoe." And if you say, "There is nothing I can do," then *"Mirizo ta nichiamu"* would translate "I am sniffing my nails." That is what I heard, anyway.

THE LUGGAGE AND THE LUGGER

At the port we lugged our suitcases through a maze of people and ships and ferries going to various places. Sandy had faced all sorts of challenges during her travels as an entertainer and wasn't swayed by mishaps or confusion.

This veteran of airports and traveling crowds around the world simply charged ahead, pulling her two large suitcases and looking neither right nor left, keeping her eyes on the prize. Meanwhile, I stumbled and struggled behind her with the other suitcases.

***

***AUTHOR/HUSBAND NOTE:** I have learned that it is best to get out of Sandy's way when she takes off like that. By the time we got to Paros, I was well aware of this, but years later I saw a port officer learn the lesson first-hand.*

He was standing there smiling and greeting the passing parade of people coming and going to ferries. "Kalimera!" he said with gusto as Sandy swept past him, innocently rolling her very large and heavy suitcase over his foot. While he hopped around in pain, I accelerated as fast I could and fled the scene.

***

As I struggled to keep up, Sandy actually found the ferry in the confusion of boats and with plenty of time to spare. But we meandered around blissfully while those in the know hurried to take up all the seats on the over-crowded ferry. There was more confusion when we tried to figure out which section we were supposed to be in and we almost ended up camping out on the lower deck, a place packed with happy young people carrying their ever-present backpacks on another leg of their exploration of the planet.

Young travelers often bond and hold hands or hug in planned or impromptu embraces and you wish them well, perhaps recalling the time you were young and wished you had toured foreign countries on a shoestring, sleeping in hostels or camping out on the beaches.

I had previously written about these young travelers in my newspaper columns for *The Dallas Morning News* and knew about the great enthusiasm and adventure of that time of their lives. Some after returning home would find that their distant reality can dim the glow of red-hot relationships established in romantic places, i.e., falling in love with the wrong people for all the right reasons. In their youthful ardor, they do not realize that they will love each other forever until tomorrow. They promised to write or telephone newfound friends and keep in touch, and sometimes they do for a while and then keep meaning to call or write but never do. The loves and friendships may fade, but that grand, inspiring sensation of an adventure when they were young never will vanish.

All of those human emotions were right there on the lower deck and mercifully, after the ferry was underway we finally found seats for our Aegean journey through the Cyclades to Paros.

STEPPING ASHORE AT PAROIKIA

Luggage that can't be carried is stashed in the belly of the ferry with trucks, cars and motorcycles. Passengers are supposed to get off first but it isn't good to tarry too long or a loud horn from a vehicle behind you could cause you to jump six feet high if you were not already anchored to the deck by your luggage.

We quickly stepped ashore at Paroikia. The first thing we noticed was the squat, white traditional Greek windmill between the dock and the actual township.

Our first ancient relic? No. That signature windmill was once an office to aid tourists. The office workers had moved on, but the windmill remained as a landmark, a reliable point of reference for travelers.

Early impressions of Paroikia were exciting, but we only planned to stay there for a short time before renting a car and exploring the island in our search for our dream house by the sea.

The dock and the area around it were crowded with some people waiting for passengers to arrive while others waited to depart. Taxi drivers were hoping to grab tourists and talk them into staying at this or that hotel, possibly because the hotel belonged to this or that relative or friend. We had no reservations at a hotel so the cabby who helped us with our luggage told us about the great attributes of a nearby hotel called the Apollon.

He even showed us a brochure picturing the Apollon, together with a wonderful view of a beach and the ocean.

A HOTEL PICTURE WORTH A FEW CAREFULLY CHOSEN WORDS?

The Apollon, back then, was a nice hotel down an alleyway just off the street that ran along the western shoreline of cafes, tavernas and places to rent cars and motorbikes.

***

AUTHOR'S NOTE: *It has since become the Apollon Boutique Hotel with a reputation for service and congeniality – a charmingly updated place to enjoy a stay.*

***

Back in those early days, the décor of the lobby of the hotel was in what we called Louis XIV style but which was more likely vintage Greek with plenty of statues. The hotel was operated by some very nice and cordial people who hoped we'd stay for more than a night.

As an enticement, they gave us "the best room," a second-floor room with a door leading to a large rooftop balcony.

There was no view of the beach or ocean from the Apollon because a building blocked it. I was a little put out by being misled by the picture on the brochure and the cabby but soon Sandy and I were joking about it. We'd rather laugh than complain.

We slept a couple of hours, then awoke hungry. On the advice of the hotel lady – still hoping we'd extend our stay – we walked down the street to get something to eat.

Most of the tavernas along the street were closed because it was the tourism off-season in Paros. Also, it was after midnight local time – I'm not sure what time it was in our bodies – way past dinnertime was my best estimate. We managed to find a small dining spot – at an outside plastic table with folding chairs. At another table, three or four men were smoking and talking and watching television – this was an ambience we hardly envisioned for our first meal in a romantic, exotic land of history and legendary cuisine.

I had scrambled eggs and pasta soaked in olive oil and Sandy had a Greek salad with lettuce, tomatoes, red onions and cucumbers topped with vinegar and olive oil. The Greek salad would become one of our staples. The food was all right but dining would become much better when we learned where to go and what to order.

We tend to make the best of things and ended up dancing on the rooftop of the Apollon under the stars with music from one of Sandy's cassettes on our all-purpose, travel cassette recorder. The sky was clear with stars and constellations, all bright and sparkling. There was planet Jupiter, the brightest object in the sky, and the glimmering Milky Way stretching East to West across the sky, with Perseus in the West and the Herdsman in the East, and suddenly, as if on cue, a falling star swept across the sky.

Yes, the hotel had indeed given us the best room.

THE FIRST MORNING AND THE TRAFFIC PATTERNS

Our first morning on Paros we walked over to the downtown beach named *Livadia,* northwest of the port and shaded by tamarisks with branches of feathery-like leaves.

It is a beach for people both passing through and staying in Paroikia. Some rested in the shade, a young man was asleep with his head on a backpack, and two couples were at water's edge in bathing suits while a scraggly dog stood nearby, willing to wait forever to be beckoned by somebody with a handy treat.

Once we'd rented a car, we were ready to move on around the island, getting away from Paroikia, which, we reasoned, we could see later.

After all, we were in search of our place by the sea.

ON THE ROAD: THE SIGNS ARE THERE

We drove away from the Apollon and immediately began learning how perplexing driving can be when you know neither the local customs nor the local roads. The language? A mystery.

"It was very confusing that first year," recalls Sandy, always our designated navigator. "It seems that the road signs we saw during our first trips to Paros were only in Greek. Unlike in some other international cities, it's difficult to untangle Greek by simple logic. For instance, in Italian '*Roma*' is Rome, '*Napoli*' is Naples, and '*Milano*' is Milan."

None of that logic was visible on the Greek road signs.

Sandy was also having to deal with the Greek alphabet for the first time, deciphering signs at turns and forks in the road while trying to efficiently discern what they read in English from a moving automobile piloted by a bewildered driver. There was no slowing down because local drivers behind us were always in a hurry and always on our bumper.

"Okay, in upper case an upside down V is an L, a triangle is a D, a P is an R," Sandy explained to someone later. "And just when I thought I was making progress the nightmare of the smaller case letters emerged. It was quite a while before I got it in my head that the o with a loop on top was one form of an S, not to mention we don't even have a loopy-looking omega and pitchfork looking letter in English. (The letter omega [Ω] looks like a horseshoe, while psi [ψ] looks like Neptune's fork!)

"What would happen at first was that Bob had already made a stab at what a sign read before I could figure it out," she said. "Fortunately, he is a *modus operandi naturale* and pretty good at it."

Sometimes I would go the wrong way on a street or road and we'd turn around and try again. Fortunately, Sandy got better at reading the street signs, and we also would become familiar with the island, although there were embarrassing situations in which the uncertain driver would guide the rental car down impossibly narrow roads that turned out to be donkey trails which would send roosters and dogs into fits and cause donkeys and sheep to turn their heads toward us with both alarm and curiosity.

But there we were that first day, on our way to the perfect place – of course, we did not yet know that, but, like the information on the roads, the signs were there. You just had to know how to read them.

CHAPTER 3
DO THE FATES WORK IN REAL ESTATE?

We decided to leave the Apollon behind and drive out of Paroikia to take in the beauty of the island of Paros. The initial drive through the mountains can be a bit nerve-wracking until you have become accustomed to it and, really, that sensation may linger a while.

When we first set out we inadvertently took the wrong road, ending up climbing terrain upward on what became more of a donkey trail than a road as it narrowed to a single lane. We feared we might unexpectedly meet a car, or worse, a truck coming around a blind curve.

Somehow before encountering calamity, we managed to get turned around and found our way to the road we wanted, the one that matched our map. How true it is when they say the map is not the territory!

And even on the main road, all is not peaceful, as oncoming traffic passes with reckless abandon or perhaps wanders into your lane and your heart skips a beat or two. So although ascending the mountains provides a beautiful view for the passenger, it is best that the driver keeps both eyes on the road.

We headed southeast over the narrow, twisting, two-lane road of winding turns through the central mountains and hills with their green patches of shrubbery, rock and stone walls and occasional *katikias* (farm houses), mostly deserted but resolutely clinging to the steep inclines. Some peaks were crowned with windmills and small white chapels like beacons overseeing majestic valleys below and the occasional villages of astoundingly white structures.

Finally, we made our way to Lefkes, a beautiful village high in the center of the island at the foot of Profitis Elias, the highest peak at 770 meters, i.e., around 2,525 feet.

We would later visit many times and always be reminded of that first time we were there.

During that first visit, Sandy suggested that we park the car and take a walking tour. She also suggested we take a right – but we ended up nowhere.

"This time let me show you how it's done," I said, taking a left turn.

So I turned down a steep hill into the center of the village feeling young at heart and… *suddenly became very confused.* I had driven us deep into a busy place on a narrow cobblestone passageway in the labyrinth of endless white residences with blue doors and shutters and people and animals. We looked around, desperately studying the next move but there seemed to be no way out – not enough room to even turn around and escape! People and animals stopped walking or whatever they were doing to stare at us. Some talked and pointed. A small child peeked out from behind her mother's leg. An elderly woman in black painfully hurried upstairs, went into her home and quickly shut the door.

"I think we're not supposed to be driving here," said Sandy.

"Well, it was your idea to take a right." I lied.

"Ha!" she answered.

We learned that even small foreign rental cars weren't supposed to be driven on narrow walkways with apartments, houses, hotels and whatever. I couldn't go forward or back out, so in order to turn around and escape, I had to move the car a foot or so at a time, backward and forward, forward and backward, on and on while Sandy tried to make herself as small as possible. This ridiculous process seemed to take days, albeit about 20 minutes in reality.

"Maybe we shouldn't come back here for a while," I said.

"Maybe we never should come back," Sandy replied.

But we did many times – and nobody seemed to protest. It was just another of the daily lessons we learned on the first trip to Greece: DON'T DRIVE on walkways in the heart of towns and villages.

I never saw a road sign and if I did, I didn't understand it, anyway.

A PLACE OF MYTH

After we left Lefkes we continued on our quest to explore the island. The road leveled out near the sea on the outskirts of the village of Marpissa. Like so many other villages on Paros, Marpissa derives its name from myth. It is said that Marpissa was named after the daughter of the River God Evynos (sometimes Evenus). Homer wrote that Apollo and Idas fought over the beautiful woman. When Zeus intervened, she had to make up her mind which one she favored and chose Idas. She feared the God Apollo would only love her as long as her youthful beauty lasted and Idas would be in for the long haul.

We were tired from driving around the island when Sandy noticed that rooms were for let at The Afentakis Hotel/Apartments on the road passing Marpissa so I turned around and we stopped there. It was a two-and-a-half story, white-stone building with large, lovely trees offering outdoor shade. Wonderful red bougainvillea accented the outside walls. We would stay there a couple of days and move on, we decided.

In early mornings while having coffee on the balcony of our Afentakis apartment, we watched the poignant, timeless ritual of men with their donkeys bringing vegetables to sell in the village. Just about everywhere we went, it turned out, in places large and small, men on donkeys would be there. I would later lament that as Paros grew and became more of a tourist destination, this sweet, simple, uncomplicated way of life in a divinely comfortable present would become yesterday, merely a passing thought or a faint memory in the rush to tomorrow.

THE SUGAR & SPICE

Across the street from The Afentakis was a place called The Sugar & Spice, which was a little misleading because it did not specialize in sweets but served such items as pizza and spaghetti. We made friends with Christina Sifakis, who ran the place.

One thing I learned early in Greece, as I had found to be true in other foreign countries, was this: If you don't know the language but do the best you can and be mannerly and respectful and learn some polite greetings, Greeks will appreciate it. They'll even speak more of the language and try to be helpful with your usage, correcting pronunciation and teaching new words and expressions. Besides, most people we met on Paros spoke some English, a language studied in the school system. Their English was better than our Greek.

I apologized for not speaking the language when I met Christina. "*Signomi...* excuse me... I do not speak Greek," I said and she smiled. I would use some words I knew and Sandy, who already was picking up additional bits of the language, would suggest phrases to me. Christina also understood some English so we were able to communicate with few words and a lot of body language.

Her husband spoke English but it was still difficult to communicate with him. One evening a man and woman came in and were obviously his friends. He sat down and the two guys started yelling and talking and pointing at each other. At first, I thought they were having a heated argument but I would later learn that Greek men gesture a lot with body language full of sound and fury but might be only saying, "It's wonderful to see you again."

VIEW FROM THE TOP

Marpissa is a beautiful village spread out at the foot of historic Kefalos Hill, which towers over the entire area. But that first year it was just a stopover for us, although we would learn to appreciate it much more in later trips to Paros.

The cone-shaped Kefalos Hill was inviting so it seemed that the thing to do was to climb up there before moving on. "Why?" Sandy asked and as I stared upward at the peak, I repeated the climber's code: "Because it's there!" I think she laughed.

Besides, I figured, we had been driving all over the place and needed the exercise. We were both wearing light jackets which weren't much protection from the strong, cold wind that felt like it was going to blow us over. I was determined to go on, whereas Sandy was a bit reluctant but she is, shall we say, competitive and a good sport, not necessarily in that order.

The upward path led through scuffy vegetation and bushes past the ruins of Kefalos Castle, built in the 15th century but little more than a stack of rocks and stones somewhat belying its place in history. Then we made it to the peak of the hill where the 16th century Monastery of St. Anthony, the *Agios Antonios,* remains in all its glory.

The view was wonderful with the white villages below and you could also see the entire east coast. You were, of course, standing where history had been played out for eons. You could almost see it coming alive from where we were standing.

WHAT REALLY HAPPENED: BARBAROSSA

A rage of distant history was in our heads as we stood and looked out across so peaceful an area that had once been a horrifying field of battle. Before we'd made the first big plane trip to the Cyclades, Sandy and I had continued to buy books at newsstands to read about Paros and other Greek islands because we wanted to learn more about the people and places and events – when we'd see it for ourselves, we'd know what we were seeing.

Some of the things that shaped the island occurred long before castles had crumbled and ferries brought visitors from Texas looking for tranquility. You can catch up on this island history by reading the different versions of "what really happened."

One thing all versions agree on is that the greatly feared Barbarossa, high commander of the Ottoman fleet, led Turkey's successful quest to conquer and claim the Aegean islands. It took him just three years. In 1537 ships brought his forces to Paros and the slaughter began.

When Barbarossa's murdering horde swept with devastation across Paros, the only surviving Parians and 300 Venetian soldiers, who had formerly controlled the island, fled to Kefalos Castle. Knowing the Turks were on a rampage, they fortified the castle but it would be the last bastion against Barbarossa's army of 1,500 determined soldiers.

After four days of siege and two unsuccessful attacks, one version had the Turks resorting to trickery. An Ottoman soldier was said to have dressed up as a pregnant Greek woman and pounded on the castle door, begging to get inside before being killed by the Turks. When the door opened the Turks stormed inside, massacring everybody in sight. Well, almost everybody.

Bernardo Sagredo, the last survivor, was supposed to have also dressed as a peasant woman to slip away and eventually flee to Venice where he was reunited with his family. Another version was that he escaped with his children but his wife Cecilia Venieri was killed or took her own life by leaping off the hill, rather than facing what the Turks might do to her.

Cecilia is well known on Paros and is called '*Oria,*' or "beauty." She also was involved in a more in-depth rendition of this event. After taking over the castle, the Turks were supposed to have gathered all the surviving women and forced them to dance so they could pick the ones to their liking. Cecilia was given to the Sultan as a present for his harem. Then he later married her.

Some 6,000 citizens of Paros were killed and others enslaved. The Ottoman conquerors thus ended the Venetian period on Paros, leading to four centuries of Turkish rule.

Keep in mind, all this mayhem and murder and terrible behavior occurred hundreds of years before Sandy and I landed on very peaceful Paros not trying to conquer anyone, but simply trying to understand the language and road signs while searching for that perfect house by the sea.

LEAVING MARPISSA

When we were leaving Marpissa, I visited The Sugar & Spice to tell Christina what a nice person she was and that I simply must have her picture. She shook her head again and, one more time, said, "*Parakalo...* please... *Oxi...* no?" I clasped my hands in front of my chin as if in prayer, bowed and said we were leaving and that not having her picture would be very disappointing. She smiled ever so shyly, pushed her hair back and stood still. I took several pictures and thanked her very much. Going out the door I looked back and she was smiling and waving.

THE ROADSHOW AT THE PLACE OF FLOWERS

After our brief stay at The Afentakis, we were driving through Dryos (or Drios as it's also spelled) on the southeastern tip of Paros. Suddenly, Sandy spotted a two-story house behind an iron gate on property that was beautifully blanketed with flowers.

The astounding scene aroused the sleeping gardener within Sandy so she wanted to turn around and check it out. We did – this time the road was wide enough to turn around without making a traffic-stopping production of it.

An apartment was available in the house that belonged to Mr. and Mrs. Caloudas, a sweet, friendly, elderly couple. We rented a nice upstairs apartment with a bedroom, kitchen and two balconies from their son George who had moved back home because his parents were aging and needed his help.

The sea and beach weren't far away and the house could serve as another base while we searched for our "Villa of Destiny."

And it wasn't a long walk from the house to the small business area with a grocery store where we could get supplies if we wanted to eat in the apartment. Plus, there was a bus stop, some shops and Anezinas, a nice restaurant we enjoyed.

Behind the shopping area was a little residential neighborhood with a path that led to a hotel with a fine patio and what appeared to be apartments atop a cliff. This vantage point overlooked the narrow beach beside the natural harbor.

The shutters were closed on the windows of the hotel and apartments for off-season and nobody was around. I walked down rock steps, somewhat steep, from the top of the cliff to the harbor and was taken by the history.

The interesting rock formations that form a natural inlet at Dryos were, in ancient times, the harbor of Paros that was frequented by, among other conquerors, the Turkish fleet preparing for rampages through the Aegean.

As I walked back in a kind of historical reverie through the residential area where people keep goats, chickens, roosters and dogs, one of the hounds suddenly started leaping onto the fence and barking excitedly and I jumped a foot back into reality.

I had forgotten that I had reminded myself over and over to expect peaceful, nice dogs but also loud, vicious-looking dogs of all sizes, shapes and temperaments. Dogs are important companions and workers on the island – we would learn this firsthand.

WORKING WITH GEORGE, DINING WITH CATS

It turned out that the Caloudas's son George had a theater group that performed on other islands. Sometimes he'd be gone for several days at a time but we were fortunate that he was home during our stay. He joined us a few times at Anezinas and asked us to please speak English because he needed to practice the language. He was unaware that our Greek was so limited that it would be impossible to speak any other way. He would ask questions about Texas – his main exposure to the state, as it is for many others in Greece, being re-runs of the television show *Dallas* and, of course, cowboy movies.

We assured George that all Texans weren't rich and/or power hungry, present company included.

He was cultured enough to know that there were no longer cattle drives across the country and that the so-called Wild West was long-ago history. Oddly enough, there were people who thought Texans were cowboys with six-shooters but it wouldn't surprise me if some American tourists looked for chariots in Greece.

At Anezinas you could dine inside or outside in a garden that was shaded by lemon trees.

The stuffed vine leaves, Greek salads and a number of other dishes were very good, but I withheld my opinion about a couple of drop-by visitors. The proprietor's two cats, free to roam inside and out, usually joined us at our table.

I liked cats okay and might have had a closer attachment if I weren't somewhat allergic to them. Sandy loves cats and would feed them bites from her plate and only smiled when I suggested that she just pull up a couple of chairs and order the house special for them.

They were table-hoppers – pretty sure that's not really a breed – but, like most humans on the planet, they seemed to prefer Sandy's company. So, they would often camp out at our table because of their friend Sandy and they would stare at me as if I were some inferior species.

Everywhere we go Sandy befriends cats and dogs. I'm along for the ride.

***

AUTHOR'S NOTE: *My Cat Lady of the Island does get carried away at times. Once on a different island, i.e., Manhattan Island, we were walking down the street in New York and met a woman with a tiny animal on a leash. Sandy bent over and said, "Here kitty-kitty-kitty." Then she petted the little guy. "Nice kitty," she said. When the woman and animal walked on down the sidewalk I mentioned to Sandy that it wasn't a cat but a dog. She smiled, slapped me jovially on the arm and we moved on, never looking back. Little did I realize then that a few years later we would have an Animal House on Paros with Sandy adopting stray dogs and cats – or did they adopt her?*

***

We loved the Caloudas's house, our apartment and the people. The flowers were beautiful and obviously the old gentleman's pride and joy. You could usually find him amid the flowers in the large field by the house. He was a retired shoemaker and a pleasant, sweet guy and certainly welcomed everyone to join him among the flowers or even help him with them.

Sandy was thrilled to get a closer look. The experience changed her life forever. She had loved flowers but, until then, had no thoughts of growing them to any great extent. After we returned to Texas, she began to plant all kinds of flowers and has done so ever since. Cut flowers are always in vases in the house and outside are garden beds and a field of flowers, her living ode to the old gentleman in the Cyclades.

NOT AS QUIET AS THE FLOWERS...

One night, however, we feared we'd blown our relationship with the Caloudas family. We bought wine and cheese and bread and yogurt at the little store by the restaurant and had dinner in our apartment. We partied too much and started singing every song we ever knew. Sandy did sing her favorite, *Somewhere Over the Rainbow*, several times and I stumbled through my Jimmy Webb medley (*Up, Up and Away, MacArthur Park, Wichita Lineman*, etc.). The later it got, the louder we got.

In retrospect, I was glad we didn't do our version of classical Italian opera, where we make up the language as we go and take 10 minutes to die when stabbed. "*Glelitteriomio!*" "*Ha-a-a-iii, blisterrocia!*"

We, the suddenly crazy Americans, were very worried the next morning about disturbing the family. We kind of tiptoed out and suddenly the woman saw us, said something in Greek and came over and hugged us and the old gentleman smiled and shook our hands.

"We love to hear happy people singing," George later explained. "This made my parents feel happy."

When we left, there were hugs and exchanges of kisses on both cheeks all around and we hated to leave such a pleasant place with nice people, good conversation and beautiful flowers. Inside we knew that if we didn't find that place overlooking the sea we would come back and stay longer at the Caloudas's house.

On later trips to Paros, we'd sometimes drive to the house of the flowers and knock on the door but nobody answered. We were once told at a nearby restaurant that George still resided there but was out of town most of the time. I never asked anybody if his parents were still alive because I wanted to remember them as they had been on that first visit, happily enjoying the show put on by the zany American performers.

LEAVING AND LAUGHING

The day we left Dryos, Sandy drove. Self-defense, maybe. As we were going back through Marpissa I decided to take some shots with the video camera.

I rolled down the window, stuck my head out and began shooting scenes.

"Slow down, please," I said. "And veer a little to the right on the road so I can get a better shot." She did. Suddenly, as I peered through the viewfinder, some kind of roadside foliage began slapping me and the camera. Startled but unhurt, I joined Sandy in some roadside laughter about the foliage attack. Maybe don't veer so far, I laughed.

I've always felt sorry for people who can't laugh at themselves, i.e., those who take themselves too seriously even when they blunder. We have no problem like that because we're always laughing at each other and ourselves. We are, after all, given ample opportunity.

THE VILLA SEARCH, LIKE THE ROAD, NARROWS

That day we took the southern mountain road, then turned north toward Paroikia. We saw some places that looked promising, though not exactly what we wanted and besides, everything seemed to be closed for the off-season. Sometimes prospective places were nestled in the hills and at other times near the ocean. I drove while Sandy carefully scouted possible houses that might become "the" villa.

"This is exciting… Look! Turn around and go back. I think this might be what we're looking for," she'd say.

I'd turn around, drive back, park and Sandy would go fast-forward, her usual pace when she's excited, jumping out of the car and racing to check out another in a series of prospects, only to find them closed until the tourist season.

Then one day Sandy wanted me to drive down a rock and gravel road that seemed to lead to the beach. You could see some white houses off in the distance. "Let's go down there," she said. "You never know. We might find something interesting."

"I don't think so," I responded. "We've already done this so many times. It's off-season. Paros is closed."

"Pleeeze! Let's just look," she urged.

"No, absolutely not," I declared as, of course, I turned the car around to go back onto that road. There was only room for one vehicle, going or coming, and even driving slowly the holes and rocks shook the small, fragile rent-a-car so severely that I feared it might disintegrate.

"I'm not going down this road. It's going to tear up the car."

She laughed. "Only you would worry about a rental car. Let's just go a little farther."

"Absolutely not," I declared, going a little farther, of course. I do love the girl and want her to be happy.

There were some people standing outside a white house on the road. We drove up and stopped. A man came over and Sandy asked about the place he was staying and the other houses in this area. He was a very nice guy from Sweden and took time to tell us about the houses, and graciously shared what he knew. And he told us the houses were for rent.

He seemed to have all the information. What were the odds? He said the person to contact was Kostas Akalestos and he gave us his telephone number. We thanked him and drove on down the road which curled to the right in front of villas located up from the shore, each with a great sea view.

The last one on the road seemed perfect and, as we could tell by peeking through the windows, it seemed so enchanting inside.

Sandy got excited at the possibility of renting the place. I was skeptical it would work out. It was such a long shot after other disappointments.

But, heck, that fellow who *might* have been from Sweden might really have been our guardian angel disguised as a real estate tipster. An agent of The Fates, no doubt.

CHAPTER 4
KOSTAS & THE MAGIC OF HOUSE NO. 5

It was on this initial trip to Paros in 1992 that we met Kostas Akalestos, the fellow we'd first heard of in a conversation with the man who was either a Swedish real estate tipster or a guardian angel masquerading as a Swedish real estate tipster.

Our introduction to Kostas was at the island's traditional "meet me there" landmark, the squatty, white-washed windmill in a high traffic downtown Paroikia area across from the constantly busy ferry dock.

After we'd discovered the seaside houses on the hill and, frankly, gotten excited about the prospect that our dream home was at hand, I'd telephoned from one of the open booths off the city square. I asked the man who answered if my wife Sandy and I could look at the houses, especially the one at the end of the road overlooking the sea – if (I thought about adding!) they were not closed for the off-season like every other piece of property on the island.

"The houses are available," the man said. "Good you are interested. We meet at the windmill in one hour, please."

It seems odd now to think that the three of us - this man and

Sandy and I – had ever been strangers scheduling a rendezvous for the sake of a business deal.

I was drinking coffee with Sandy in a sidewalk cafe when the time came to meet Kostas, so I walked over to the edge of the street where drivers were speeding around as if this landmark were the center of a carousel. Soon a young man on a motorcycle circled the windmill and skidded to a stop in front of me at the curb. He'd probably picked me out as the American caller named Bob. There were clues: I was wearing a baseball cap, faded jeans and the confused look of a tourist.

"Hello, I am Kostas," he said, smiling. "Do you have the car?"

"Yes, the little red rental car right over there," I said as Sandy joined us.

"Good you do," he said. "Now, follow me, please."

Kostas revved the engine of his motorcycle and off he went with us racing along behind him. I was afraid the small red car with two people and huge, medium and small suitcases might be too much if we had to drive up a steep road. We might start rolling backwards before I could down-shift. No problem, the little car was up to the challenge.

Kostas led us back past the windmill along the waterfront and then upward and around the Pandrossos Hotel on a hill at the top of Paroikia, overlooking Paros Bay. Then we followed him on a descending road that connected to the winding two-lane main road that led southwest out of Paroikia. We covered the five-plus kilometers, more than three miles, to the area called *Agia Irini* (Saint Irene) in not much more than 15 minutes. He slowed and hooked a right off the highway onto a narrow road of dirt and rocks, and we followed him past several of his rental houses to No. 5 located farthermost on the road at a dead end. Mercifully, I thought, no cars were going to be driving by "THE villa."

THE STERN NEGOTIATIONS

It was like we'd written this place into existence. House No. 5 was on a short rise with a clear view of the sea below, and the northern and southern hills spreading along the coastline in each direction. We'd been anxious when we first bungled onto the property, but now we were eager to see if we could rent this particular white villa.

I had read in one of the guidebooks that Greeks liked to negotiate prices so I'd cautioned Sandy to be cool, that we must play good cop/bad cop when haggling on the rental for House No. 5. I was confident that the hard-edged negotiation plan was in place.

We went in with Kostas, looked around and, before I could say a one word with even a hint of haggling, Sandy enthusiastically declared, "This is wonderful! We'll take it!"

When Kostas left us our first day in House No. 5 after making sure everything was all right, we became totally absorbed with the villa by the sea and the enchanted surroundings.

And near dusk out on the veranda, Sandy and I hugged and then hugged again as I almost stumbled and Sandy, who can be very excitable, might have jumped into my arms and likely put both of us on "injured reserve." We'd just found House No. 5; we didn't want that!

Sandy said excitedly, "Can you believe this? We're really here!"

"Yes, we are!" I agreed, and added, "Maybe the Greek Gods we read about favored us to find such a perfect place."

And we couldn't stop looking around, exploring here and there and everywhere.

We soon realized Kostas was different and didn't care about haggling over money. And, we had the beginning of a wonderful friendship, too.

AUTHOR'S NOTE: *One reason I think that Kostas and I became such good friends is that we have some similar values. We both admire fairness and honor. For example, one year the* *assistant of Tom Hanks called Kostas.* "My client is Tom Hanks, and he will be visiting Paros," he said. "I would like to rent one of your villas for him." And he gave the dates. Kostas replied, "I am sorry, sir, but the villas are full then." The assistant emphasized, "But Tom Hanks is my client. Don't you know who Tom Hanks is?" With equanimity Kostas replied, "Yes, of course, I know Tom Hanks,… and my villas are still full."

THE HOUSE THAT KOSTAS BUILT

Inside the house that Kostas built were wooden blue doors and floors of marble tile with white ceilings and walls with alcoves for candles, trinkets, pottery, flower vases and, soon, Sandy's artwork. All the rooms had wooden blue shutters over glass pane windows; the two windows in the living room wonderfully overlooked the sea.

The bed in the master bedroom was near a pane glass door just behind a louvered blue door that opened onto the veranda. Sometimes on mild evenings we opened both doors and listened to the night sounds and felt the sea breeze.

A short walkway in front of the house led to stone steps through a tall, statuesque white arch, opening onto the veranda and, on each side, walls of rock rose from the ground to about two-and-a-half feet above porch level. Kostas also painted the front door blue and added a touch of magenta Bougainvillea that grew from the ground in the corner of the veranda to the top of the door and spread along the wall to the bamboo roof that sheltered the veranda.

We became so enthralled by all these touches over the years that when we were remodeling our house in the woods of Northeast Texas, we had a white arch built in the living room to remind us of Paros.

Over the years, Kostas had gradually purchased this prime land at *Agia Irini*. When the property was his, he began building the houses, doing most of the work himself. He constructed eight villas in *Agia Irini*.

Most of these houses, like others on Paros, are basically built from the vast source of white marble stones on the island. The stones are crushed into a kind of sand and then formed into building blocks and heated at very high temperatures for hours. The stone becomes even whiter in the process. A white cream made from the marble is used to give the blocks an even more distinctive quality and is also employed in painting the houses, inside and out.

Kostas's dad, Michalis Akalestos, who we all knew as "Mr. Michalis," had suggested that Kostas build square houses in the Greek cubic style that is widespread on the island. But Kostas decided he wanted two different styles of artistic houses.

"I was giving it (the project) so much money," Kostas said, "No, I did not want to make them square but to be different. For me it was like playing a game, making the curves and arches."

THE 'NO DEADLINES' SENSATION AT HOUSE #5

One of those villas with the "curves and arches" turned out to be House No. 5.

The wonderful veranda was our vantage point when Sandy and I watched the sun setting on Paros for the first time. Kostas had created an outdoor auditorium and now we had front row seats to this majesty, to this magnificence, as the sun descended, creating displays of color dancing across mountains and land and sea. Red, pink, yellow, silver – all glimmered on the water. It was magnificent.

The prevailing northern wind, the *vorias*, also known as the cooling wind *meltemi* in summer, can be very strong at any time of year. When the weather was cold and the wind high and the waves roaring and wooden blue shutters rattling in the windows, it was the perfect atmosphere for bundling up in blankets and reading paperback novels by P. D. James and Anne Perry and John Grisham and John Irving and, of course, the works of my favorite, Hemingway, and F. Scott Fitzgerald and on and on. On our first visit, we'd packed hardback editions, making our suitcases even heavier. After that, two much wiser travelers bought paperbacks and whatever we found at airport and island newsstands.

There were evenings when the weather was fair and a translucent moon would begin to take shape and a multitude of stars would glow so brightly and constellations, such as Hercules, the Lion, Cassiopeia and the Big Dipper and Little Dipper, and so many other celestial images would be vividly discernible across this pure Parian sky.

Neither the lights of big cities nor smog were around to obscure the beauty of the heavens. Sandy, who has traveled the world as an entertainer on cruise ships, said such bright stars over Paros reminded her of the brilliant canopy of lights seen on clear nights from an ocean liner far out at sea.

There was, here at House No. 5, something new in my life: time to enjoy such things as the stars. Sandy continued to inspire my interest in the constellations and movement of the moon and sun as the earth turned and the sunset cast a wide yellow trail over the sea. I'd never taken the time to consider all that back in busy Dallas at the newspaper – there was always a deadline.

In early evening, slightly swaying fishing boats could be seen heading for home port in the channel of the blue Aegean Sea that separates the islands of Paros and Antiparos by only about a mile.

Lights appeared suddenly, glowing like diamonds from houses and spreading along the coastline of the nearby island's port city, also called Antiparos, meaning "the other Paros." From our vantage point, the scene across the channel looked like a miniature city strung with Christmas lights.

Just to the south of us at Pounta, a small and old and creaky ferry became ghost-like in the darkness as it crept away from the dock on another of its 15-minute commutes across the channel between Paros and Antiparos.

We were seeing our new world in our old world setting, thanks to The Amazing Kostas and his determination to create a "different" home for visitors.

SOMETIMES MISHAPS MAKE FOR A GREAT MATCH

I was feeling especially chipper one morning in the vibrant fresh island air. I was even uncharacteristically whistling a tune when I just stepped over a low fence with rocks askew near the house and began to walk toward the northern hills.

Suddenly, something stung me just above the ankle. I figured it was just an ant or some other crawling bug I'd disturbed and didn't think anything more about it.

The following day Sandy noticed two tiny red holes an inch or less apart on my ankle – the pattern looked like a snakebite. Sandy, who tries to be my much-needed keeper, was a little worried but figured I'd have already died if the snake had been poisonous.

"Poor snake," she said grinning, "*IT* probably died."

One evening, Sandy was sitting on the couch next to the fireplace and sketching a nearby vase. She has incredible power of concentration when she's working on her art. She rose and stepped closer to the vase, looked very carefully at it, then backed up to sit down but she missed the couch and fell on the edge of the brick extension of the fireplace, hitting her back smack between the shoulder blades.

She's a trooper and she went on with her art and our vacation and still laughs about missing the couch. I've noticed that, since that episode, she will look back at her target before attempting to sit.

We're both injury prone but she is more creative, although I'm catching up.

If I'm nearly finished reading a book, I'll continue at night in bed. Sandy chuckles and we joke around when I try to explain to her the proper position for reading in bed. We are of two schools. She's all over the bed, reading on her stomach or side or just sitting up.

In the *Bob St. John Handbook for Efficient Reading*, the proper way to read in bed is to assume a flat position on your back with elbows braced on the bed and a pillow or two or more behind your head. Then you hold the book at just the right distance to focus.

It is easy, comfortable and all is well with the world, I lectured, and the next thing I knew was that I was reading along, yawned, and somebody must have slugged me in the face, mostly my nose. It wasn't a cowardly intruder attacking in the night. It wasn't Sandy, who was laughing. It was self-inflicted. I'd dozed off and the book fell and smacked me in the face. Timing – the great key to marital comedy.

Playing sports, I had broken my nose a couple of times, an injury that was at least manly. But if someone noticed my nose was swollen this time, what was I going to say? "I was doing heavy reading and a book busted me on the nose."

Sandy laughed. I did, too, through my ironically damaged nose. I'm thinking of inventing a reading helmet with a headlight and a nose-guard.

THE VILLA AND ITS PLACE

On the northern and southern sides of "our" villa are hillsides of rock and marble, where ceaseless waves for eons crashed against the lower surface, created crevices and left remnants of caves and fallen boulders by the sea. Tough, greenish shrubs, some of which have tiny purple and yellow flowers, grow in and about the hills where erratic paths cross the terrain.

In March and April the wild red poppies begin, to use a fitting term, popping up here and there and brightening the landscape.

In certain places near the villa, the southern hillside drops almost straight down into the water – the area isn't quite as high as the northern incline of some 60 feet. In the north, a mile or so from the villa, the hill veers west past a white marble section of the terrain that comes to an end above a narrow, seldom used harbor and a small beach backed by tamarisk trees.

About three houses over from No. 5, there's an opening in the rock fence. From there it is five steps down to a natural cove nestled at the base of the beginning of the southern slope. There are places to sit on large rocks or stone benches that Kostas, not willing to wait eons for nature to do the work, carved out, and below, in the shallow water, fragments of white stone can easily be seen beside the dock Kostas built for his boat.

There have been times down in the cove when I will be in a kind of fugue, staring out to sea but then snap out of it when spray from wind-blown waves brushes across my face. Sandy stays busy in the cove, swimming and picking up small white stones for souvenirs and laughing when the cold spray brushes my face.

Just below the peak on the far side of the northern hills are ruins of an old rock house, maybe owned by a sheepherder. It was without a roof but with weeds growing through the walls and a cracked and a broken stone fireplace that might still work. Over the years more houses have been built on the far side of the hill and a dirt road tracked to the old place if someone were interested enough to make the climb.

Sometimes I find myself waking at dawn and going outside on the veranda in hopes of experiencing another sunrise over the mountain range far to the east on the other side of the main road. It is a yearning to see slanting, newborn shafts of light painting the clouds the softest rose madder and, with luck, I'll catch sight of an elusive streak of yellow light crossing the inside of the arch at the entrance of the veranda.

Back home in Texas, even if I were up early, I'd only experience reading the morning newspaper while drinking coffee in an easy chair.

On Paros a day might be calm with the sound of the sea whispering and the water glassy with only occasional ripples. If this happens on fading afternoons, it's easy to doze off in a chair on the veranda, then wake up thinking only minutes have gone by when an hour or more may have passed.

So we viewed sunsets and sunrises, and the sea about us – these interludes became important times of tranquility on our early trips to Paros, and those thereafter. That special villa would become like home since we could move around in the dark without stumbling or bumping into a table, lamp, chair or each other (unless we wanted to).

We quickly, happily, learned to appreciate the simple things of life and we do not mind being without a telephone and machines and gadgets that do our work for us. We expect delightful times in the bliss that is House No. 5, like enjoying our candlelight dinners by an open window with the sound of the ocean providing accompaniment or, perhaps, the two of us dining at the large table in the dining room.

All the while we'll be listening to the wonderful soprano voice of Greece's Nana Mouskouri, the international star with the trademark eyeglasses, or other favorites, such as Tony Bennett on tape or CD or radio. And sometimes we slow dance across the living room floor.

But sometimes I just get out of the way and watch Sandy dance like someone in a Broadway show and listen to Sandy sing like the professional she is.

That is all part of the joy of House No. 5.

It gives us the place, the opportunity to focus on the depth of our love. We dance, we laugh, we look into each other's eyes and, because of the mood-setting magic Kostas built into House No. 5, we find each other and draw closer than might have been possible the day before.

The hearts are there; they needed a place. House No. 5 is that place.

CHAPTER 5

A NEW WORLD & THE LAUNDRY

House No. 5 is close enough to Paroikia to quickly, easily drive to get groceries and other supplies. In our early island days, when Paroikia's population was about 3,000, we'd never see a billboard or traffic light because there weren't any.

There were stop signs but other drivers interpreted "stop" as a mere suggestion. Many drivers saw them as a reason to slow down. It's a driving style you get used to after a while. Plus, you learn to watch out.

Our habit in those early days, was to finish our shopping and, before going back to House No. 5, we'd go to one of the newsstands and buy the *International Herald Tribune* (renamed the *International New York Times* in 2013). It was our favorite newspaper abroad, publishing a variety of stories, columns and editorials about America and Greece and elsewhere in Europe.

On Paros it also came with an English-language insert called *Kathimerini* [i.e., *The Daily*] with stories about Greece and the islands. An edition in English of the *Athens News* was available and also *USA Today* so we could keep up with what was happening at home, especially in sports. The delivery of *USA Today* could be erratic due to the not always predictable ferry-from-Athens's habit of bringing all sorts of things but sometimes not the newspapers.

At other times in Paroikia, we would just walk around town – we were not in a hurry to be anywhere or do anything unless the mood struck us. Through our many years of visiting, I've continued to enjoy sitting in an open-air café near the downtown windmill and watching people of various nationalities get on and off the ferries.

I try to imagine where they're from and what they're like by watching body language and, if they take a table nearby, listening to the cadence and tone of their voices. I'll jot down notes in a booklet while sipping coffee or beer or a glass of wine. Meanwhile, Sandy will be off on a sketching tour around town. We always make sure we designate a place to meet in case one of us wanders off.

Reading books, magazines and newspapers becomes an anticipated enjoyment. Time is measured by mood or whim, not by minutes or hours or even days.

Sure, there were many other vacations that were respites from work and the fast pace and many photographs that were taken and "stored." The photos we have taken on Paros are in albums and various drawers and on desks and tables because they summon us at a glance to the fine days we have enjoyed on the island with its people. They matter to our hearts.

When I was writing columns for *The Dallas Morning News* and, on my own time, writing for magazines and writing books in my office at home, I would usually arrive weary at Paros and carrying not only luggage, but the enormous personal baggage of workplace and deadline-pressure stress.

When I'd reach this boiling point, Sandy would always say, "Well, it looks like I'll have to put you in a basket and take you to Paros."

After being at House No. 5 for a while, I would feel totally relaxed, and Sandy would claim I looked years younger. The mirror demonstrates that the "spell of youth" doesn't last, but trust me, the emotional joy of the island is enduring.

WINGING IT THAT FIRST YEAR

On that first trip to Paroikia, and on others to come later, we bought wine, cheese and yogurt and loaves of bread not only for our meals but also for picnics on various beaches and excursions around the island. And we also dined out at times.

We were admittedly winging it for a while that first year. Once after, uh, vesper martinis, at my suggestion and with my unfortunate help, Sandy created a dish that looked a bit odd and not-of-this-world. When she left the kitchen for a while, I cautiously approached the dish and said, "We won't hurt you. We are your friends. We come in peace."

It turns out the mystery dish was quite good, though I am still not sure what was in it. Sandy was a good sport, so we laughed as usual.

She read Greek cookbooks, practiced on me and actually became such a successful chef that we didn't go out for dinner very much when we were at House No. 5.

We enjoyed the scenery, martinis, wine, meals and each other at House No. 5.

VERMOUTH IS FLUENT IN THE GREEK

Once when we were looking for a place to dine, we found Parostia near Market Street in Paroikia. That was on our second visit to Paros in the Fall of 1993.

Parostia had excellent ambience whether dining inside or outside under trees in the garden. The property was bordered on the back and both sides by stone and rock walls and remnants of old buildings.

The Greek dishes and wine were good, and there was always fresh fish and it became our favorite restaurant and we were sorry when it closed a few years later. Island restaurants come and go, but they frequently leave pleasant legacies of great times and meals to match.

Sandy studied the Greek language, often interpreted for me, and knew much, much more than I did or ever would, but as she often said of my skills, "You get more mileage out of a limited amount of Greek words."

For example, as we were leaving Parostia after dinner, in my very limited Greek, I thanked the manager for a delightful meal and asked her name, "*Pos sahss lehneh, parakalo?*" (What's your name, please?). She responded in words I didn't understand, so I told her, "*Onnommahzommeh Bob*" (my name is Bob) with a knowing smile.

The manager seemed so delighted to find an American who apparently was fluent in Greek. She immediately invited me to her reserved table to meet her family and friends without noticing Sandy, who is usually ALWAYS noticed wherever we are.

I was having my unfair moment in the flickering limelight, smiling politely and nodding knowingly when somebody said something to me in Greek I didn't understand. So I mumbled, cleared my throat and finally said, "*Kallinichta*" (which I think was "good night"), bowed slightly and left. I found Sandy waiting at the door and shaking her head in disbelief.

"Listen," I said to Sandy, who was making an effort to learn Greek, while I was not so industrious and so knew about four phrases, "If I can find time, I'll try to help you with your Greek." She smiled, thankfully.

The only shortcoming to dining in a number of places abroad, including Paros, was ordering martinis. The first night we dined at Parostia, we wanted to order them, but I was worried that in Greece they would not know how to make a martini. Sandy, the world traveler, laughed and said, "Why everyone everywhere knows what a martini is!" So we ordered martinis. When they arrived, we sipped them only to discover they were straight vermouth. Martini is a common brand of vermouth. Sheep-faced Sandy swallowed her pride – as well as an entire, unpleasant glass of vermouth.

THE TERRIFYING LAUNDRY INTRUDER COMES CLEAN

That first time we were on Paros and adoring House No. 5, we probably could have taken our dirty clothes into Paroikia to be washed, but that seemed silly and lazy so we just decided to do it ourselves. We'd wash our dirty clothes in the sink or bathtub and hang them out to dry on the clotheslines that Kostas had installed next to the utility house he built on a rise behind the villa.

This would become a chore we'd share on Paros over the years, although I suppose some men working for Kostas around the property might have wondered about my sanity when they observed me hanging clothes on the line while whistling a happy tune.

One problem we had was that after we washed them, the clothes never really smelled all that clean. Naturally, Sandy claimed that when she washed clothes they smelled cleaner than when I did. She also cited the fact that bees swarmed around her socks hanging on the line, whereas they didn't come near mine.

"Bees are attracted to the cleanest clothes because they smell sweeter," she explained, smugly. I argued bees are attracted to things that smell funky.

But I have to give her credit. Our clothes did come out smelling much better when she washed them.

When I asked what she had done differently, she replied proudly in her typical animated fashion as she stood over the kitchen sink preparing to wash clothes.

"I act like I'm a washing machine," she explained. "I just jiggle the clothes when I'm washing and then jiggle them again for the rinsing cycle."

I stood behind her and observed the method. She began jiggling the clothes with her hands and arms and then her whole body while emulating the cycles of a washer. She heard me sigh, stopped and looked back.

"Don't stop! For goodness sakes, don't stop!" I said. She shook her head and went back to the chore at hand.

When Kostas learned we weren't using the washing machine in the utility house, he explained that it had been put there for us to use all along.

There was a problem, however. The instructions were in Greek. But, I didn't need to translate. Somehow, I figured out how to get it started by pulling and pushing and turning knobs. Then, it took a while of trial and error to shut down the thing. (Just one more example of how I can conquer the Greek language whether in restaurant or utility room!)

Kostas also explained that if the door of the utility house happened to be locked, the key would be under a rock beneath the window near the front door. About a year later, one evening at dusk I decided to give the washing machine a try. The door was locked and the key wasn't under a rock near the window.

I shook the window, hoping it wasn't locked – maybe I could just open it and crawl inside. It was locked tight. No problem. Utilizing my burglary skills, I would just go through the door.

Perhaps I'd been a thief in my other life, because after locking myself out back home a few times, I'd become adept using a credit card to slip a lock. Oops, the credit card did not work on Paros. So, I really got physical with the door, at first just pushing and shaking it with my hands and then hammering on the door with my fists to loosen it up and even talking loudly to the door. "I'll open you yet!" I declared to the door.

Then, suddenly, something stirred on the other side of the door and startled me!

Unbeknownst to us, Kostas had hired a young woman from Bulgaria named Miglena to do washing, drying and folding clothes for villa residents. She also would live in the small utility house.

Gradually, she opened the door just enough to see this

crazy-looking bearded man in a baseball cap and she seemed to back up a bit before regaining her composure.

At first, I feared she was going to scream.

When I tried to explain and apologize, I thought she couldn't speak English or understand my English but fortunately she could. I told her I was so very sorry and meant her no harm and wasn't aware anybody was living in the house and just wanted to use the washing machine and, and, and – In desperation, I bowed, tipped my cap and hurriedly jogged back down to House No. 5, slightly stumbling en route as if a martini might have tripped me up.

I told this story to Kostas and asked him to please explain to Miglena, a petite, pretty young woman, how I'd made the mistake and that I meant her no harm.

He laughed and laughed and promised he would explain me to her. For a while she seemed to take a wide path when she saw me – my imagination, I'm almost sure.

Soon we would speak to each other and she would even smile and wave when she saw me nearby and sometimes we'd chat.

Sandy and I found a kind of peace in the dreamlike villa, watching sunrises and sunsets and the hypnotic ocean, experiencing the wind and its power and meeting people such as Kostas, for whom acts of benevolence are simply a happily chosen way of life.

There is a slower rhythm to life on Paros and you soon become part of it. Memories made there linger and, of course, I hope first-impression memories I've made for some other people, such as Miglena, don't linger.

The truth is we had found our dream home by the sea, that special place on Paros, a relaxing lifetime away from our homegrown stress. And with freshly laundered clothing that smells good – could it get any better?

CHAPTER 6
A MAN WHO KNOWS HIS WORLD

Kostas Akalestos is unforgettable, someone who realizes the significance of the past, is cognizant of the present and comprehends the importance of the future. He is the epitome of a Renaissance man. He is introspective, funny, thoughtful and has a youthful enthusiasm for life and, also, for simple things such as helping wounded birds and animals and growing all sorts of flowers, shrubs and plants to beautify his villas of Agia Irini.

One afternoon we were driving "home" on the road to House No. 5 when Sandy saw Kostas kneeling down beside a bush as a few people stood behind him and watched him intently. I parked and we walked over to see what was happening. There was Kostas, moving very slowly in a crouched position while whispering warmly as he moved closer and closer to a small bird that was quivering on the ground in an opening beneath the bush.

It was as if Kostas hypnotized the bird. It appeared to have a damaged wing, yet he was able to hold the fledging and gently stroke it. After he introduced us to his tranquil bird friend, Kostas took it to his friend Marios at the non-profit Aegean Wildlife Hospital in Paros. The wildlife hospital treats injured wild animals and birds with the intention of returning them to health so they can be released back into their natural habitat.

Once Kostas even had to deal with what was a lynx of some sort – it's like a Texas bobcat, at least twice the size of a robust housecat and known to be dangerous at times. He couldn't let it go running loose in villas with his clients. He chased down the cat, trapped it and humanely put it down but the entire incident bothered him.

"It was sad to have to kill such a marvelous animal," he said. Some people would be gloating over a prize kill but not Kostas.

He is a man of perpetual motion and many talents, doing all sorts of things around the villas to make sure they're in top condition and still finding time to operate his travel agency, Paroikia Tours, while tending to the family's ice business and devising an agricultural drainage system so his plants, flowers and small exotic trees will always be watered.

After getting to know Kostas, which certainly didn't take very long, I agreed with what John Pack, director of the Aegean Center for Fine Arts in Paroikia succinctly told me: "Kostas is just one of those rare individuals."

And, oh yes, he also has a keen sense of humor. And isn't afraid to use it.

READING OTHER PEOPLE

On one of our trips to Paroikia we finished shopping for groceries and stopped by the liquor store on the way home to *Agia Irini*. It was during mid-afternoon heavy traffic, a time when fearless local drivers are traditionally darting in and out and creating some weirdly askew parking opportunities. I got lucky and maneuvered into an adequate space by the store. Inside, I bought wine and, of course, gin for our beloved martinis and then loaded our supplies into the small, red rental car.

Just as I was about to start the engine and move on, a guy in the car behind us not only bumped our car but shoved us a couple of feet forward. I kept telling myself that I was in a foreign country and I needed to be cool. And besides, I thought, it might have been accidental and, clearly, I needed to be calm and unruffled.

Then he bumped us again. This was no accident.

I jumped out of the car in a rage and charged the car that was bumping us, and then froze in my tracks since Kostas was the driver! He had their son Michalis and daughter Alexia with him, and they were all laughing. So was Sandy. And I joined them after, momentarily, covering my face with my hands. I had blown my cover as a mild-mannered, easygoing man. Kostas isn't opposed to playing tricks and I admitted that was a good one. But he knew his target; he saw through my disguise!

THE DAREDEVIL BEEKEEPER

Kostas is also a bit of a daredevil and his playground is the water in the channel between Paros and Antiparos. He'll be windsurfing and doing all sorts of tricks and twisting and turning or heading lickety-split toward us as, from the veranda, we are watching him get closer and closer toward the shore until, at the last second he suddenly turns away. Sure, he might flip over and crash majestically into the water, but he gets right back up and starts all over again.

"Kostas and Bob always seemed to be kindred spirits and share boyish madness and mischievous qualities," Sandy once explained to someone. She then proudly cited evidence that convicted me. "Bob keeps playing basketball no matter how old he gets or with injuries to his wrist, neck, back and counting. This is the same person, who in his younger years got on a bull at the Mesquite Rodeo, was thrown and tried to get up again but, mercifully, Don Gay – an actual bull-riding champion – wouldn't let him. He also sparred with world welterweight boxing champion Curtis Cokes. Bob ended up on the floor. He said he was just resting."

I was. Honest. Of course, I needed rest after taking that punch.

Kostas would bring us fish he caught for lunch or dinner, and if we arrived late on one of our trips to Paros, he would leave orange juice and breakfast rolls and fruits by the door. Sometimes he'd leave his special treats – jars of pure honey from the beehives he kept back in the hills.

The hives were in a quiet, isolated place and one day I went along with him to see the honeybees at work. He drove up the hill as far as he could and then parked and we walked the rest of the way on a rocky path.

On the way, we passed remains of a rock and stone house with the sides and roof practically gone and foliage growing through the openings.

"It was in the early 1800s that a family came into the mountains to escape the Turks," Kostas explained with a reference to long-standing conflicts with Turkey. "There were nine who lived here in the small house. I am not certain but do not believe they were found."

I wondered how they lived in such a crowded space, perhaps taking turns outside as lookouts to watch and listen for the Turks, knowing that if captured they would likely be enslaved or killed. There are a number of remnants of rock and stone houses on the hills and mountains of Paros forever holding secrets.

We could hear the honeybees buzzing as we got close to the hives. We put on the traditional netted head covers and I reminded him, "I'm sorry, but I'm somewhat allergic to bee stings."

"Do not worry about these bees," Kostas said. "They are harmless and will not bite you unless you try to bite them first."

We were laughing and naturally a bee landed on my arm and stung me.

"Very sorry," said Kostas, and he added with a straight face and a twinkle, "The bee made a mistake."

"One of the worse bee stings was when I was a kid," I told Kostas. "With some of my buddies, we stirred up a nest and tried to swat them with a wooden paddle, pretending they were enemy planes. This practice ended for me when a bee stung me on the nose. It swelled up and never went back down."

We watched the worker bees build rows of waxy, hexagonal honeycomb cells to store honey they made. And Kostas pulled some delicious honeycombs.

And the next day I got an injection because my forearm was swelling. I'm sure the bee regretted the encounter.

A MAN OF PAROS, THROUGH AND THROUGH

Kostas and I were having a beer in a taverna in Paroikia when I noticed a photo of James Dean hanging on the wall. There was a striking resemblance between the 1950s movie star and Kostas. And, as I would later learn, in his younger days he had been called the "Greek James Dean." It embarrassed him when I brought up the subject.

Kostas is a nice-looking guy, about six feet tall with the wiry build of a long-distance runner and the dark eyes of his countrymen. At one point, he wore his black hair short in what used to be called a "flat top" in the United States.

He was living history on Paros, a man of the island. He was born and raised on Paros and, consequently, was very helpful with information about Paros, its history, its treasures and its residents. He hadn't talked much about himself, but when I asked him if I could tape an interview with him on what it was like growing up on Paros, he agreed. My recorder didn't bother him at all, plus he spoke as if he were an anchorman accustomed to talking into a microphone all the time.

It was from these "interviews" – really just conversations between friends – that an understanding of the island began to form. Kostas provided a history not just of events, but of sensations and experiences. From him we learned of the evolution of this beautiful island.

THE ISLANDER'S HERITAGE

Kostas Akalestos grew up in post-World War II Paros when walking and riding donkeys were the main modes of transportation and automobiles were only seen in pictures in newspapers or magazines. There were no supermarkets but there were small, scattered shops – "Mom and Pop stores" in the States – on or around Paroikia's appropriately named Market Street.

Occasional ferries brought a few tourists to Paros and when no lodging was available, the Parians invited these visitors to stay in their homes. People from New Zealand and the United States lived with Kostas' family for a while.

It was from that experience, he remembered, that he grew to like the idea of getting to know people from other countries.

There was no electricity on Paros until the early 1960s. Farming and fishing were the leading occupations and people made their own wine and olive oil and were generally adhering to the old habits and didn't worry much about tomorrow because it would probably be like yesterday. Kostas learned to love fishing and water sports and exploring the sea around the island.

His father, Michalis, was a prominent man on Paros. Mr. Michalis had been a radio operator who worked for a couple of years at the Athens airport and then for 11 years elsewhere. He also spent two years working with his brother in Argentina and they were successful running various companies. Mr. Michalis was financially secure and lived with his family in a nice house and was able to buy a boat and automobile.

"Until I was six years old there were no cars on Paros," Kostas recalled. "My father bought the second car on the island."

About six months later Mr. Michalis was involved in an automobile accident. His wife, Frederica, was pregnant with Kostas' younger brother Euripides and was in the car. Fortunately, nobody was injured. But Kostas says it took him a long time to get over being haunted by the terrifying memory of the accident.

THE LONG SUMMERS

"The first thing I remembered when I was growing up were feelings of happiness and freedom when summertime came and school was out," he told me in a conversation one afternoon in the living room of House No. 5. "It seemed like summertime would last forever."

During the summer months when Kostas and his friends were in their early teens, they would wake in the morning at 10 o'clock and hurry down to the port. When one of the ferries would arrive, the youngsters would sneak around the outside gate to the dock and wait for passengers to embark. As the ferry began to leave, the kids would rush out and jump into the water and swim near the departing ship to both challenge and enjoy its powerful wake and the waves.

"Stay out of there!" the port officials would yell at them. "You might drown! Get out of there! Crazy kids!" They would get out, but they'd always sneak around and leap back into the sea to ride the waves as the ferries left. Perhaps this reminded port officials, who had more bark than bite, that they had done the same thing as carefree kids.

"It was so hot that the concrete passageway going back home would burn the bottoms of our bare feet unless we had been in the sea to get them wet. Then we'd have to run like crazy," Kostas laughed and added, "We all became faster! Then after lunch we were FORCED to have the siesta."

When the kids were older and their parents allowed them to stay out at night, they would wake up from their afternoon naps at five or six o'clock and rush back to the port and toss lines on bamboo poles into the water and catch or try to snare fish near the shoreline until dark.

"We were not afraid to be out at dark," said Kostas. "There was no danger on Paros."

When Kostas and his friends were 16 or 17, they would sometimes venture out at 9 p.m. to watch international films at the only cinema in town. When they weren't interested in a film, there was always the sea in which to swim and play games and feel that special delight of the freedom of youth.

"Yes, it was a very good time to grow up here on Paros," Kostas recalled somewhat wistfully all these years later.

The sea had meaning to the family. Kostas recalled the fun they all had when his father bought a traditional wooden boat and in the summertime would take the kids out into the inlet to fish. Kostas was already skilled in handling boats.

"Yes! Yes! Freedom!" declared a smiling Kostas. "The only restriction was just not to hurt yourself doing crazy things.

"Of course, I was always active and trying some trick or something crazy and sometimes getting hurt. Once I even went into a coma for two days after falling and hitting my head on the walkway."

Teachers at school told his mom Frederica that her boy Kostas was too active, very accident-prone and that, if he didn't calm down, he would be lucky to grow up.

After getting to know Kostas, I could imagine he was something of a daredevil back then. He clearly carries on this way as an adult, sometimes throwing caution to the wind as he darts and jumps and crashes on his windsurf board.

THE ACCIDENTAL RUNNER

In the first class of the Lyceum High School, Kostas became what you might call an "accidental" champion in long-distance races. In school, he paid no attention to the runners because possibly, he might admit, he was preoccupied with the girls.

So he didn't have any experience running races until he simply decided to join a group of boys who would go to Parosporos Beach, near Paroikia, and race three kilometers (about two miles) back to the school. Kostas was 16, and was running with some boys his age, but others competing were the more mature 17- and 18-year-olds.

Once, Kostas remembered, he was running along with the others and was suddenly surprised to realize that he was in the lead after one kilometer. "I was asking myself, what is this? How can I be in the lead? It must be a mistake. Don't they run a little better than this?"

About halfway to the high school, he was in front when he noticed a large group of boys had begun to drop back, leaving him with a dozen other runners and in front of the pack. Then that smaller group started to fall behind even more. He thought, *"Only one kilometer left, when are they going to start running the race?"*

He effortlessly left the remaining runners behind and easily won.

One of his professors witnessed the finish of the race and said, "Wow! You're one of those kids in school who doesn't smoke and that's why you are so good."

Kostas shrugged, still puzzled by his success.

The most amazing thing was that Kostas never really trained for the races. Aware that others were jogging, running and getting ready to compete he decided, "OK," telling himself, "I'll go practice a little bit." He stretched and ran around a little bit.

And he won the long-distance race again in Paroikia the next year and then a third straight time in his final year in school. Somehow it was easier than ever for him.

But the competition became stronger when runners from other

islands in the Cyclades competed against him. And the distance was four kilometers (2.5 miles) instead of three.

"In the middle of the distance I remember I was feeling my limits," he said. He recalled thinking '*What is this… why are they pressing me when that had never happened before?*'

"And then there were four or five of us pulling out ahead of the others," he said. "My throat was dry… my heart beating so fast. I had to press my luck to keep up with the leaders."

Then Kostas passed them and pulled up even with the lead runner from nearby Naxos, and they had a big lead on the rest of the runners with 500 meters left to the finish line. With 100 meters left Kostas was two meters ahead and he pressed on to win the race.

But he was completely exhausted. "The race was over and one of my legs was still trying to run," he said, laughing. "Then the next day neither of my legs could move!"

In his last years in school, he was winning all the races, but his treasured freedom was often interrupted by interest in girls.

Once, when I asked him why he had become a runner without caring that much about it, he grinned and said, "I did not like doing it so much, but to get attention of the girls."

Of course, that would stop when he met Karine. And by the time we met Kostas, he was solidly in love with his beloved Karine, soon to become engaged and then married. He would go on to become a man dedicated to the island's strongest tradition, that of family and fatherhood.

CHAPTER 7

NO JET LAG: THE VATICAN, PRELUDE TO EASTER, A SOARING ZAPATO & SURGERY, ALL ON THE WAY TO PAROS

IN APRIL OF 1995 on our way to Paros, Sandy and I planned to spend a week in Italy where she, an experienced world traveler, had already been but I had not.

She especially wanted me to see Venice although, operating in her traditional fast forward, we would also spend time in Milan, Lake Como and, certainly, Rome.

After all that, we would go on to Paros and House No. 5, our special place that was becoming our second home. There, we would rest and relax.

As it turned out we would be celebrating Easter twice that year.

We hadn't given much thought that the Easter holidays come at different times in Italy and Greece and hordes of young people, out of school for the holidays would join the ever-multiplying crowds in Rome.

There are those who practically ruin exotic trips for themselves and others because if things go wrong they pout, have temper fits, arguments, threaten to eat worms, want a divorce, hate where they are and wish they'd never gone there in the first place.

We are not like that. After fleeting sinking spells, we move on, enjoy the challenge and end up happily making fun of ourselves. That was a good philosophy to have in Italy that year when our best-laid plans often went astray.

The night we landed in Milan, we were both tired but we also were happy because we were, indeed, *in Italy!*

NO JET LAG? REALLY?

After long, tiring flights across the ocean, I become zombie-like, but Sandy snaps awake all happy and smiling and announces her usual refrain, "Why, I don't even have jet lag."

Yeah, sure.

We claimed our baggage, which included Sandy's well-packed two large blue suitcases and my even larger black one with everything crammed inside without rhyme or reason. I had surmised that one huge suitcase was easier to handle than two large ones, not thinking that the black one would be as heavy as two blue ones put together. Like I said, Sandy is the veteran world traveler.

We got in long lines to be checked by immigration and customs. "Isn't this fun?" Sandy said, all perky. I managed a weak smile. The couple in front of us scowled at each other.

"I don't even have jet lag," Sandy cheerily announced again. I managed a faint smile.

When it was time to collect our baggage, Sandy grabbed her

suitcases and was heading off into the sunset, so to speak, when she tripped over her own carry-on, stumbled a few feet and then walked right on as if nothing had happened.

No jet lag.

"It's just my way of walking!" she grinned, using a line she'd stolen from her perpetually clumsy husband.

You cannot stop her once she starts charging through a terminal, not even if she's down to wearing just one shoe.

BEFORE WE EXIT MILAN, A BOGOTA ZAPATO ADVENTURE

Among the many shoe adventures Sandy had during her years as an entertainer on cruise ships was a very public incident in South America.

It was at the airport in Bogota, the capital of Colombia. She was trying to catch a flight to Cartagena where she would board her cruise ship. Just about everything that could go wrong did. The flight was delayed, there was a chance she'd miss the cruise and she couldn't find her luggage or anybody who could speak English. Just a few setbacks.

She was the frustrated traveler, walking through the airport terminal when her inner entertainer executed a magnificent high kick – that's her way of coping with tension and frustration.

Her right, high-heeled shoe came off at precisely the correct moment to be launched up, up and away and it did NOT come down but lodged dramatically and perhaps permanently in a high-level passageway. As she hobbled along, people kept helpfully pointing at her feet and saying "**Un** *zapato*.... **Un** *zapato*," sincerely indicating that she had but one shoe, as if she did not know it!

After hours of frustration and a successful connection with the cruise ship seeming impossible, she actually made it. But she had learned two words in Spanish she'll never forget. And I would wager to this day she holds not only the South American but also the international altitude record for high-kicking a high-heeled *zapato* in an air terminal. *Si, un zapato! Magnifico!*

BACK TO MILAN AND THE CAB RIDE

At last, without injury or loss of shoes, we exited the terminal in Milan just in time to get into another long line waiting our turn to catch a taxi. While we were waiting, we got busy checking to see if we had not only our suitcases but also our camera and video equipment, and coats, purse and billfold and carry-on books to read while traveling.

"Isn't this great! I don't even have jet lag!" Sandy gleefully repeated.

This time I pretended I didn't hear her.

Why is it that every time we get in line for a taxi, we end up getting the undersized ride? No way our luggage – reminding you: two large blue suitcases packed meticulously by Sandy and my double-large black one with everything crammed in it at the last minute as usual – will fit in the trunk.

"That's OK," Sandy told the driver. "We'll get the next cab. It's bigger."

"No, No *mamma-mia*! I have the, uh, *ropa, signora*! Please allow me."

We succumbed. The driver started ramming the luggage into the trunk. Push, smash, slam, bam!

I started to grab the camera and video cases but the driver smiled and said to Sandy, "*No problema, signora.* Allow *me*."

But I went ahead and took the camera and video equipment into the cab. The trunk was quickly full and there was no room for more luggage – even the lid was tied down by, yes, "*un cordón,*" yes, a "*ropa.*"

We were placed in the back seat with the remaining luggage stacked on top of us.

Finally, against what I will describe as incredible odds, we arrived at the San Francisco Hotel. Exiting the taxi was less challenging than the loading.

Mercifully, at the San Francisco, we had a nice room with a garden and trees outside. I was so happy. "This is great," I said. "Let's go find a place to eat."

No response. "Sandy?" I said. "Sandy?"

But she was motionless on the bed. Fully clad. Sound asleep. Yes. No jet lag.

We saw bits of Milan the next morning and then rode in a regular-sized taxi to the station to catch a train to where we'd been told was a beautiful Lake Como resort. We would stay there for a couple of days on another leg of our seven-day, fast-forward tour of some of Italy's high spots. It was a string of challenges, beginning before we ever got started way back in the USA.

THE GALL, THE NUN, THE TRAIN & THE BELLHOP

Five days before we were supposed to leave for Italy I wasn't feeling very well and, never mind packing that big black suitcase, I ended up having surgery to remove my gallbladder.

But after a lifetime of throwing caution to the wind, there was no way I was going to mess up our trip even though logic, somewhat a stranger to me, suggested a delay. My loving wife, the veteran traveler, was concerned enough to suggest that we should postpone this journey.

If I insisted on going, which I did, the surgeon and Sandy, not necessarily in that order, cautioned me to be very careful traveling because I might mess up the successful surgery. I promised I would.

I was determined to be careful and when I make up my mind there's no way I'll deviate. I am almost certain.

So, travel we did and, yes, there were some iffy moments. For example, the train station in Milan was crowded and I sure didn't want anybody to bump me and pop a stitch.

Then I encountered a pathetic scene: A tiny nun was struggling with the largest suitcase I'd ever seen, larger even than my super-sized black one. When she reached the flight of stairs, a guy passing her nearly knocked her over and the giant suitcase wobbled as if it might fall and take her with it.

'This is crazy,' I thought. *'That poor woman.'*

"No! Don't even give it a thought," warned Sandy, easily reading my mind. "You've just had surgery, for heaven's sake!"

"I can't help it," I said and my Texas-raised manners and personal mission of always being helpful rushed me over to the poor woman.

I grabbed the nun's suitcase – so heavy it almost jerked me inside out – and carried it up the stairs. She thanked me and then said, "Bless you, sir," which apparently carried some value because there was no damage to my recuperating body.

Sandy then spoke a recurring declaration: "You're crazy, and you know it! Definitely your Irish side!"

This was only the beginning to the day's excitement. Next, we wrestled with the confusion and hustle-bustle of Milan's beautiful but intimidating train station. Finally, after purchasing our tickets to Lake Como, we had no idea at which platform the train we were taking would stop. Such uncertainty never deterred Sandy. She revved her motor, said, "I bet it's over there to the left," and took off, leaving me in her wake. Then she stopped, reconsidered and said, "The right, for sure. I'm sure of it."

We wandered left and right, up and down, in and out trying to find the right platform. Sandy started out one way, and I thought she's usually right and I followed and, even if she's wrong she "means well."

We picked up that phrase from what my mother used to say about me when I was growing up and did something stupid. "He means well," she'd lament. My mother said that about me a lot.

When Sandy's ideas and suggestions failed, I turned to my own devices of body language. My favorite and most successful ploy traveling is to put on this pathetic, helpless, woebegone face. Suddenly, as if responding on facial cue, a quaint, elderly Italian woman walked up to us.

"*Signore*, surely you need help?" she said. "What is the *problema*?"

"Which platform is for the train to Lake Como, please?" I asked.

"It is the number eight," she answered. "Just over there."

I started walking with Sandy and the luggage in tow but paused because I wasn't sure I'd understood the woman. She had been watching us and easily noticed my uncertainty. She frowned and shook her head at me and said, "I take you there. Follow me."

And so, we did follow our patient guide, straight to platform Number 8.

"This is where I was going next," said Sandy with her innocent look. "Honest!"

We lugged all three of our suitcases onto the train where, against doctor's orders, I strained and put them into the overhead rack while other travelers were passing and staring, figuring correctly that we were tourists.

Luckily, the effort and strain didn't mess up my gallbladder surgery. It was, however, the beginning of my shoulder problem.

Then, alas, we settled into our seats, opened our books and were just relaxing when a man came through, yelling in Italian and pointing at us. I had no idea what was on his mind but it turned out we were in the wrong car.

So there we went again, taking down the big, big and bigger suitcases and hauling them to another car, then finally relaxing and watching the beautiful scenery until we arrived at the station at Lake

Como. We got a taxi but the driver said, "*Signore*, maybe you want to get back on the train."

"Why in the world would we want to do that?" I asked. "We just got here."

"Of course, *Signore*. It is tomorrow they have the train strike. No trains maybe two, three days or more."

"Great!"

We went back into the terminal and the ticket manager confirmed there would be a train strike.

But you have to look at the good side, which kept moving farther and farther away, almost vanishing in the distance. We could go ahead to Venice instead of stopping. There were no strikes there, we were told, so we called an audible and got on the train to Venice. We arrived without incident, got our luggage and ourselves over the bridges and cobblestone walks and made it to the water taxi station.

Things were looking better. Looking, I emphasize.

Now although Sandy has a quick mind, she has never been one to catch the fine print nor pour over details. She got it in her head that our hotel was at Venice's Campo Santa Margherita. Toting our luggage through the cobbled streets, and over arched bridges we managed to find Campo Santo Margherita, but not our hotel. When I asked a man where it might be, the gentleman kindly said, "Signore, the hotel you are looking for is in Mestre."

Then I remembered we'd had some problems with our reservations and the travel agent had changed them from the heart of Venice to nearby Mestre on the northern side of the district. Great!

Now the neighborhood next to Mestre is called Marghera. Marghera – Margherita! Somehow that must be how Sandy got Santa Margherita in her mind.

We dragged our luggage to the bus station. On the bus to Mestre even Sandy was losing her perky disposition and my shoulder and allegedly healing incision from the operation were both bothering me.

At last we arrived in Mestre, not far from the Marco Polo Airport, and checked into the four-star Michelangelo Hotel, a very nice place with an excellent restaurant.

So we got into our room and ordered ice and martinis. When the bellhop brought our drinks, I became confused over the exchange rate for *lira*. When I tipped him, he smiled, and I thought he was going to hug me. It turned out I'd tipped him about $40.

"You need anything, just anything at all, *signore*, I am right here. Just call."

The day had come to a rightful conclusion: Without busting my stitches, I'd made both a nun and a bellhop very happy.

A CONCERT IN VENICE

During our stay, we'd get on a bus each day for a short ride into Venice and then walk the montage of narrow streets over bridges, such as the towering, arched Rialto Bridge, one of three spanning the Grand Canal. We spent time at St. Mark's Square, *Piazza San Marco*, with the massive basilica, the Doge's Palace and the Bell Tower looking down on the entire area and throngs of people, including youngsters on spring break singing, laughing and celebrating life. And, of course, we rode in a gondola and, of course, the gondolier was singing and certainly added joy to our happily traveling spirits.

Once during an excursion, we were walking down one of the many narrow streets when we passed a window with its shutters closed. Inside, a woman was singing her heart out as if in an opera and it was such a wonderful surprise that we stood there for a few minutes and I taped it. I hope many others have gotten to enjoy the voice of this unseen performer as they visited Venice, or as she tours with a major opera! Who knows who she was – she may have been a star escaping the stress by visiting Venice. It happens.

After touring churches and historical sites, we somehow found

Harry's Bar, Hemingway's haunt when he was in Venice. I've always been a fan of his writing and his memory lingers at Harry's Bar where his favorite Montgomery's Martini, mentioned in *Over the River and Into the Trees*, is still served. It was named after the World War II British General Bernard Montgomery, who never attacked the enemy unless he had them outnumbered 15-1. Thus, Hemingway's original martini was 15 parts gin and one part vermouth, but later the house special was changed to 10-to-1. Maybe at 10-to-1 people had a tendency to order a second and add to the day's profits.

Venice was fantastic, beautiful and, yes, we mostly had good meals, including Italian pizzas, thought to be the best in the world. But, now that we are long gone from that excursion in Italy, Sandy and I think the pizzas on Paros are better.

THE VATICAN: WE EXIT TO ENTER

While in Rome we tossed coins into the famous Trevi Fountain – people who do that get to return, the legendary wish says – and we made other now-forgotten wishes.

The only disconcerting thing I saw in Rome was a big McDonald's sign in the heart of the city – for goodness sakes – selling hamburgers and wrecking my image of "The Eternal City."

Other fast food places have since joined the Golden Arches in the city where now, I guess, all roads lead to a drive-up window.

It was the Thursday before Easter when the road led us to the Vatican where the most surprising, unlikely things happened. A travel guide listed St. Peter's Basilica as likely the largest church in the world and said that St. Peter's Square could accommodate 400,000 people. That Thursday, counting us, there must have been 400,002. We joined throngs of people in St. Peter's Square. I couldn't figure out what the big deal was. Guards and security-types were searching everybody, some over and over. We then saw that there was a pretty good "why." We learned what "the big deal" was: Pope John Paul II was there.

Mostly, we wanted to see the Sistine Chapel with Michelangelo's gigantic paintings on the ceiling, a project that took him at least four years to finish in the early 1500s. Our wait would not be that long. But with the hordes of people this particular Thursday, there would be at least a four-hour wait to see the masterpiece and the chapel.

"A four-hour wait? I guess we won't be seeing the Sistine Chapel today," Sandy exclaimed.

"Well, what do you want to do today?" I asked Sandy.

"Oh, I know. I was here once before and went to the Vatican Museums. There was one wing I didn't have time to see then."

"Alright," I replied.

So I followed along with Sandy and she set off, quickly walking along with her typical, irrepressible enthusiasm. We walked on and on, down a long hall. A few visitors trickled past us coming from the opposite direction.

"I think we should go this way," said Sandy.

Now more people headed toward us. "Come on. I think there's something this way."

Now we were curving around a wall, as what seemed a multitude of people had to squeeze past us from the other direction. I noticed that a few seemed to scowl at us.

"Maybe we shouldn't go on," I said.

But Sandy's curiosity was driving her, "Oh, let's just see where this leads. Please."

"This is the craziest thing you've ever done, which takes some doing," I said. "We're going to get arrested or trampled."

My protests were to no avail. She charged onward.

At last there was a door. We entered a room as people filed out, heading the other way. Inside, it took a moment for our eyes to adjust to this new space. And then – then – then our jaws dropped. Without knowing it, we had come in the back entrance to the Sistine

Chapel! The wonders of the newly restored Michelangelo frescoes filled our vision. It was in innocence that we had arrived here. Again, The Fates!!!

It was so mind-boggling to actually see the real thing and imagine how even a Michelangelo di Lodovico Buonarroti Simoni could paint all this magnificent work – *The Last Judgment, the Fall of Man, the Creation of Adam*, etc. The time we were spending there was being well used because no matter how many coins we tossed into Trevi Fountain, we might never pass this way again.

After this artistic adventure, we continued wandering and suddenly found ourselves in St. Peter's Basilica where services were underway. We saw the man on the podium and then looked at each other in disbelief.

It was Pope John Paul II. We were THERE when the Pope was saying Mass!

"Can you imagine what my sister would feel like being here?" I whispered, feeling my traditional guilt for being the one who actually was there. Being there to see and hear Pope John Paul II in person would have been the highlight of her life.

If I ever needed a priest to whom I could confess my guilt, I was in the right place to find one, but I didn't bother to check. Based on the size of the crowd, I figured they all had a waiting list.

THE EASTER CONSIDERATION

Taking part in the Roman Catholic Easter in Italy and then being in Paros for the Greek Orthodox services were reminders that these two religious branches are still at odds after many centuries.

In 1015 AD the differences were so heated that the papal representatives in Constantinople excommunicated the Greek patriarch of the Orthodox Church. The Greeks immediately burned the document and the Greek patriarch in turn excommunicated the Pope's representative.

Roman and Greek Christian churches couldn't settle their differences, and in 1054 when Rome insisted its Pope would be supreme over all Christian churches, they split in what is called "The Great Schism."

As historian Will Durant put it, "Greek and Latin Christianity were fully divorced."

Greeks have long memories, passed from generation to generation. In the summer of 2001, many members of the Greek Orthodox Church didn't exactly welcome Pope John Paul II as the first Roman Catholic leader to visit Greece. Pope John planned to kiss the soil of Greece when he arrived but there were protests against this and even his coming to visit in the first place.

However, Pope John Paul II did ease tension to a degree when he asked God to forgive the Roman Catholics for sins committed against the Orthodox Christians in the past 1,000 years.

With the crush of the crowds and our unauthorized exploration of Vatican City and with the visit to Venice and its canals, Italy was interesting and the people there treated us well.

But we were more than ready to return to Paros, freshly departing from Italy and never dreaming that, after this amazing papal encounter at the Vatican, we would also get to enjoy this astounding Greek island's wonderful celebration of Easter.

CHAPTER 8
OUR SPECIAL EASTER

SANDY AND I were indeed fortunate when our friend Kostas invited us to spend Easter with his family. To us, it quickly became more than a social invitation. It was, indeed, an honor. As we learned, it is considered an extraordinary privilege for "foreigners" to be asked to share this holy occasion with a Greek family.

It would prove to be an unforgettable evening in the large crowd gathering outside the historically significant and renowned *Panagia Ekatontapyliani* (Church of 100 Doors) while waiting for the bells to ring at midnight and welcome Easter Sunday as the most revered, celebrated holiday in Greece.

In villages large and small on Paros, the excitement builds throughout Easter week and climaxes with lighting the darkness with candles and greeting one another with a joyous *"Christos Anesti"* (Christ has risen) and responding with the also joyous *"Alithos Anesti"* (Indeed, He has risen).

The domed, stone and red-tiled *Panagia Ekatontapyliani* stands behind a stone wall in Northeast Paroikia and reigns as perhaps the earliest remaining Byzantine church in Greece. Inside are treasured artifacts, some of which date back to the 6th and 7th centuries.

SETTING THE LOCAL STAGE: FACT AND FICTION

Greece is a country where folklore, facts and semi-facts intermingle. Truth becomes legend and legend becomes truth if you wish it to be. And there are many folk legends surrounding Panagia Ekatontapyliani.

Flavia Iulia Helena, later to be known as St. Helen, was the mother of Emperor Constantine the Great, and in 326 AD she took a ship to the Holy Land in quest of the True Cross upon which Jesus had been crucified. A violent storm interrupted the trip, causing the ship to seek safe harbor at the nearest coastal town, a village now known to modern travelers as Paroikia.

Helena came upon the remains of one of the pre-Christian Age temples on Paros and while praying she had a vision that if she found the True Cross and returned home safely she would build a fine church on the location.

There are several versions of how the True Cross was found after she reached Jerusalem. One was that she believed the Jewish rabbis knew how to find the cross. Helena pressured them and was told that a man named Judas (NOT Judas Iscariot) knew where it might be. He thought the cross was buried under three centuries of debris where the body of Jesus had been placed in a cave, and when Helen ordered excavation three crosses were discovered.

In order to tell which was the True Cross, a local woman dying of leprosy was allowed to touch each of the crosses. When her lesions were instantly healed, Helena knew it was the True Cross, the cross upon which Jesus had been crucified.

By the time Helena was 80 she had built a number of Christian churches but she died before she could build the church in Paroikia. Her son, Constantine, had a small, domed basilica constructed on the spot in 328 AD. Two centuries later Justinian the Great, ruler of the Byzantine Empire, rebuilt the church with a huge dome.

Then there is this element to the story: Justinian appointed a famous builder named Isidore of Miletus to oversee the construction.

In turn, Isidore sent his apprentice Ignatius to Paros to do the job because he had other plans. When Isidore came to Paros to see what Ignatius had done, he was shocked at the fine workmanship and became very jealous. He lured his apprentice to the roof under the pretext that he wanted to inspect his work. Once there he shoved Ignatius, causing him to lose his balance. But Ignatius grabbed Isidore's leg as he began falling and they both plummeted to their deaths. Within the complex, a sculpture caricatures the two men, showing them as two fat guys, one pulling his beard with remorse and the other holding his injured head.

The artwork is there, whether the truth is or not.

Another story holds that pirates who frequented the coast of Paros decided to enter the church and steal the altar. But as they attempted to carry it to the door, the altar became bigger and bigger until, finally, it was too large to pass through. In anger, the pirates smashed the altar.

When the Turks sacked Paros in the Cretan War (1645-1669), the church was pillaged and, through the years, had been damaged by time and culprits until, finally, in 1773, it was devastated by an earthquake. The church took on several physical forms over the years, never being restored to the appearance it had during the rule of Justinian. One guidebook says it was renovated in 1959 and another source declared the restoration occurred in the 1960s.

No one has actually counted more than 99 doors in the church, but tradition has it that when Constantinople becomes Greek once again, the 100th door will be discovered.

A GOOD FRIDAY MOMENT

On Good Friday, a day when shops are closed, we drove in our small rental car around villages where church bells were ringing and priests were chanting in cadence over loudspeakers. In places such as Naousa, fishermen listened as they worked with their nets on the waterfront. On the beach of Kolimbithres, where time and the ocean have sculpted huge rocks into what appear to be futuristic shapes, we could hear the resounding, haunting, echoing chant of a priest from across Naousa Bay. I stopped the car on the road back to the main highway and the voice of the priest seemed to be everywhere while coming from nowhere in particular.

And once again, as is tradition, in the village of Marpissa, on the late evening of Good Friday, a procession of residents and visitors filed past Biblical scenes acted out by costumed people portraying events in the final hours of Christ.

THE PRACTICAL CANDLES

On Saturday afternoon, we walked around the old domed section of *Panagia Ekatontapyliani*. We encountered a wonderful sight: An old gentleman and a youngster were on the roof by the great dome and dropping white flowers that descended like softly falling snow into the sanctuary. I waved at them and they waved back happily and unlike I might have done, neither fell off the perilous roof.

Because we'd lingered in fascinating Paroikia, we were late getting ready to go to the Akalestos house Saturday evening. We'd forgotten to get Easter candles and the stores were probably closed, we feared. But I drove back into town and got lucky and found candles in a liquor store and hurried back to the house. The way it turned out, this wasn't necessary because Kostas had candles for everybody. Anyway, in the process of rushing to get ready we would give a neighbor we'd never met a surprising thrill and darken the lives of others nearby on *Agia Irini*.

DARKNESS ON THE BRIGHTEST ISLAND

Especially in those early years of our visits to Paros, you had to be careful not to operate too many electrical gadgets at once or you'd knock out not only the electricity in House No. 5 but that of every house in the entire neighborhood. So, with the circuit breakers turned on for heating water and lighting the house and with our special dinner invitation looming, Sandy clicked on the switch for an outlet to plug in her curlers and hair dryer and *POP!* all the electricity went out and the whole *Agia Irini* area was pitch black.

Kostas would later tell us that a gentleman next door to House No. 5 had been relaxing in the bathtub, perhaps singing a happy song, when darkness engulfed him. Was it doomsday? Was he drowning? Was he afraid to move in the darkness because he might stumble and land in some unfortunate place? A swarm of fears raced through his mind and he did the smart thing, Kostas told us: He waited out the darkness, thus survived uninjured and clean!

Meanwhile in House No, 5, standing in the darkness, I eased our panic by saying to Sandy, "Great, you've brought darkness to the brightest of islands," and she laughed.

Then reality hit. "I can't go," she declared. "Not with my hair looking like a scarecrow."

"We've got to go," I said. "They're expecting us. My hair's a mess too."

I knew what she was thinking, that I didn't have enough hair to worry about. We dressed as best we could in the dark and we were walking out the door when *POP!*, the lights came back on. Perhaps the man in the tub next door thought he'd had a religious experience.

As it turned out, Sandy looked just great, as always. And we weren't terribly late and Kostas and Karine, his parents Michalis and Frederica and his brother Euripides were glad to see us and the Easter celebration with the Akalestos Family was beginning. With reliable illumination, of course.

EASTER, AS IF THERE WERE NO STRANGERS

While Frederica stayed home to prepare the traditional post-midnight meal, Kostas, Karine, Sandy and I walked to *Panagia Ekatontapyliani* where we discovered that the Church of 100 Doors was filled to capacity. So, by default we joined the crowd outside – scores of people gathered on either side of the street and quietly awaiting the midnight hour and the lighting of candles and the religious procession.

The long-haired, extremely animated conductor of a young people's orchestra had begun directing his musicians with intensity and we watched and listened to this wonderful performance. Kostas, who never misses much of anything, immediately spotted the director's resemblance to the big-haired, animated actor Tom Hulce as the title character in the 1984 film about Mozart and stage-whispered amid the reverence around us, "Look. It's *Amadeus*!" We muffled our laughs as best we could.

As midnight neared, the electric lights were turned off and the orchestra grew silent. When the hour struck, the bells pealed and a priest lit one candle, representing Christ as the Light of the World. From a single candle, the flickering lights were passed from person to person and, soon, all the flickering candles spread through the crowd and brightened the night.

I even got a feeling of being back home in Dallas on a holiday when I set off Kostas' laughter as I automatically ducked when unexpected but apparently holy firecrackers startled me in the midnight reverie. I defended myself by explaining that at midnight on some holidays in Texas, those firecrackers can be wild gunfire.

This night in Paroikia, the young and old, healthy and lame were there. We saw a teenaged boy helping a crippled man light a candle and another young woman in a mini-skirt was arm in arm with a middle-aged woman dressed in traditional black.

Across from us, I watched a little girl holding a lit candle as she stood by a man, probably her father. She was waving the candle a bit too vigorously and inadvertently moved the candle into the man's crotch. He jumped, quickly recovered his dignity and spoke to her in Greek. If I could have translated, he might have said, "Now, dear, be careful. You nearly caught your father on fire." (In Texas, the reaction to a candle in the crotch might have been similar to my reaction to unexpected Easter fireworks!)

The procession from the church included clergymen and altar boys carrying gold crowns, icons and a coffin representing Christ's tomb. Other participants were dragging a wooden cross down the route while a priest, adorned in his most celebratory vestments, sprinkled blessings of holy water toward members of the street-side crowd.

With our candles flickering and as if we were veterans of this event, we joined the joyous crowd and became one with the procession, a virtual river of candle flames lighting the way down from the church to the landmark windmill in the center of town. Our procession was met at the windmill by people from two churches on the other side of town. And above this scene, on the deck of a ferry at the nearby dock, passengers held their lighted candles. (To use an American's perspective, the candles, flickering on deck and reflecting in the waves, made the ferry looked like a giant, floating Christmas decoration. Our American Easters tend to be less of a magnificent demonstration – in contrast, we have church services followed by Easter egg hunts – in the daylight. Not a lot of hugging and kissing, but some frustration upon not finding "all the eggs.")

Throughout this wonderful Paros gathering on land and on the ferry, people were shaking hands, hugging and kissing each other on both cheeks European style, and feeling love and fellowship for others and greeting one another with the traditional "*Christos anestos*" and "*Alithos anesti*" and I thought I saw, in the crowd, familiar faces and it was as if there were no strangers.

THE RED EGG TAPPING TITLE

We walked back to the house, and when we arrived at the archway in front, Kostas used the soot from his candle to make a cross under it. This is a Greek tradition, signifying that the spirit of resurrection has been brought to the homes.

Kostas gave the candle to his mother, Frederica, who used it to light the candles on the dining table, then placed it in a sconce on the wall with the icons of Christ.

Then we enjoyed an after-midnight supper with the traditional soup *magiritsa*. The meal was delicious and the soup was quite good, and I had seconds and then found out it was made from lamb offal and vegetables and I was done with that.

We also took part in the customary observance of the "Tapping of the Red Eggs," a tradition that is thought by some to date back to the time of Christ. In Greek, this game is "*tsougrisma*." And the eggs are dyed red to represent the blood of Christ.

In the preliminary round, each person taps his red egg against another's red egg while saying "*Christos anestos*" and "*Alithos anesti*" and those of us whose eggs broke (sometimes everybody's breaks) were eliminated. However, if your egg does not break – and there are some tricks to avoid that – the tradition is that you will have good fortune for the coming year.

Kostas kept winning that night but apparently had weakened his egg with so many challenges. Sandy, who knew no insider's tricks, had fewer challengers and, in a bit of Easter Rookie luck, actually beat him, becoming the International Red Egg Tapping Champion of our family.

EASTER WITH THE NEIGHBORS

On Easter Sunday we went back to the House of Akalestos for the special Easter meal.

While we waited for the food to be prepared, Kostas took us to meet some neighborhood friends. They were celebrating outside in the beautiful Paros air and cooking lamb on a spit. These very friendly and hospitable people insisted that we eat a little something, which we did and that proved to be a mannerly challenge later in the day. But, neighborly is neighborly in Texas or on Paros.

I also made friends with a little girl, perhaps five or six, who stood by my chair because she thought I looked so different – people said it was my blue eyes that caught her attention. I hope that was the "different" she saw, not like a kid at a zoo staring at a monkey.

Soon the women at this gathering formed a line with their arms around each other and began kicking in the ancient tradition of *Bouzouki* dancing. Throughout history the people of Paros have established an excellent reputation as dancers.

And Sandy has, too, so naturally she joined them and got right into step without a single lesson.

Asked to join the dancing, I politely declined because, as I've explained in many nations, I've had problems with even the basic Texas two-step since high school and I never want to injure anyone who is simply trying to have a good time dancing!

I may not have danced, but I did manage to smile and make funny faces for the little girl and inspire her to laugh. Afterwards, however, I worried that she might think all Americans make clown faces or that, perhaps, "clown" is our true look. It's not – not always.

THE FEAST OF PAROS

As we were finally leaving the neighbors' house, I worried that we would be late for Frederica's famed Easter meal. Also, I feared some of us – especially me – would not have a proper and respectful appetite because we'd eaten so much lamb on the neighbor's spit.

Indeed, we were a bit late and Frederica did call her son, the gregarious Kostas, aside and scold him, and he listened, shrugged, grinned at his mama and joined us once again. The meal was massive with breads, potatoes, salads, cakes, cheeses, more lamb, plus an endless supply of wine and more. I wasn't that hungry after eating too much at the neighbors' but I manfully stuffed myself so as not to hurt anybody's feelings.

By the end of the long meal I figured I had eaten enough to last the winter.

That was the only Easter we spent on Paros. Later, in 2008, Kostas sent us an e-mail saying that he and his family were talking about us and that it would be good to enjoy Greek Easter with us again. We felt the same way, though I wasn't sure I could ever again eat that much food in such a short period of time.

That Easter, perhaps the last we'd ever spend on Paros, was magnificent and to apply Hemingway's reflection of life in Paris to our Easter in Paros, it was unforgettable, genuinely "a moveable feast."

CHAPTER 9
BEFORE THE STORM

The fishermen began their day shortly after dawn on a calm sea between Paros and Antiparos. Dragnets were out and one boat dropped anchor in the sea down the hill from our beloved House No. 5. The boats were funky and different – extremely unlike the boats we're accustomed to seeing on the "fishing lakes" in the United States. I was watching from the veranda when a boat came barreling from the direction of Antiparos and swept past. It was painted like a rainbow and displayed the blue and white flag of Greece. Also among the vessels was a boat flying the skull and crossbones. There were several other flags I could not identify.

The sounds carried because of the calm of the sea, so voices of two men on a boat with many flags were very discernable. They sang happy songs at the tops of their voices and the mood was contagious. I smiled, yelled a hello and waved to them and they waved back, and I thought again how much I loved this place and these people. And I suppose whenever I see a fisherman anywhere on any lake or stream or ocean I will always think of Kostas Akalestos.

***

Kostas Akalestos loves fishing more than anyone I have ever known. And he is an expert fisherman with knowledge of all the species in and around the inlet and out in the open sea. He installed radar and other equipment on his boat and seldom needed help or advice repairing the motor or whatever problems might arise.

Sometimes in fading afternoon light he would stop at the little dock he built below House No. 5, and, standing tall in his boat, yell, "Come! Come see! It is a big one!" Sandy and I would rush to see his catch and, indeed, he would have caught a big one.

In a perfect world, Kostas would fish all day, every day. "But how does Karine react if you are gone fishing too much?" I asked him. Kostas shrugged, grinned with a sheepish look on his face, and then stomped the floor and said, "She puts her foot down!"

Knowing Kostas, Sandy and I couldn't help laughing at a letter Karine once sent us. "It is very hot in Paros lately, about 33c degrees (just under 90 degrees Fahrenheit) every day, but we are surviving and our fisherman is not losing the opportunity to escape from the office to go into the open sea. He has been quite successful saying he would like to quit the travel agent chair for the life of a fisherman. Let us see!"

Kostas' love of fishing rubbed off on his family. When we were back in the states, Kostas would email photos of the larger catches, often picturing members of his wonderful family. The photos became part of a large portfolio of our friendship. Along with all the fishing pictures was a different one that I know delighted him when he sent it to us. It showed two Greek soccer stars in action. Then I noticed he had substituted his face and that of his son Michalis on a newspaper picture of the national players. I sent him an email congratulating him on his newfound stardom.

One of our favorite fishing pictures shows Kostas sitting in a chair holding a fish above his head with one arm while cradling baby Michalis and trying to somehow control young Alexia as she reached for the fish. A family moment in time. And there were other photos of Kostas holding up a fish with his children on each side of him – Alexia looking up at him while Michalis was hanging onto his leg.

When I wrote to ask him how the children were doing, he wrote back, "The children are getting more and more wild, trying to eliminate us."

There were countless boating and fishing trips with his family and there was one Michalis would never forget.

THE NIGHT CHALLENGE AT SEA

Kostas, his friend Akis and Michalis were on a fishing trip during the tourist off-season of 2005 and had gone about three miles out from the island of Serifos on the far western side of Antiparos when they encountered a school of dolphins that began playfully showing off beside the boat. They were laughing about the dolphins and talking as they moved two more miles toward Sifnos, some 20 miles from Paros.

Then, as the sun set, there was movement of something that didn't seem playful coming toward the boat, and Kostas knew it was very big because of the way the sea was swelling. Thinking that it could be very dangerous, he got a spear, lashed it to the boat by a fiber cord and threw the spear toward what he then realized was a ray, probably a Manta Ray. The spear appeared to hit the target.

"The line was moving with a lot of friction, deeper and deeper, and here I am trying to bring him up little by little," Kostas recalled. "We thought we were pulling the fish closer to us. But I realized what was happening, that the fish was pulling us!"

The ray took them on a ride of around 32 miles in the darkness. Along the way another manta ray appeared and stayed with the one that had been "hooked" until morning.

Michalis was very excited and trying to stay awake. Kostas made a small tent on the deck for Michalis and the very tired boy crawled inside and went to sleep.

The diamond-shaped manta ray was an awesome but beautiful giant of nature with "horns" and black eyes on each side of its head and, on the bottom of its "face," a gaping mouth – for plankton, not people! Such rays are usually black with a white underside – they can dive deep or leap out of the sea and move gracefully by flapping their giant, triangular, wing-like fins. Oceanic mantas are large – the "smaller" variety being in the neighborhood of 15 feet across though the large version may approach 25 feet across and weigh up to two tons.

And now, in a night in the Cyclades, Kostas was connected to this giant of the sea. It was strong, but Kostas is amazingly strong, too. He shows that strength in the way he pulls the big catches onto his boat in spite of having a bad back. But this "catch" was different. "It was close to 9 p.m. when I realized I could not take this one," he said. He used the boat's mobile phone to call back to Paroikia for another friend to come help them. This manta, he estimated, was 5½ meters (16 feet) across and a meter thick – a massive, heavy force in its watery home.

"Sure," said his friend who confessed he didn't think it was possible to get the beast.

No matter what the experienced fishermen did, the fish would not come to the surface.

After 18 hours, the cord on the spear snapped.

"My son and my friend were so disappointed it got away, but I was only living for the experience," said Kostas. "The fish was a monument of nature. There was no blood to speak of so the fish wasn't damaged. It happened the best way for a fish like that to go on living free."

BIG FISH STORIES

Kostas had experience with big fish. In the summer of 2003 Kostas had hooked what looked like a monster grouper – it is called a "wreck fish" by the Greeks. This fish was bigger than Kostas, weighing 70 kilos (about 154 pounds), yet he was able to pull it up from a depth of 190 meters – nearly 520 feet!

"I felt my limit for the first time with a regular fish," he said.

He's also brought in some huge tunas, various types of sea bass and red snappers, a real delicacy on the island after being depleted by fishermen using nets over the years. I suspect Kostas has caught a catalogue of species and, whether the catches are big or small, he always seems so thrilled, exhibiting an excited and almost childlike enthusiasm, another trait that makes him special.

If Kostas is going to take me fishing he will yell as he takes the boat past House No. 5 toward the small dock. "It is time because the fish they are waiting!"

He will call, and I will join him, although he is a master fisherman and I'm on the opposite end of the scale. However, life is not fair because in spite of lacking skills, I have been a lucky fisherman.

I confessed to Kostas that the best example of my undeserved fisherman's luck occurred when I was covering Super Bowl X in Miami for *The Dallas Morning News* on Jan. 18, 1976. (Dallas lost to Pittsburgh, 21-17, but the weekend was a win for me!)

The days before a Super Bowl are traditionally a festival – not always a smart festival, but a festival nevertheless. The Cowboys and media were staying in nearby Fort Lauderdale for the game. Four reporters, including my friend Frank Luksa from the competing *Dallas Times-Herald*, woke me. We had partied the night before and I did not want to get up. But they practically dragged me out of bed because they needed me to help pay for the charter. I did not feel very good and knew for certain that jumping on a charter to go deep-sea fishing on a rolling sea off the coast of Florida wouldn't help.

Once aboard, they agreed I should take the first turn in the fishing chair and then get out of the way for Luksa, a real sportsman. Not feeling well at all, I hoped I wouldn't even catch a tiny fish. So, I immediately caught a nine-foot, 11-inch white marlin, the catch of the week and one of the largest whites ever caught in the area. The Associated Press wired the picture around the country. I wore my celebrity status bravely with a grin.

Kostas has been very patient with me. But he fished with a line and spool, and I'd always used a rod and reel and was certainly clumsy at first. If I happened to snare a big one, as inept as I was, I'd probably end up cutting off my hand with the line.

Naturally – and accidentally – I once hooked a large barracuda. Kostas, rightly so, was afraid I'd lose it so he took over the line, and brought it in. Kostas thought this might have been the largest barracuda caught that year in the waters near Paros. Kostas was thrilled. So was I.

Sandy joined us once when Kostas caught another barracuda, unhooked it and dropped it on the floor of the boat. It began snapping near her foot. I was always surprised how quickly Sandy could move when necessary. She jumped to the back of the boat and nearly fell into the water. Later she decided that it would be best if we'd leave her out of fishing expeditions.

CALAMARI AND ME

Near dusk late one evening Kostas took me fishing for *calamari* (squid) north of the house near a huge rock sticking up out of the ocean. He showed me how to fish for *calamari,* dropping the bait straight down into the water with a number of hooks attached. "You will be able to feel one on the line," he said, then warned, "But you must be careful of the hooks."

The first time I tried, I thought there was a bite. So, I pulled up the hooks, one of which stuck in my hand. It was embarrassing to catch only my hand instead of squid, but Kostas was busy fishing on the other side of the boat and didn't notice when I silently grimaced as I pulled out the hook. It was getting late when I finally felt another slight tug on the line.

"I don't think the pull was strong enough to be anything," I told Kostas.

"Let me check," he said, moving over beside me. "Maybe… perhaps you bring it up."

I did and there was a large *calamari* on the line. *Calamari* is a staple on Paros and is included on menus in tavernas and restaurants everywhere. It's slender and small, maybe four to six inches, with ten arms and a pair of triangular fins on its tail and two eyes that stare out of its head, right behind those tentacles. It does not look like it would be good to eat but it is.

Later, as Kostas was letting the *calamari* and me off at the dock below the house, he explained that to soften *calamari* so it could be eaten, I should pound it on the rocks. So, I pounded and pounded without rhythm or technique. Kostas had assumed we knew how to cook *calamari* but he was wrong. Let's just say we weren't exactly Julia Child.

THE FISHERMAN AND THE FOG

On a December day in 2006 Kostas had finished fishing near Sifnos and was headed back to Paros when he experienced a rare occurrence, a "phenomenon" as he called it. It was a windless day and in the distance a cloudlike mass above the sea was coming toward him. "I realized it was fog, something that was practically unknown on Paros," he recalled. "It was like being inside a gigantic ball of cotton. I couldn't see the front part of the boat. The moment you get inside it is shocking. It became colder and so wet that everything was dripping with water, including me."

He couldn't see where he had been or where he was going but suddenly he could see the sun outside the "roof" of the fog and realized where he was. "It was like summertime had suddenly appeared," he said. He was about a mile from the port of Paroikia. His mobile phone rang and it was his friend Tasos of the port police calling.

Frequently, when people were lost or having trouble at sea, the port police of Paros would contact Kostas for rescues and other challenges. He was a natural "go-to" rescuer because he knew the sea so well and was an experienced hand in a seagoing craft.

"Kostas, where are you?" Tasos asked.

"I'm at sea coming back to the port," Kostas told him.

"Ah, that's good," Tasos said. "We need some help. A guy from the village who is diabetic is lost in the fog and needs his insulin. Night is coming and he can't come back. So, we must find him."

Tasos met Kostas as he pulled into port at Paroikia. Tasos called the lost man and asked, "Can you give me your coordinates?"

"I have no idea," the guy said.

"Let me talk to him," Kostas said, and Tasos quickly, happily handed over the phone. "Tell me exactly what you did before getting lost."

"I went to the Mermigas reef and then started coming back toward Paros and was cruising for about 10 minutes when I got into the fog and realized I wasn't doing very well. I was holding my position at 130 degrees. I ran out of fuel. When I was trying to put the fuel in the boat, the boat turned around a couple of times and now I'm completely lost."

In order to figure the distance the guy might have covered, Kostas asked him the speed he had been cruising. He wasn't sure.

Kostas figured the distressed man was in a certain area and told him he would come in that direction. On his sea chart, Kostas made a square of the area where he expected to find the lost fisherman.

"We used a very high-tech method of communication with the guy," smiling Kostas told me later. "It is called 'whistling'!"

He told the man what he was going to do. "I will make zigzags in your area and I will keep whistling very loud and you keep listening. If you hear me, immediately call me so I will know how close you are."

"All right," the guy said.

Then they started their search and Kostas told Tasos, "We're getting close to the fog. Take off your glasses. Put your radio inside."

"Why?"

"Just trust me. Do it!"

"Come on, what for?"

The situation was swiftly explained by experience. Tasos obviously didn't think there was any need for precautions. Then, suddenly, they were in the thick fog and Tasos immediately got soaking wet and started dripping, as did his glasses and radio.

"That is why!" Kostas told him.

Kostas had piloted them into the area where he believed this man was stranded. He began whistling. Tasos started whistling and making all sorts of loud noises, which cannot be translated into English. It was like he was calling "GGGRRRRR! BBBRRRRR! WHOOOO!..."

They were whistling, BBRRRRing and sometimes cussing as loud as they could every 10 seconds for 30 minutes.

The ocean was rough and it wasn't easy to control the boat so Kostas called the guy again. "What is happening?"

"I heard you!" the guy shouted.

"Okay, why didn't you call me?" said Kostas.

"I couldn't call you because I couldn't remember your number."

"Of course you know my number!" said Kostas, getting more frustrated because they knew each other and he knew the man had his mobile phone number.

Kostas gave him his number again. "Just write it down," he

urged. "Just remember it. It's a very easy number.... When you hear us whistle, you call back to us."

Kostas guided the boat in the direction he'd put on his chart, this time over increasingly rough waters. They zigzagged around the area, phoning and whistling. When the guy hadn't called Kostas phoned him and asked what was the problem.

"I heard you but I forgot your phone number again."

"AHHHH! Scratch it on the boat!" Kostas told him.

Kostas, tired and frustrated, sent Tasos into gales of laughter when he added, "WE WILL FIND YOU AND I WILL SINK YOU!"

"Now I can hear you," said the troubled man.

"On which side can you hear us?" asked Kostas and the guy told him "the right side."

"This is not helping," Kostas told him. "On which side of you is the breeze coming?" The guy told him and said the wind was getting stronger.

"Okay, I'm going to turn off my engine," said Kostas. "And then you whistle very loud."

"I don't know how to whistle," said the guy.

Kostas told him, "We will definitely sink you! Do you know how to scream? You do. Okay, scream with all your might."

They heard this faint scream and found the guy. "Follow us back," Kostas told him.

He didn't follow well. The guy was behind them and little by little pulled up beside Kostas' boat. Then he took over and passed them as if they were in a race. "Look at him," Kostas said to Tasos. "It is really funny what he is doing. He is turning right now and leading us AWAY FROM PAROS TOWARD SIFNOS AGAIN!"

Kostas pulled his boat beside the guy. "Where are you going?... You are going to Sifnos. GET BACK BEHIND ME AGAIN! Just follow me."

They finally got back to the port and the guy told Kostas, "Thank you so much. I'm going to kiss you. You brought me back."

"Go, get away and be quiet," said Kostas, the heroic sailor of Paros.

There is no doubt Kostas is a real man of the sea. He knows the waters, the trends of waves and where there are dangerous reefs, those that can and cannot be seen on the surface. He knows when and why the currents can be dangerously strong in certain places at certain times. And, of course, he is an excellent boatman.

The time would come when Kostas' expertise and knowledge of the sea around Paros would be the difference between life and death for many people on a bitterly cruel night.

CHAPTER 10

THE PAROS FERRY: HEROES AND HELL

In the fall of 2001, my friend Kostas took me in his small boat to The Portes where the two giant rocks rise from the sea and form "The Doors," the famed "entry" to Paros. Kostas believed quite correctly that taking a trip to The Portes, seeing where the ferry Express Samina *had struck a reef, then following the ship's path of death would give me a better feel for what had happened and what he had experienced a year earlier. I would get an understanding of how life or death was measured in such a narrow distance and time for 80 of the 540 passengers in the worst Greek ferry accident in three decades. If you go to such places and truly clear your mind, concentrating on what happened rather than what you assumed happened, sometimes the reality of the past will whisper its truth through your imagination.*

***

SHORTLY AFTER 10 o'clock on the night of Tuesday, Sept. 26, 2000, gale-force winds were whipping the waves into white-crested natural forces that became more and more violent as the *Express Samina* neared the brightly lit, well-charted Portes.

The vessel was only three miles from the port at Paroikia. The familiar Portes were not ominous to passing ships but had served for centuries as a traditional landmark so safely distant on that final stretch of the journey. Chances of a ferry, operating under normal conditions, striking the rocks seemed unfathomable. But we know that the odds don't matter to Fate.

On the island, people would soon begin to gather at the wharf adjacent to the windmill in the heart Paroikia to wait for the ferry that was bringing friends, loved ones and tourists. Some people were standing outside the fence that separated the docking area from the public area. Others watched from tables at sidewalk cafes or stood close to buildings for protection against the wind. A dog slept in a doorway and two others wandered through the crowd, befriending anybody who patted and/or gave them scraps to eat. Sure, it was a high wind, stronger than usual, but of course the 345-foot ferry was so large, so controlled, that the elements would only be bothersome at worst.

Near The Portes, passengers on the *Samina* would soon brave the wind to go topside on one of the decks or, in the shelter inside the vessel, crowd against circular windows to see the warm, flickering lights of Paros and, tired as they may have been, feel a sudden uplifting emotional surge because they were reaching their destination.

There are modern, streamlined ships that carry passengers from Piraeus, the coastal city adjacent to Athens, to Paros in three hours but they operate less frequently and are more expensive. Ferries such as the *Samina* cover the distance more often, although the trip consumes five to five-and-a-half tiresome hours to Paros before continuing to nearby Naxos, Samos, Ikaria and Lipsi. There are airline flights from Athens – just 45 minutes to Paros – but, yes, the traditional journey beckons and the ferry carries your car, too.

AN AGING VESSEL AT SEA

The *Samina* was in its 34th year at sea, although many believed it already had outlived its time. The guidebook *Greek Island Hopping* described it as arguably the worst of the ferries. "A large grime bucket with a reputation for running late… for most of the time she shuddered along. She is definitely a boat to be avoided… an accident waiting to happen."

However, the ferry operator of *Minoan Flying Dolphins* would later claim the *Samina* was seaworthy after being cleared by an inspection by the Merchant Marine Ministry – ironically, only a few days before the tragedy.

Sandy and I were among the many who had made the trip on the *Samina*. We had been on ferries, sometimes in rocky seas, but it never occurred to us that the ship might sink. That just doesn't happen.

Early accounts varied as to just how many passengers were on the *Samina* because children were not required to be counted. It was only after that night of September 26, 2000, that officials determined those 540 passengers included children. The travelers included tourists and people returning home from far and near and anxious to see loved ones no doubt awaiting them at the pier. Some traveled alone and others with their families.

And there were young people with their ever-present backpacks on another leg of their explorations abroad.

Had the sea been quieter and the wind calmer and the weather not so cold, many travelers would have slept outdoors on deck. But weather forced these young adventurers to congregate with passengers in the deck-class seats.

And there were four young Greek Navy commanders and 17 Army conscripts, ages 19 to 25, returning to duty on nearby Naxos.

As we had seen many times in our travels, no doubt some passengers who were stretched across seats or even napping in the empty aisles were awakened from travel fatigue by the chatter and stirring around them. They stretched, rubbed their eyes and gathered their backpacks and prepared to exit because it was September 26 near 10 p.m. and their destination surely was near. This must be Paros and perhaps a baby cried after awakening and a small boy ran up the aisle between the seats, bumping into passengers just getting up, and his father yelled for him to come back. "What is this I see? Why are you running out! Do you think you are equipped to walk on water?"

An old woman, wearing the traditional long black dress, struggled to her feet to stretch and almost fell because her legs were out of rhythm with the swaying of the ship but a young man, standing nearby, grabbed her and said, "Let me help you, mother," even though she wasn't his mother and she smiled and thanked him. The young in Greece are very polite and respectful to the old.

MAKING READY TO DISEMBARK, WATCHING THE GAME

It would not be long before those getting off at Paros would prepare to make their way down to the belly of the ship, where their suitcases and boxes tied with string or rope were stored. And there they would wait for the creaking sound as the giant door was lowered, giving off a loud thud when dropped onto the pier. Then they would walk onto the ramp along with exiting cars and loaded supply trucks and people on motorcycles dodging between the vehicles.

But that "routine" arrival never came.

As surviving witnesses would report, many of the ship's crew of 64 were watching a soccer game on television and became excited or upset, depending on which club they were for, although soon they would need to prepare for the monotonous ritual of docking. Of course, the old and the young – the fathers and mothers and children and lovers and officers and army conscripts and ship's officers and crewmen – would not make it to the pier this time and so many would never make it anywhere, ever again.

German passenger Christa Liczbinski would recall, "Everyone was watching the game… I joked with my husband, 'Who's driving the ship?'"

Samina Captain Vassilis Yannakis would later testify that he was ill and taking a short nap for "only ten minutes" and that he had left the ferry in control of First Officer Anastasios Psychoyos, who in turn had placed the ship on automatic pilot. Capt. Yannakis said crewmembers told him that Psychoyos had taken a keen interest in a passenger in the lounge and did not care about napping or watching a soccer game or taking the wheel of the ship.

***

After Kostas and I reached The Portes in his boat, he recalled, "Two weeks before the accident I was out in my boat and very strong currents from Naxos to Sifnos occurred here. We had not had such currents in a year. It was the same that night of the ferry and it would have been difficult navigating. The winds would have pushed the ferry off the course that the automatic pilot had been set for. Without the strong currents, they would have missed The Portes by 300 meters (almost 1,000 feet) even on automatic pilot. But, of course, they had radar and should have known."

CHALLENGING NATURE

In Greece, the Beaufort Wind Scale (from 0 to 12) is still used to measure wind force, whereas knots are most commonly applied internationally. Anything over Force 12 on the Beaufort Scale is classified as hurricane strength. If the wind is Force 9, constituting a strong gale, there is a ban on shipping. That night of the *Samina* tragedy winds increased from Force 7, a moderate gale, to force 9 with long streaks of white crests on dangerously high waves of 13 and 14 feet and some claimed they even reached 20 feet before the night ended. Obviously, as investigators later found, the elements did force the ferry, traveling on automatic pilot, off course toward The Portes.

First Mate Psychoyos noticed the winds might be causing problems and woke Capt. Yannakis. The captain then hurried back to the bridge and was shocked to find that the ferry had drifted off course toward the rocks. In later testimony, Psychoyos said, "When I saw that we were headed for the two rocks I ordered the helmsman to turn the ship. Then I grabbed the wheel myself and turned hard left. The bad thing happened though. It was my fault."

Meanwhile Captain Yannakis recalled, "Before I managed to get to the bridge, I heard a boom…"

***

We circled The Portes, then Kostas killed the motor and we drifted within less than seven feet of The Portes as he showed me just how close the ferry had come to missing them. "The rocks go straight down 30 meters so the bottom of the ship would not have scraped them," he said. Then he added, "Had the ferry had only minutes, perhaps a minute more power, it would have made it closer to shore and perhaps more would have survived."

We moved close enough to the rocks that we could reach out and touch them. There was a dark place where the ferry had scraped them. Kostas was silent for a while as his mind drifted back to that terrible night.

NO CHANCE TO STAY AFLOAT?

It sounded like a mammoth clap of nearby thunder, loud and vibrating, as the starboard side of the ferry hit and ground against the rocks, cutting a hole 10 feet long and three feet high in the hull and passengers lost balance and fell and, as the ship began tipping to one side, water rushed in and strong winds and high waves took control and there was panic of the unknown which quickly became the known. Likely, flashes in some of their minds were of the still-popular 1997 movie *Titanic* and the horror but this was too real to be true. Surely.

What? What has hit the boat? Sinking! It must be sinking!

Imagine the tumult and terror as passengers and crew panicked. Their world was suddenly in threatening disarray.

Unknown to these passengers and perhaps some of the crew, the watertight doors, designed to seal off the flooding compartments and prevent sinking, had never been closed so there was no chance of the vessel staying afloat for even minutes. Just minutes. That might have been enough to save lives and this would have become just another part of a story of what might have been, but the ocean was coming through the huge hole in the side of the ship, flooding it with chilling water as the vessel began a death-fall on its side.

Life was suddenly a rushing jumble. People were stumbling, falling, grabbing as they lost control of their footing and there were screams, cries and no doubt hurriedly uttered prayers of "God save us, God, please save us," and so many crewmen were scrambling with passengers who were trying to find loved ones, and where were the life jackets and life rafts and exits and somebody should help us and the ship became a giant slide into an unforgiving sea and people crushed against each other on narrow stairs leading to the decks, and they were hanging onto the seats to keep from sliding but some were falling and unable to climb back up and the ship as it sank on its side seemed as if it had a mind of its own, veering desperately, hopelessly away from the port at Paroikia and angled south toward the nearer beach at *Agia Irini* and a better chance for survival for passengers. Sadly, for many of these innocents even a better chance was still no chance at all.

SO MANY CHALLENGES, SO MUCH ANGER

In the aftermath, survivors were angry at crewmembers, claiming they failed to help passengers as the 345-foot long ferry with a 10-foot rip in its side sank. They said customs of the sea certainly weren't followed for women and children to exit first and that, as passenger Lisa Torrance of Scotland said, "People were hysterical and the crew did nothing, as nearly as I could tell, to help."

Some were trapped inside the ship and others made it to the upper deck and fell or jumped into the ocean with or without life jackets which both saved and caused deaths because people wearing them became tangled in the rails and were wedged helplessly as they sank with the ship. Survivors would later claim there were even life jackets filled with blocks of wood and why, why, why was this but it was too late for an answer.

Christian Shannon, an artist and teacher from Seattle, was on the main deck when the ferry struck The Portes. "I saw it hit. It was well above the top of the deck… like in the movie *Titanic*. Nobody told us to do anything. They were just yelling and pushing. We were handing out life vests. People were starting to jump off the boat without vests. I thought we were going to die but we managed to get into a life raft that they were letting down into the sea."

Marianne and Stephen Richards, both 47, a British couple married only two months earlier, had not planned to disembark at Paros and were sleeping in their cabin. Perhaps their dreams were of an extended honeymoon – until they were jolted awake by a tremendous shock, a shattering noise and the unmistakable and terrifying sounds of pandemonium. "We knew instantly we had to get out," she said. "We pulled on our clothes and we could feel the boat tipping. There was no one giving instructions and there was no organization. We saw none of the crew but someone gave me a life jacket."

Her husband had no life jacket.

"We got to the top of the deck and it was in panic, complete chaos, and we were looking for some sort of direction but there was none. I was pleading for somebody who spoke English but couldn't find anybody who did and I did not know the words they were speaking."

She said that men, shouting, pushed in front of them while other passengers were panicking. "I was walking on my hands and knees as fast as I could and all the time you could hear glass breaking and water rushing in and the boat tipped and tipped. Then I was hanging onto the rails for dear life and my husband was clinging to me.

"We were holding onto each other and I could see the underside of a tremendous wave and we went down."

The couple lost touch as they dropped into the water. "I went deep down and it was all black and I had this pain in my lungs and I thought, please, let it be quick. In the next moment, I was rushing up and I saw stars and it gave me a new lease on life." A fishing boat picked her up but her husband who had no life jacket was gone. She cried, called to him and then knew he must be dead.

"The life rafts were in shambles and the crane couldn't move to get them out into the sea," said passenger Panayiotis Spanos, who plunged into the ocean with his mother as the ship was sinking.

And Effi Hiou said she scrambled out of bed and made it outside only to be thrown off the ship because of its severe tilt. "The ship's side was touching the seas and it turned into a slide. One after another, we fell into the sea."

And Zoe Kolida said, "The ship fell apart as it sank. There were people hanging onto the railings. Children were crying and old people were screaming. I jumped in the water and looked back and the ship was gone."

"The collision was very strong," said Stamatis Delavinias. "I thought of the *Titanic*. There were old women and others who kept hanging on because they were afraid to jump into the sea." He said the boat sank in less than a half-hour. Others said less, others more. Time stopped, then raced.

Nicola Gibson saw somebody pass a baby down from the ship to the life raft but did not know if the baby survived. And George Kioulafis had jumped into the water and said, "I heard the cries of a baby in the water. I managed to save the baby but his mother drowned."

Grigoris Bertakis, one of the soldiers aboard the *Samina*, saw a Navy commander named Georgiadis jump into the sea while holding a small child. He then swam toward an elder woman and gave her his life jacket.

He kept reassuring the child. "Don't be scared. Don't be scared. I won't let go of you."

Others saw this, too, and other heroics and cowardliness and did not know who survived and who didn't. And Mrs. Richards did not know about her husband, her beloved Stephen.

THE HEROES OF PAROS

A newspaper in Scotland quoted survivor Lisa Torrance declaring, "A Greek boat came and pulled us out of the water. Those fishermen were real heroes."

***

Kostas Akalestos and his friend Akis had been windsurfing that day and were exhausted. When Kostas got home that night, he went straight to bed. But within only a few hours, he was awakened by his mother.

"Wake up! Wake up! Something has happened!" she said.

"Wha… What is it that has happened?" the startled Kostas asked.

"There is trouble with the ferry."

The house in which Kostas lived with his family and parents at that time is on a hill near Paroikia so he could see the distant Portes and harbor where the ferries move into port. When he went outside to look, he recalled, "I could see the lights by The Portes and did not notice anything wrong. I could not believe the ferry had a problem at The Doors." But he realized something terrible might be happening because the ferry seemed to be listing to one side and veering away from Paroikia. His father, Michalis, watching television and listening to the news, told him, "The ferry has crashed into The Portes!"

The excitement of the moment seemed to lift the heaviness of fatigue from his body and the adrenaline was flowing and he quickly telephoned Akis, who had a fine 40-foot sailboat, the Katerina. Kostas told him there was trouble with the ferry and that he and his brother Euripides would meet Akis at the boat. They had to hurry – every second counted!

"Put on your wet suit," his brother cautioned. "It will be very cold."

"It would take four minutes to put it on," answered Kostas, grabbing an underwater flashlight and the wetsuit and moving out the door. "There won't be time for that."

They all arrived at the boat at the same time and quickly jumped aboard and cast off into the strong, blinding wind and mounting waves. Other pleasure craft and fishing boats, large and small, from Paros and nearby Antiparos, joined the rescue effort. The Greek Coast Guard and three British ships (the HMS Liverpool, HMS Cumberland and the aircraft carrier HMS Invincible, with helicopters aboard) were on exercises in the area and hurried to the scene. Helicopters scanned the sea and a plane from Athens served as a spotter for survivors.

When the Katerina was about 660 feet (200 meters) from the scene, the electricity had gone out on the ferry – it had sunk below the surface and those in life jackets were bouncing in dangerous waters in the distant darkness.

Kostas realized that a helicopter with searchlights was looking for survivors in the wrong area of the sea. He radioed his father and gave him the proper coordinates, which Mr. Michalis in turn relayed to Athens and the problem was corrected.

***

Kostas and I followed the ferry's trail of death. Near Agia Irini on Paros were four reefs, two rising prominently out of the water and the others barely showing just under the surface. Kostas explained that there were two currents that meet in the area and cause irregular waves. One might be six or seven feet and suddenly another would reach 13 feet. More than life, the reefs were death.

"One more mile," Kostas said softly, "and they would have been past the reefs close enough to shore to make it safely."

SO MANY DANGERS

Stamatis Kotsornithis, 33, believed circumstances might have contributed to saving his life when the *Samina* struck the rocks. He thought the ship had only scraped a reef and would be fine so he didn't panic. Then he knew it hadn't and he dove into the sea, surfaced and started swimming toward the lights of Paroikia. Seeing the lights, a beacon of hope, kept him going and he was encouraged that there were many other swimmers around him. So he was among those able to make the agonizing three-mile swim to shore in the cold, raging sea. "Even if for a moment I had been left alone, I believe I would have drowned," he recalled.

People dove or were thrown into the Aegean, so beautiful and blue in the light of day but so treacherous this night with dark, chilled waters. Some passengers were tossed against the reefs with killing force. Others were able to climb onto the reefs, hoping they would be safe, only to be swept back into the sea by waves which also slammed them back fatally against the rocks.

Katrina Wallace and Nicola Gibson talked to the BBC about their ordeal. "Luckily we found a lifeboat to get on despite all the screaming and chaos. It was just like on the *Titanic*, I guess," said Ms. Wallace.

"When we found the lifeboat, we thought we were safe, but then we had a hassle getting it down the side of the ship and then away from the boat," said Ms. Gibson.

Ms. Wallace added, "Once in the water, the lifeboat hit one of the reefs. So, then we had to clamber onto the rock with waves crashing around us. We were terrified, cold and just waiting for help. We could see boats and lights on the island in the distance but we could do nothing but wait."

One of the helicopters from the carrier *HMS Invincible* rescued a dozen people stranded on a rock. Capt. Rory McLean of the *Invincible* said, "The people we brought in alive after three hours in the water were suffering from hypothermia."

And those determined men in the miniature armada of pleasure craft and fishing boats from Paros and Antiparos, looking so inadequate in the raging cold sea, put their lives on the line by braving the elements around the dangerous reefs and trying to control their boats in the currents and wind. One boat sank and Dimitris Malamas, the port-master at Paros, died on the job that evening – heart failure from stress in the office of the Port Police.

***

We went between two of the reefs and Kostas, the former Navy man and experienced fisherman, was very familiar with the waters. "Yes, I knew the place around the reefs and was confident we could handle the waters," he said. "Those in the fishing boats from Paros and Antiparos had the best chance, also being familiar with the waters. If you weren't familiar with the reefs – they were practically invisible in the darkness – they held more danger than the winds and churning sea.

A VIOLENT SEA CHALLENGES THE HEROES

A number of small craft had to turn back but the Katerina was still out, steadily but gradually progressing against the elements, enduring the deafening roar of the wind, and clashing waves gone mad that climbed higher and higher and reached over a dozen feet before crashing down and, in their unpredictability, climbing again and dropping again with terrifying force. Amid all this fury of nature, there was a wailing chorus of the desperate, their pleading cries becoming faint. People witnessed the deaths of others in this horrifying needless spectacle. All the while, men on boats were searching desperately in the darkness to locate anybody and then, sadly, watching them disappear into the horror.

"We were trying to save children and others when we could, but the treacherous rocks were a problem," said Kostas. "The wind was Force 7, 8 and our boat was being lifted high and dropped as it moved toward the rocks. If we came in incorrectly while trying to collect people we might cause them to be thrown into the rocks."

Kostas grabbed the hand of a man in the water just as a wave lifted the sailboat and the man slipped away, disappearing as suddenly as he had appeared, and Kostas thought, oh no, oh no, but there was no time for regrets nor laments because others were out there. "I could… not hold on," Kostas recalled, his heart burdened with the sadness.

THE RESCUES AND THE RESCUED

Passenger Effi Hiou recalled, "I saw a flare after I fell into the sea and a fishing boat from Paros was in the distance. But one of the ferry's lifeboats had been lowered. I called out to the people in the boats to take us as well. People young and old were calling out. I was swimming. I was wearing shoes and pajamas. I started to get cold… but kept swimming for one and a quarter hour when I saw this plank of wood and held on. Big waves were coming and a suitcase hit me in the head. We kept swallowing water and we said this will be our tomb. We carried on, calling out for help to the fishing boat.

"The fishing boat approached. Just before midnight it came to us. It was full of people. The people were piled like sheep. They were all soaked. Three boys on the boat threw me a rope and pulled me in. I was shivering, along with everyone else."

Mrs. Richards, who'd been ripped away from her husband, Stephen, believes she was in the sea two hours before she was hauled aboard a fishing boat. "I was praying all that time," she said. She also knew that if Stephen, who had no life jacket, were still alive, he also was praying.

Kostas, Akis and Euripides saw people being swept off a raft into the ocean as it rose and dropped with a wave. "A man was hanging onto the raft by a rope but we could not get him… and then he was gone with the others."

A helicopter hovered over a reef and was able to rescue some people there, clinging for dear life, in fear of being washed away. And there, over there looked like – it WAS another raft of people propelled by the waves and wind toward a reef and rescuers on the chopper watched helplessly as the raft crashed into the rock, apparently killing all aboard.

***

Kostas steered us near the shoreline inside the reefs, perhaps a mile and a half from the site where the ferry sank, so close… so far. We were there more than a year later, but in a nearby cove there were still sad remnants of the tragedy: scattered plastic bottles, pieces of torn cloth, a youngster's Teddy Bear, etc. – the confetti of death.

For me it was aftermath; for Kostas it was still real.

Still there. He could see it. Floating objects – bottles, plastics, clothes, boxes, suitcases strewn over the sea and there were struggling people and there were bodies, some wearing life jackets, and others smashed against the rocks, lifeless as rag dolls. And these heroes were pulling people out of the water and struggling to keep the boat a safe distance from the reefs and there, over there, was another raft of people being tossed madly by the ocean. All that a scene of horror burdening the heart and memory of this good man, Kostas Akalestos. This hero.

THE RESCUERS KEEP TRYING AND TRYING

"I got smashed on the head by a piece of ship and I think I was trapped under something but managed to swim clear and climb onto a lifeboat that was floating upside down," Michael Beaten told the BBC.

And the crewmen on the Katerina were soaked and tired and chilled and blinded by the wind and sea crashing into the boat and over the bow. Throughout this assault they were filling the boat to capacity with people they'd rescued and in the background they were hearing screams of others. "Here! Here! Help, oh, help!… Oh, God! Ohhh, God!"

Euripides became sick and vomited but gamely continued to grab people out of the ocean while they all slipped and slid on vomit and the water coming over the bow into the boat.

Zoe Kolyda, 42, had jumped into the sea and held the hand of another woman, swimming and trying to stay above the surface. She recalled a sailboat, perhaps the one belonging to Akis, tried to rescue them but the waves were too high, the wind too strong and the boat almost sank. The sea and the wind took the women closer and closer to the rocks, which seemed certain death, but the sailboat returned and managed to get them aboard just in time.

LISTEN... SOMEONE IS CRYING!

The Katerina crewmen were throwing ropes to those too far away to be grabbed and also toward the uncontrollable life rafts. The tragic drama was happening so quickly. A raft was near them but they could not see it because it was leaning to one side and blocked the lights on the life jackets of passengers aboard and… And they would have missed it completely if not for a cry of terror that could be heard nearby in the darkness through all the elements and it sounded like… In the middle of all this came a caution: "Listen… a crying, someone is crying," yelled Kostas.

"It was a baby who could not be silenced," he said. Then they saw the raft and tried to maneuver toward it. "It was very dangerous because we were being tossed and turned and sometimes lost our direction because we couldn't see the lights of Paros," Kostas said. "If we were turned wrong and a wave hit the back of the boat we could capsize and be thrown over ourselves."

They were within maybe 60 feet of the reefs when Kostas tossed a first rope toward the raft. It landed on the target but quickly slid away. They got nearer and again a rope was thrown to the people aboard and it landed on the raft but the raft was moving and it slid away.

They threw the rope once again. "Grab the rope!" Kostas, his brother and friend pleaded toward the raft. "Grab the rope!"

But the people on the raft were exhausted and could hardly move to get the rope and the baby continued crying and the rope kept falling out of their reach into the sea so the crew knew they must bring the sailboat closer.

They tried circling between the raft and the rocks. At about 50 feet from the rocks, they tried throwing the rope to the raft again. "Grab it! Grab it!" they all called.

But again, the rope slid away.

They were only about 40 feet from the reefs and the wind and waves could toss them into the rocks but, in a determined moment, the rope was thrown again. This time someone on the raft grabbed the rope. Another was thrown and someone grabbed it. The ropes were secured to the raft and the Katerina began pulling the raft out of danger toward the shore at *Agia Irini*. By now, the Katerina was packed with 32 survivors and there was no more room.

"There were others in the water, calling for help but we had no place to put them," recalled Kostas. "This was a tragic thing but nothing could be done."

They were making headway but there was another unexpected challenge when they were some 120 feet from shore. The engine stopped. They weren't sure what happened but quickly realized a floating rope from the raft had become tangled in Katerina's propeller. "Now we were in the same situation as the life raft," Kostas said. "I was fortunate to have brought the underwater flashlight."

Kostas and Euripides, wearing a wet suit, went overboard into the dark, blind waters of the churning sea and dove below, using the flashlight to find their way to the motor. Kostas cut the rope with a knife and freed the prop. They surfaced and climbed back aboard the boat.

Ropes again secured the raft to the boat and they continued toward shore. But the waves were so violent, picking up the raft and then dropping it, causing slack and then sudden tension on one of the connecting ropes that it snapped.

These men worked fast and hard and soon had two ropes connecting the raft and boat once again. Fearing a rope would again snap, Kostas grabbed both ropes, wrapped them around his back, and, holding one in each arm tried his best to act as a kind of shock absorber between the boat and raft so the ropes wouldn't snap again.

He had been yelling and straining so much that Akis told him, "Kostas take it easy! You have foam coming out of your mouth!"

Kostas' face was bloody, his back bruised – a day later when he could not move his right arm, he would learn that he'd torn a tendon.

But on this violent night, he had no time for personal injuries, he was trying to save lives. He would not let go and the ropes held.

They fought the elements for at least an hour before making shore north of the reefs at *Agia Irini*. After the survivors were unloaded, this brave crew started back out in what seemed by then a hopeless attempt. But they had to try. They went back out to search for survivors in almost impossible elements. Winds reached Force 9, over 50 miles per hour, and cresting waves began to appear eerie white in the darkness as they soared even higher. The crew searched from midnight until 2:30 that morning but could find no one. The Katerina and other boats returned to shore.

THAT NIGHT ON THE SEA

The boats, ships and helicopters had rescued many, while other people had managed to swim to shore. In all, 460 survived.

But 80 drowned in the Aegean that night, some going down with the ship and others being lost in the water or smashed to death on the reefs. The *Samina* was found on its side in sand in 115 feet of water less than two miles from shore. Estimates were it had sunk in just under half an hour.

The rescued were treated by medics on the military ships and taken to medical facilities on Paros and nearby islands or flown to Athens. Some had been in the water three hours and suffered various injuries in addition to hypothermia.

In this odd storm, it had taken the Katerina an hour and a half to get back to shore. The people who had been waiting on Paros for a ferry that never came went to the hospital and to the authorities to try to get information about missing friends and loved ones and some waited on the shore as the last boats returned. Among those standing on shore, still hoping, still praying, was a man with whom Kostas had gone to school.

"Kostas, how does it look out there?"

"Not good. I'm afraid that many are dead."

The man, his head bowed, slowly walked away. Kostas learned later that the man's father had been on the ferry. He was one of the 80 killed.

A SURVIVOR

Mrs. Richards was among those taken to a hospital in Paroikia. She still believed her husband Stephen was dead, their happiness shattered after such a short time.

But there had been a miracle.

A doctor told her he was alive. Stephen, without a life jacket, had washed onto a reef and managed to hang on until he was rescued by one of the boats from Paros. He was treated for a broken collarbone and severe effects of inhaling seawater. But they were together.

"The real heroes were the fishermen and local people from Paros who rushed to help us," said George Kioulafis. "We owe them a big thank you. The waves would have thrown us (to our deaths) against the rocks had it not been for them."

For two days, gale-force winds and strong currents prevented divers from descending to the wreck and when they were finally able to work, 20-foot waves and high winds hampered them. The underwater current was so strong that it ripped a body out of one diver's grasp.

Diver Lazaros Christodoulouo was among those searching for bodies. "We found three people wedged in the railings, stuck by their life vests as they tried to squeeze through," he said. "There was another woman dead in a life raft. It was shocking. With all the debris, it was just chaos down there."

***

Kostas wanted to show me the ferry and, after circling the area for a quarter of an hour, he found the wreckage of the Samina *buried on its side in a constantly shifting grave of sand just off the coast at Agia Irini. The ferry's huge shape was distorted by the moving current. It appeared almost ghost-like and the current created the illusion that the vessel was moving ever so gradually. Staring and searching in the empty windows, I let my imagination see distorted faces trapped in such agony. I felt dizzy, had a sudden chill. After a long while of quiet contemplation, we headed back to shore and I looked at The Portes in the distance. All of it was incomprehensible.*

THE KATERINA'S LEGACY

One day over a year after the ferry tragedy, Sandy and I sat with Kostas on the veranda of House No. 5. Sure, Kostas was proud of what he, his brother and friend had done but he was still upset with himself for what had not been accomplished.

"We were not efficient," he said softly, pain still evident in his heart. "We made mistakes. Missed boats with rope. We made a hundred mistakes."

A couple from Switzerland, clients of his travel agency, had been among the survivors on the *Samina*. They returned to Paros the following year. But he only heard from one of the people saved by the crew of the Katerina.

"I answered the telephone at the office and a man said, 'Oh, my boy, I finally found you'." Obviously, the man was very grateful.

The Katerina had stayed out the longest, was responsible for so many rescues and was frequently seen on television in the news stories. Kostas' family had watched an Athens interview with one of the survivors who said he was very grateful but, "It took too long to get us to shore."

"My daughter yelled at him on the screen," said Kostas, who is very aware of the dark side of human nature.

The coastal authorities said Kostas, Euripides and Akis should be among those recognized for what they had done, for the lives they had saved. But Kostas told them, "I do not want an award. I do not want to be honored. I do not even want to talk about it."

AFTER THE FACT

Critics of the *Samina* and its crew abounded. They declared angrily that there was no way the ferry should have hit The Portes, very familiar to ship captains, well-marked on nautical maps and illuminated by a beacon.

Authorities in the European Union, which bars vessels older than 27 years from circulation, were especially critical. Greece does not adhere to the standard.

"The *Express Samina* was operating illegally and was not up to par with strict European regulations on passenger safety," said European Union Parliamentarian Alekos Alavanos.

John Gopoulos of the Greek Coast Guard said The Portes were "quite conspicuous to be identified and avoided by everyone… A blind man could have avoided the outcrop."

Greek Merchant Marine Minister Christos Papoutsis said that the ferry hitting The Portes was "incomprehensible and totally inexplicable in an area that any captain sailing the Aegean is familiar with."

Shortly after the tragedy, the guidebook *Greek Island Hopping* posted this on its website: "If there has been a high loss of life, then the age of the *Express Samina* (34 years) and questionable standard of her facilities might have played a part. Her 1960s design – with comparative lack of exit facilities – would make it very difficult to escape from inside the vessel in a rapid sinking. The only exits for deck-class passengers were at the stern (other doors are usually kept locked on vessels of this age to prevent deck-class passengers invading high-ticket price areas)."

Authorities of the *Minoan Flying Dolphins*, a subsidiary of Minoan Lines, issued a statement after the tragedy that the *Samina* was checked thoroughly and found seaworthy four days before it sank.

Nevertheless, during a 10-month probe it was determined the *Samina* would certainly have sunk more slowly and perhaps even have been able to make shore had the watertight doors, which can be closed manually or electrically, been activated to seal off flooded lower compartments.

In the inquiry Capt. Yannakis was blamed for this "critical oversight" and failing to call for an abandoning of the ship. He testified he pressed the button to shut the watertight doors but the mechanism did not work.

Capt. Yannakis and first officer Psychoyos were jailed and charged with manslaughter with possible intent and malice aforethought. Two other senior officers shared blame for not shutting the watertight doors.

Within weeks of the *Samina* tragedy, another ferry of the *Minoan Flying Dolphins* ran aground near Naxos, an island just across a channel from Paros. Ships rescued 1,081 passengers and took them to nearby ports. Just before the *Samina* sinking, one of the company's hydrofoils caught fire and 75 passengers abandoned ship. Company officials changed the name of the line to *Hellas Flying Dolphins*.

Lawsuits abounded from relatives of the deceased and survivors of the *Express Samina*.

In numbers, of the 540 aboard the Samina, 287 of the 357 Greeks survived; as did 120 of the 122 foreigners and 53 of the 61 crewmen.

GOT OUT ALIVE, BUT NOT OK

Sandy and I were on Paros on Sept. 26, 2001, a year after the tragedy, as memorial services were held for those who perished. Survivors, relatives and friends of those who died came to the island to join mourners from Paros.

People in all of Greece were touched by the tragedy. A month after the memorial services were held and the Olympic flag arrived in Athens for the summer games, Greek athletes dedicated the 13 medals they'd won at the previous Olympics in Sydney to the *Samina* victims.

Mostly the tragedy will haunt the survivors, the people who lost family members and/or friends and the heroic boatmen and residents of Paros. The terror and loss will dim with the years but will always be there, a thought away. This will be true for those who risked their lives by going out in small boats to try to save as many people as possible because it was the only thing to do… because *they must try*.

Survivors living in Athens were interviewed by the Greek newspaper *Kathimerini* a year after the tragedy. "As soon as I board a boat, my eyes impulsively turn to the places from where I can jump into the sea if necessary," said Stamatis Kotsornithis, 33. "I haven't developed any phobias, but I still have the same nightmare: that I am on a ship that sinks. But I always survive."

"I've stopped traveling alone," said Zoe Kolyda, 42. "I am too scared."

Dimitra Kastani, 26, was still having problems a year after the tragedy. "I haven't gotten over it. I frequently have nightmares. How can I forget the people who drowned right before my eyes?… I may have gotten out alive from this story but I am not OK. My life has changed dramatically…. The only thing that helps me are the conversations I have with those who were also there, because they're the only people who can understand me.

"As for my fears about traveling, I am trying to overcome them. I have been on a boat again out of necessity because I have a house on Samos and travel often. But…"

On Paros, Sandy and I saw people who had been touched by this horrific tragedy emanating from human error.

At dusk, two women stood by the harbor looking out toward The Portes. They stared silently, then began to cry and hugged each other tightly. Ever so tightly.

Another woman sat alone, looking out to sea as if expecting someone, perhaps a son or daughter or husband, to suddenly appear. Perhaps next year there would be a miracle. She would return the next year, too, and if more time were needed to win this miracle, the next.

BOOK II
AMONG THE MONUMENTS: AMERICAN HISTORY ON PAROS

CHAPTER 11
THE FATES' LONE STAR INFLUENCE

On the evening of March 5, 2005 in Galveston, Texas, Sandy the Artist and her work were the focus of a show at the Mosquito Art Café. Among her many paintings on display were several she had done on Paros.

There was quite the congenial crowd with people meeting people and examining Sandy's paintings and speaking favorably about her work. I was, of course, quite proud.

And I was talking with a nice couple, explaining that Sandy and I had been to Paros many times, how much we loved it and that we were making a return trip in a few weeks.

It was at this point that The Fates from Greece made their presence known on a Texas coastal island half a world away from House No. 5 on Paros in the Cyclades.

The woman I was talking to nodded discretely toward a woman standing nearby and confided that the woman had actually lived on Paros and, since I was working on a book about Paros, I should meet her. And with just a few steps, courtesy of The Fates, I made an important connection into a world I'd been trying to find.

This Galveston resident had, indeed, lived on Paros for seven years. She genuinely spoke so lovingly of Paros and its people and said Sandy's paintings brought back memories – she even identified by name the places Sandy had painted.

I explained that I'd been having problems getting information about a man named Brett Taylor, who, while still in his early 20s, had founded the Aegean Center for the Fine Arts on Paros in 1966.

Enter The Fates *dramatically*: This woman, Gail Wetzel Taylor McAdoo, was Brett's widow! She was married to him when he died in a Philadelphia hospital in 1983 at barely 40 years old. He had lived, she said, a genuinely full 40 years. We made an agreement to talk later and I made a note to send a thank-you card to The Fates – apparently, they can get their mail anywhere, Texas or Paros.

As it would happen, Gail filled in the blanks about Brett Taylor's life. And we agreed our chance meeting was mind-boggling. When Sandy and I returned to Paros, we discovered that there were certainly a lot of people who knew and liked Gail.

In conversations and interviews, Gail shared with me history and stories that she learned from Parians and things she'd experienced after arriving in 1971 and easily becoming part of the group at the still-evolving Aegean School of Fine Arts. That's what the Center was named when Taylor founded it in 1966. She also told me of the experiences and ambitions that brought this young artist Brett Taylor to the Cyclades in the mid-'60s, one of the most interesting and turbulent eras for rebel-minded youth in what has been labeled "the American Century."

He was a rebel who was focused on an artistic quest.

THE TAYLOR MISSION OF ARTISTIC FREEDOM

By the time Taylor rode a ferry to Paros late one evening in 1966, he had already visited 14 other Aegean islands in search of the perfect place for the art school he was determined to found.

As he arrived, there were only a few lights, scattered and eerie, struggling to illuminate the dock and only a handful more strung along the street facing the pier. Taylor had no idea what to expect, and not even an inkling that his search would end and his longtime dream would become reality on this small Aegean island.

His ambition was to establish a school of art that operated contrary to the traditional flow of teaching in American schools. He envisioned a style of instruction in which students would be freed from the group boundaries of their classes and distanced from a familiar environment. These artists would be in a place where they were more likely to reach fulfillment as individuals. With his quest fueled in part by his frustration in the American method, and after visiting those 14 unsatisfactory Aegean islands, Brett insisted he must establish his school on an island with a telephone system, a doctor and a building for the school – a building that he could rent inexpensively.

He also wanted residents to take students into their homes. That way the students could soak up the customs and language.

On Paros, Brett Taylor was about to make that fortuitous connection that gave his ambition the proper time and place.

THE YOUNG MAN, THE ARTIST, THE DREAM

Brett, a master artist and classical musician, had graduated from the Tyler School of Art at Temple University in Philadelphia and supported himself by working as a student-teacher. Once, when asked why he was playing music at an art school, he replied, "Music IS art." He was, however, completely disheartened with what he saw as the regimentation in art education in the United States. And he certainly didn't keep his feelings to himself.

Travis Wagner, one of the professors he befriended at Temple, asked Brett what he would do differently if he could create his own teaching philosophy and curriculum.

"I would take each student at his or her level of mental development in art and build from there," he said.

Wagner agreed that, as far as he knew, there were no colleges or universities in the United States that taught the way Brett envisioned.

Brett believed that somehow, someway he must follow his theory of teaching and adapting art studies that coincided with the skills of the individual. But he didn't have the finances needed to follow this dream in the United States. So Wagner offered to give Brett the money to go outside the country, perhaps to Canada or Europe, to try to establish the kind of art school he wanted. As it turned out, Wagner also had a passion for the Aegean Islands and suggested one of them might be a good place for that special art school. Rent was cheaper in Greece and so was the available Greek food.

Before this geographic consideration, Brett's closest connection to Greece had been one of parental fate and location. His parents were struggling artists during the Great Depression and lived in the Greek section of Philadelphia. His father was an artist and his mother a poet so the fine arts were certainly in his blood. And, growing up in a creative environment had introduced something special and fundamental to Brett's pursuit of art.

So in 1966, Brett, recently married, took his young wife Nina with him in search of a functional place that satisfied his criteria and empowered his ambition: Start a school in Greece's beautiful islands. He and Nina flew to Athens, then boarded a ferry at Piraeus and they were on their way.

Wagner, in anticipation of Brett's drive leading to success, had already advertised that an art school was available in the Aegean and four students had signed up. So there was some pressure on Brett to find the ideal island swiftly.

Fourteen had failed to meet his needs. Then he found Paros.

ELECTRICITY WAS NEW, BUT THERE WAS A PLACE...

The ever-present white, squatty windmill was there near the dock on Paroikia but the island he saw on arrival had little to do commercially with what it would become over the next decade.

Electricity was still new. It had been a mid-'60s introduction to Paros and came with frequent setbacks and blackouts. The only paved road on the island was from the main village of Paroikia on the western coast to Naousa on the north of the island and Pounta on the southwest. Other passages were still just rough dirt roads established through the centuries by carts and animals on practical agriculture routes. Farming was a primary profession and the major mode of travel was donkeys.

There were, on this island, only four private cars, one taxi and a single bus from Paroikia to Naousa. There were some public toilets in the cities and outhouses by the homes and not all of those homes had running water.

That was the world the Taylors found that night when they got off the ferry and immediately went to a café across from the windmill. The people in the café welcomed them. They brought the Taylors wine and Greek food – it became a festive evening. One Parian couple took them home with them until they could find a place to stay. The Taylors experienced for the first time the wonderful, warm hearts of the people of Paros.

Everything Brett asked for to start a school was there: a phone system, a doctor, an appropriate building for the school, plus a hardware store with canvas for painting and other art supplies. (He also suggested students bring what they could for their art projects and he knew they would: After all, *they were artists*.) He was ready to start his extraordinary school.

There was only a summer session that first year. But it was a beginning. Brett Taylor had founded what was, in 1966, called the Aegean School of Fine Arts. There were about a dozen students that year. The number would continue to grow. And, of course, even a pure-of-heart art school is not immune to legal wrangling, so thanks to some previously unknown Grecian regulation about use of words, the Aegean *School* of Fine Arts became the Aegean *Center* for Fine Arts.

Brett had wasted no time learning the rudiments of the Greek language on that initial trip through the islands. After he had been on Paros a couple of months, the Parians would hear him speak and they would say, "Oh, you are from Paros."

Gail, my Galveston connection to Brett, recalled that his language skills were so good he could even carry on conversations about philosophy and other lofty topics.

"He did believe it was all-important that students actually live with Greek families and become a part of a different culture," Gail told me. "He was convinced that in order to grow in art the students had to change their orientation, their perception of art, and that by doing these things they would progress."

During his third year, there was only a summer session at the Aegean Center, but some of the students wanted to stay for the winter. Brett was still linked to Wagner and the art school in Philadelphia – it supplied publicity and advertising but no funds. His only income was from application funds and fees from students and other incidental contributors. He wanted a winter program but couldn't afford it. So some of the students paid their own way for what would become the first winter session.

A MUSICAL ENDEAVOR

In early autumn of 1969 another American came to Paros, although it would be a while before people realized that Robert Stallman wasn't just a visitor but was, in fact, the world-renowned flutist, a virtuoso who had been soloist for many international orchestras. Probably he'd heard that Paros was an excellent getaway, a reprive from the crowds and noise of cities.

Gail recalled that Stallman was there to practice for an international competition in Europe. "Brett got to know Bobby because he found a sheet of paper with music on a pathway between his home and the one Bobby was renting," Gail said. "He saw Bobby standing nearby and asked him if the paper might be his. It was and Bobby thanked Brett, a classical guitarist, and from that meeting they became close friends."

They practiced and performed their music together and Stallman decided it would be nice to bring an ensemble to Paros. Brett agreed. No doubt it might just be the first time people on the island would have the opportunity to hear such classical music.

The musicians in the ensemble used their own instruments and also began playing the pear-shaped, stringed Greek instrument, the *bouzouki*, and entertained the islanders with dance music. They performed before farmers, laborers and young and elderly Parians from all walks of life. They wouldn't accept money but only asked that they get a place to live for the summer.

Stallman went on to gain even more fame as a flutist, and also as a teacher and author and contributor to a number of books, and the popularity of his music spread.

Inspired by what he'd seen, Brett decided he wanted to add music to the curriculum at the Aegean Center.

About that time his partners at the art school in Philadelphia indicated they were sorry but they could not continue supporting the center. So, in 1970 Brett took on the added duties of advertising and became independent from sources in Philadelphia. This meant he could add what he wanted to the curriculum at the Aegean Center. He was achieving his goal.

AFTER THE MUSIC

Brett was a tall, thin handsome guy with an auburn mustache and hair that he wore long in the look frequently favored by intellectuals in those days. As one of his friends would later tell me, he certainly attracted women.

He and Nina divorced and she left Paros. It was after that when, in the summer of 1971, Gail, a young physical therapist from Philadelphia, enrolled in the school.

"When I arrived, Brett was applying for tax-free status in the United States," said Gail. "There was a lot of writing and things to do, so he gave me a scholarship and some extra money to work in the office. By the time he got the tax exemption I was hooked on the island and hooked on him, so I stayed instead of going back home.

"The people were just wonderful to me. I lived in Paroikia, which at that time was little more than a village. Brett lived in a place we called the 'by-pass' near a hotel and the Church of 100 Doors, which wasn't even inside the village at that time."

Gail was very fortunate that a neighbor had a 12-year-old girl who wanted to learn English. Gail was trying to learn Greek so they taught each other the basics of their languages. They would do things like pointing to a fork so Gail could say the word in English and the girl could say it in Greek.

"One day the girl's mother came to visit when I was making spaghetti sauce," Gail said. "She took a bottle of olive oil and poured half of it into the sauce and then some oregano. I did find it a bit oily…"

"Okay, you come to my house every Friday," the woman said. "Then I will teach you the Greek recipes."

"All of this was just hospitality," Gail said. "No money ever changed hands. And some of the women included me on their May Day walk into the country where we picked beautiful wild flowers and made wreaths to put over doors and for use in June for celebrating the summer solstice."

Gail was a quick learner, adapting to speaking Greek soon after she came to Paros. But language and culture are two different challenges.

For example, a woman in the neighborhood had given birth recently. When Gail saw the woman holding her baby she went over and said, "Oh, he's soooo cute." The woman reacted by spitting on the ground three times and rushing away with her baby.

The stunned Gail later learned that by saying the baby was cute before he'd been baptized and named, she had put the "evil eye" on the child.

From then on, Gail said, she "never noticed babies unless the mother came up and said 'Oh, his or her name is so-and-so' and then it was okay to say how cute the baby was!"

SERIOUS CONVERSATION, SERIOUS TIMES

Gail cherished the wonderful times and lasting memories from the seven years she lived on Paros. But she also recalled that during a serious wife-to-husband conversation she told Brett that she would not want to die on Paros, preferring to go back to the United States. Brett wished to die on Paros.

"He was the most avid pacifist I've ever known," Gail declared. "He did not believe in war or aggressions by one country against the other, but he said if war came to Paros he would fight for the island. He would give his life to protect it."

Even in paradise, sadly, humans can find frailty. In the early 1980s, Brett became ill. In fact, he became so ill that the Taylors went back to the United States and stayed from September 1981 to March of 1982. Brett seemed to get better, and when they returned to Paros in March, they fully expected the life they had cherished would continue.

Then a doctor on Paros discovered Gail had a lump in her breast and suggested she go back to the United States for the surgery. The doctor believed she would be more comfortable in the U.S., i.e., waking from anesthesia to someone speaking English. In the United States, a physician determined that the lump wasn't cancer. By that time, Brett had returned to the States to be with Gail.

But he was again facing his own medical challenges and would not get his wish to die on Paros. Her health was improving but within two weeks, in the spring of 1983, Brett Taylor, the American teacher and artist who would become an Aegean legend, was dead.

His theories and his work live on. His school, growing in reputation and in curriculum, celebrated its 50th anniversary in 2016.

Gail took his ashes back to Paros and scattered them. She continued to be drawn to Paros and is listed on the school's website under "people who have taught" at the Center, specifically in printmaking and administration.

It was after the mourning that she discovered an old love. And that is how The Fates put another writer from Texas in touch with the dramatic history of a legendary art school on his adopted island home of Paros.

Gail's high school sweetheart, David McAdoo, a successful scientist and academic in Galveston, called her. She said he'd wanted to marry her when they were in high school but she wasn't ready.

"What are you doing?" he asked Gail in their first phone call in years. "I'm living, what are *you* doing?" she answered.

This time she was ready. They married and lived in Galveston which, coincidentally, is on an island, Galveston Island. Not in the Aegean, but on the Gulf of Mexico on the Texas coast.

"I will always have an affinity for a lot of people on Paros," Gail said. "When I talk to people on Paros now, such as writer and poet Jeffrey Carson, I find the feeling to be mutual. And as they say, Paros stays with you forever. It will with me."

Brett Taylor reached his goals for students. "He wanted an unfamiliar and very different setting which fostered a fresh perspective and independence and that's what he got," Gail said.

Brett was an accomplished artist with hundreds of prints, canvases, drawings and sculptures. Gail and Wynn Parks, who was interim director of the Aegean Center after Brett died, were exhibitors of the collection of Taylor's artwork displayed in the United States. The art was seen in Brett's hometown of Philadelphia and elsewhere, such places as Texas, New York and Alabama. With the arrival of the computer era, his work can be found online and appears on clothing as well as in exhibits.

In 1996, photographer John Pack, who had become director of the Aegean Center in the mid-'80s, created the "Brett Taylor Painting Scholarship" and other student grants.

He also maintained Taylor's philosophies of art instruction and freedom of expression not only at the Aegean Center for the Fine Arts, but also at the sister campus in Pistoia, Italy, in the Tuscan Hills.

It is through this effort of others that Brett Taylor's energy and inspiration live on for the sake of not just young artists, but also other artists who after all this time may not be so young except in their ideas.

CHAPTER 12

A POET, ART & ISLAND IMAGES

Jeffrey Carson had come to Paros in 1970 and stayed. When I met him, he was nothing like I expected. He had a reputation as a scholar and teacher at the Aegean Center for the Fine Arts. But it was all packaged in a burly guy with a bushy beard and the appearance of a wrestler or a mountain man reincarnated from the Old West.

His appearance belied the fact that he is a scholarly, sensitive, philosophical man who also is a noted poet, journalist, teacher, translator of Greek to English and Classical Greek historian with expertise in music, art history and probably a few other things that might have slipped my mind.

After several attempts over a few months to get in touch with him, I'd finally reached Jeffrey by telephone in the fall of 2002. I identified myself as a retired columnist at *The Dallas Morning News* and author of a number of books. I told him I was writing a book about Paros, the island and its people, and I wondered if we could meet.

The ensuing brief silence led me to fear he was going to hang up because some crazy guy had gotten through to him on his personal phone. But, quickly enough, he was friendly and soft-spoken and he agreed that we could get together the next morning before his writing class at the Aegean Center for the Fine Arts.

And that was when I expected to meet a very proper gentleman with a scholarly appearance. But here came this Hemingway-esque fellow zooming up on a motorbike and stopping (without skidding!) for my interview appointment. We said our hellos with handshakes and nods and names and I followed him up the steps to the second floor of the Center.

The Center is just off Market Street, a once-tranquil passage that has evolved into in a prime commercial area of cafes, tavernas, banks, shops, etc. This vibrant area now stretches all the way north to the ferry dock, a distance of several football fields, as a busy crow might fly. Takes longer by car.

When we started to go inside, Jeffrey looked back briefly at all the commercial endeavors in the area and, in a bit of a lament, said, "When I was first on Paros there was nothing between here, where we're talking now, and the waterfront except the ground and trees."

He seemed to wish it still might be that way.

We sat at a long table in the room where he held classes and we chatted about literature and writers, such as Pat Conroy, the celebrated Southern author of *The Great Santini* and *The Prince of Tides*. And we discussed psychology, the people of Paros, and how he loved the island and its people.

Jeffrey was a New Yorker – so how did he end up on a Greek island called Paros?

FROM HARLEM TO PAROS

Jeffery lived with his family in New York, and after he graduated from New York University (NYU), he was looking for work while managing to avoid the military draft in the Vietnam War era. He married his girlfriend Elizabeth and wanted to get a teaching job. At that time, you could get an occupational military draft deferment if you were a teacher. There was a teaching job in Harlem, then regarded as a high-crime, low-potential section of New York City. He took the job.

"I was teaching music in a junior high," he recalled. "They should have given me combat pay. I stayed there a year and learned how to survive but really wanted to get out of there."

Leaving Harlem was the first step toward Paros.

Jeffrey eventually came to Paros because of a gentleman named Ralph Hicks. He'd met him while attending NYU. "Ralph had been to Paros and kept telling me I must go there so I finally told him, 'OK, I'll go to Paros.'"

Jeffrey liked the idea, too, that a trip to Paros could also be his year abroad as a writer.

Mr. Hicks came back to Paros again, then retired on Naxos, the largest island in the Cyclades and east of Paros, just across a relatively narrow bit of the Aegean. "He drank, smoked and was sharp as can be when he was 100 years old," Jeffery said with obvious admiration for Ralph Hicks. He paused briefly, then continued, "He was a special man. He was 101 years old when he died. I still miss him."

When Jeffrey first came to Paros in 1965, the island was not the tourist attraction it has become. Though there were few cars, the Greek drivers already had a reputation for being terrible. Jeffrey joked that the drivers didn't really bother him since he traveled by donkey.

After a short while on the island, Jeffrey felt attuned to Paros, liked the looks of the island and its slower pace of life. And, as others before and after him, he believed the island was where he wanted to be.

ON THE ISLAND

Jeffrey's wife Liz was also working so they could save enough money to live on Paros for four years.

The Carsons were both 25 when they moved to Paros in 1970. "When I came to Paros that year, I wanted to study Greek poetry that I could read in English and also avoid the draft and the Vietnam War," Jeffrey explained.

People did have shops in town but "it seemed to me that just about everybody was still a farmer in those days, growing fields of olive trees and grapes for wine. They still do.

"The old people worked with their hands and knew how to handle animals. I remember helping my landlord reap. I lasted about an hour. He was an old man, yet he worked all morning, took off an hour for lunch, and then worked until sunset."

Jeffrey felt attached to Paros's culture because older people were still a part of it. "I was in my 20s when I first came here and continually met and talked to people in their 70s and 80s and still do. They were what I call traditional people. They didn't go to high school and might be thought of as illiterate but they knew a lot of things."

He has pinpointed a moment when change came to Paros. "Once farming became mechanized, it changed everything here. Now a lot of farmers use machinery and drive pickups. The fields that can't be reached by tractor aren't farmed much now, but everybody is still growing olives for olive oil and grapes for wine.

"I like the looks and the pace here and the village life. It's like small towns in America in a way. You know just about everybody – like the name of the person who checks you out at the store. You might not like some of them but you know who they are. The small-town mentality is also here. Do something and everybody knows about it."

ECONOMIC PRESSURE

When Jeffrey and Liz began to worry that they'd run out of money, they took action. Jeffrey started doing various things to earn money. He was building quite a resume on the island.

"I had a little music school for a while. But we barely had enough to get by so I was teaching at the Aegean school, writing journalism stories, acting as a guide around Paros, and hustling all sorts of jobs."

Elizabeth, a noted photographer, became a teacher of her trade at the Aegean school.

There are Greeks and other expatriates who are writers on Paros, but Jeffrey certainly qualifies as the poet laureate of the island. He joined his friend James Clark in writing the first foreign language guide to the island in 1977 – it was in English and simply called *Paros*. Then it was translated into German. They added material and updated the book and, in 1986, it became *PAROS: Roads, Trails & Beaches* and included maps of the roads, trails and beaches plus historical information for visitors interested in excursions.

Jeffrey also published *JEFFREY CARSON POEMS: 1976-1996* about which renowned Greek poet Odysseus Elytis said, "They are full of Greece, a handful of sea-pebbles that are sensitivities and meanings granted by contact with Greece's nature."

Jeffrey, aided by his friend Nikos Sarris, translated into English *The Collected Poems of Odysseus Elytis* and released it in 1997, a year after Elytis died at 84.

Dorothy Gregory of Ionian University in Corfu wrote of his translation: "Jeffrey Carson, a poet himself with a kindred sensibility to Elytis, has admirably succeeded in bringing across the Greek poet's lyrical voice and the richness of his diction."

Jeffery had studied other poets, yet he loves poetry written by Elytis because he believes it "captured the essence of the islands, far beyond anything I was trying to produce."

Jeffrey and Elytis had met thanks to an introduction some of his friends set up at the Hotel Grande Bretagne in Athens. During their discussions, Elytis read some of Jeffery's poetry and was very impressed and praised him.

Odysseas Elytis' surname was Alepoudellis, but he changed it because he didn't want his work as a poet to be confused with or connected to the name of the popular Alepoudellis soap manufactured by his family. He is generally considered the finest poet of modern Greece. He was relatively unknown outside his own country until he was awarded the Nobel Prize for Literature in 1979.

The Swedish Academy presented the Nobel to him "for his poetry, which against the background of Greek tradition, depicts with sensuous strength and intellectual clear-sightedness modern man's struggle for freedom and creativeness."

Elytis and poet George Seferis, described as one of the most important poets of the 20th Century and winner in 1963 of the Nobel Prize for Literature, are the only Greeks, as of 2018, to have won that honor.

Incidentally, Seferis thought Paros to be the loveliest of the Cyclades islands and was said to have found inspiration there.

Elytis wrote of such things as history and myth and of Greece and its magical light, the Aegean Sea and suffering, grief and war and the search for paradise.

He had joined the resistance force during World War II and, while he lived in France, came under the influence of surrealism. He was later active in cultural affairs, such as the Greek National Theater. His final years were spent in semi-reclusion.

THE FAMILY

In a later discussion with Jeffery, I asked him for his thoughts on how some national cultures are family-oriented more than, perhaps, the modern U.S. culture.

"Greeks do not place themselves by generations like the Americans and a lot of Europeans do. The entire family in Greece is still very important. The families stay together," Jeffrey said, then explained that the feeling of connection is a two-way street from older to younger and younger to older.

"Young people don't mind at all associating with the older generation, and a 16-year old also doesn't mind if his 14-year old brother tags along with him," Jeffrey said.

Family bonds notwithstanding in Greece, this interview with Jeffrey, conducted in 2002, may have occurred as Paros, affected by outside influences, was experiencing a change in attitudes and ambitions. Jeffrey said then that on Paros he sees more young people moving forward and trashing some of the old values, attitudes and customs just as is happening elsewhere in the world. The older generation has no choice but to accept the inevitable march of time, the looks and fashions of the new generations, he said. Growth and progress open the door to the outside world for young people.

"The young people around the world now see the same ads in the media… the DVDs, television, magazines and so forth and try to emulate the people in the ads," he said. "They want their hair and complexions to look like these people."

Jeffrey was young during the Hippie Era in America and when young people revolt from the norm and cultural changes explode, it is *déjà vu* to him. As far as some of the attitudes are concerned, he says he sometimes talks to youngsters but they don't listen – just like he didn't listen when he was a young rebel in an America when generations were becoming disconnected.

Jeffrey pointed out something else I hadn't thought about. If you're not a Parian, you don't have and can't acquire the same status as a genuine Parian.

"The first thing people my age want to do when you meet them is talk about genealogy," he said. "You're considered a foreigner if you're from Thessaloniki and open a restaurant on Paros. Most of them don't think much about going to that restaurant. But if some Parian has one, he's all right and they go to his place to dine."

After our interview, we began exchanging emails and sending each other the books we have written.

But our age of newspapers, books and non-amplified music was drawing to a close. The new age may be an improvement, although I, approaching senescence a bit further along into the sometimes inexplicable 21st century, cannot imagine it.

Whatever happens, there will still be monuments to history on Paros.

CHAPTER 13
A MYSTERIOUS FIGURE, AN ANCIENT QUARRY & THE FATES AGAIN

At mid-afternoon under a partly cloudy sky, the woman in the light-colored Greek island dress that moves with the wind, walked almost soundlessly over the rocky pathway leading to the ancient quarries, and I could not help but stare because there was something both surreal and serene about this stranger's certain calmness.

She paused ever so briefly as she met Sandy and me on the pathway and then continued as if she had not seen us. She had the palest of blue eyes, a light complexion and the appearance of listening to faraway music.

Hours later, as we were driving back to Paroikia, I saw her again, this silent figure walking along the road, looking neither left nor right but steadily straight ahead.

I started to turn around and offer her a ride to wherever she was going but I didn't want to interrupt her reverie. Besides, wherever she was going might not have been where we could take her.

From then on, each time we went to the quarry or passed by it

I always looked for the woman with the pale eyes but never saw her again – not at the quarries or on the road or anywhere else. Sandy and some of our friends thought I might have been dreaming. Maybe so. After all, this is magical, mythical Greece.

THE BEAUTIFUL STONE

The ancient quarries are the major source of the white, translucent Paros marble that brought fame to the island. They are around six miles from Paroikia. To get there, you take a curving, climbing interior road on the western slopes of the central mountains that takes you to the neighborhood of the village of Marathi. The Paros stone – Paria lithos – was used for vases and figurines believed to date back to the Proto Cycladic period (2000 B.C.) and also for one of the earliest sculptures, "The Keros Harpist" from the 3rd millennium B.C.

Over the astonishing ages, this beautiful, bountiful marble was used in statues of Aphrodite, Venus de Milo and Hermes of Praxiteles (also known as Hermes and the Infant Dionysus) as well as in the temple of Apollo and the Parthenon in Athens and beautiful churches and chapels.

Organized excavation in the quarries began in the 7th century BC but was periodically interrupted and exploited by foreign countries. Work was especially disrupted during the Turkish occupations (1649-1669 and 1684-1699). In the days of the Roman Empire it is believed more than a thousand slaves were used to work these "open pit mines."

These quarries were still active in the 19th century when a French company built mining installations and became successful at exporting the stone from 1844-1877. The company was even said to have furnished marble for Napoleon's tomb in Paris. It also brought tourists from France to see the quarry and the stone that was used for the emperor's resting place.

A railroad was built to move the marble from the quarries to the harbor. And Nikolos Crispis, who headed the quarry, employed so many miners from other places on the Continent that his company was called "Little Europe." He also printed his own money for payrolls and other expenses. There is one story that says a Belgian Company took over the quarries in 1878, but if that were true, being "under new management" didn't last very long.

INTO THE CAVERN OF THE NYMPHS

There are three remaining tunnels into the slightly sloping hill. The longest tunnel is 190 meters (623 feet); the deepest descends to 91 meters (300 feet). The best-known cave is the "Cavern of the Nymphs." Why? Because on the wall just inside the entrance is a Hellenistic relief from 350-325 B.C. that is dedicated to the mythical, beautiful, graceful young women said to inhabit the sea, rivers, trees and mountains.

The Cave of the Nymphs is in the southernmost cavern at the bottom of a steep marble and rock hill that is angled just enough to allow a careful human – or a confident goat – to make a safe descent over stones and loose rocks. Looking from top of the hill, facing the downward slope, you see a large black hole that is both inviting and foreboding.

I had not planned to go into the cave on this particular trip but the attraction of the Nymphs was too great and I decided I would attempt the climb down even if I didn't have a flashlight and in spite of the likelihood that I could possibly re-injure my left foot. I almost never go anywhere without a sports injury.

I'd broken the foot a month or so earlier while, ignoring age and common sense, I tried to play basketball with all the skill and energy I'd enjoyed decades earlier. After the unfortunate and painful break,

I'd repeated my traditional refrain, "It isn't easy being me" and Sandy replied, "It's more like it's impossible being you."

Sandy was not about to go into the cave, which she feared might be dangerous and also might harbor snakes like one we'd seen earlier while climbing another nearby hill.

I made it down to the cave more easily than I expected and stood there for a while in awe of ancient history. Sandy watched from top of the hill and later said the cave opening dwarfed me, making me look like a really tiny person. When I started inside the cave, Sandy yelled down, scaring the heck out of me and I jumped haphazardly because I thought she'd spotted a waiting snake just daring me to tread on him. But she was just warning me not to go inside. My panicked jump slightly aggravated my damaged foot, but I manfully limped on.

It was worth the limping. Just inside the cavern on my left and behind modern iron bars (no doubt to deter tourists from inscribing their initials) were the remains of the relief, rust-colored with men or Gods and nymphs in some kind of celebration. Greenish colors were on the wall above the relief. Farther into the cave, the ceiling was a mixture of rust, dark and light green. Grayish rocks covered some of the pieces of translucent marble of various sizes all over the cave entrance and going onward into the darkness. Visitors had made inscriptions near the relief, such as the inexplicable "Paros 90/91 and 95." These were absolutely art-free scribblings, the international language of thoughtless people intent on degrading treasured objects.

Supports and solid rock walls shored up this ancient cave and, on the ancient walls somewhat deeper into the cave, were old etchings of roughly drawn faces and something that looked like a large animal. I stood still and briefly felt a chill of silence and sudden dissociation. Then I continued, moving deeper, slowly, and sometimes ducking the "ceiling" and also tripping over rocks that had fallen from that very ceiling onto that path – and I didn't know how recently or if more were about to suddenly drop onto the foolhardy human. But, without lantern or flashlight, I'd gone as far as I could into this cave's intimidating darkness.

Later I found out the inner cave was narrow and perhaps four feet high or less. I wanted to go back with a flashlight and enjoy being surrounded by this combination of manmade art and natural beauty. Sometime, perhaps, on another day. Mercifully, there always seems to be another day, another time on Paros.

THOSE GREEK FATES – AGAIN!

I'd already benefitted from an accidental encounter in Galveston with Gail Wetzel Taylor McAdoo, widow of The Aegean Center for The Arts founder Brett Taylor. How much good fortune could the Greek Fates visit on one writer from Texas?

It was appropriate, perhaps, that another episode of Parian happenstance occurred during our 2005 visit to the ancient quarries.

From my busy writing life a half a world away from him, I'd been unable to re-connect with John Pack, the knowledgeable director of The Aegean Center for the Fine Arts since 1984. This particular season, he was very busy with a new class of students arriving for one of the three-month sessions. I desperately needed to get in touch with John to update a chapter for this book.

One day, as I twisted myself into a mental pretzel over trying to pursue some facts about the famous Center, Sandy and I decided to take a relaxing drive on the mountain road to check out some of the villages near the quarries.

En route to the villages, we ignored our plan and stopped at the ancient quarry and explored the area. Nobody was around but a silent donkey and an active sheep, bleating what sounded like "baa-baa" on a hill on the other side of a crevice that possibly was once the path of a rushing river. Sandy "baa-baaed" back at the sheep. And I walked ahead while she and the sheep carried on their conversation – I couldn't speak Greek; there was no way I could speak Sheep.

If some tourists or islanders had passed, there's no telling what they would have thought of Sandy confidently exchanging "baa-baas" with a sheep. She also meows with cats and they seem to understand what she is saying. Sandy chooses not to bark with dogs – she and the dogs simply communicate quietly with each other.

As we were moseying along, we were surprised to see a woman standing alone beside a car parked on a hill near the ruins of the old mining company. We waved and she waved back. Sandy is ever-friendly and meets no strangers. So she hiked over to the woman, introduced herself, and they started talking. The woman's name was Jane and when Sandy asked where she was from, she said, "Colorado… but I've been here for years."

"What brought you to Paros?" Sandy asked.

"It's a long story. You see there's an art school here…"

"The Aegean School?" Sandy asked

"Yes, my husband is the director."

"John Pack!" Sandy exclaimed.

"Yes."

By this time, I'd managed to wander over and join them. I couldn't believe my luck. As I was telling Jane that I had given up trying to reach John, suddenly there he was, proudly bringing new students to the quarries at the same time Sandy and I had simply stopped for an unplanned visit!

While we waited for John to emerge from the quarry, Jane said she and John always brought the new classes to explore the Cave of the Nymphs and see the relief at the entrance.

John, by now very familiar with the cave, always introduced his students with visits to the main cave and its several passages. Someone not familiar might have gotten lost forever. But John knew the historic site.

John would later tell us that when he had his group deep inside the cave, he turned off the flashlight so the students could experience total darkness for five minutes. He would also pick up a loose piece of marble and shine a light on it in the darkness, showing the group its natural transparency. Each student was given a piece of marble to remember the experience. The shards and pieces of white marble from ancient times are easy to find everywhere around the quarries.

Jane, an open, friendly person, is a celebrated artist who also teaches at the Aegean Center and helps John when needed. (She was head of the center's studio arts program for more than two decades and is a painter, printmaker and sculptor who maintains her American connections.)

The first person out of the cave this fateful (perhaps "Fates-ful") day was the Pack's son, Gabriel, a friendly youngster of 13 that year. He gave the three of us figs to eat and chatted with Sandy and me as if he'd known us for years. The Packs had sent him to a Greek school but then decided to also get him a private tutor, feeling it would be more beneficial toward the goal of learning to think for himself.

His tutor, a young man named Brett, came out of the cave and climbed up the hill to join us. He wore an American-style baseball cap with a "D" on it.

I wondered: Could it be for Dallas as in the Cowboys football team? No, the D was for Duke University in Durham, N.C. Brett was an avid fan of the Blue Devils basketball team. And during his travels to Mexico, Argentina, Italy and Paros, he always checked to see how Duke's basketball team was doing. In the pre-internet-everywhere days, he'd call home back in the U.S. to discuss the situation with his brothers – supporting Duke was a family tradition.

Because I've been visiting Mexico for decades, both as a vacationer and a journalist, I was interested to hear about his travels to the nation where, in recent years, things had not always been as safe for gringos as they'd once been.

His experience had been one of armed isolation.

"In Mexico City, I was hired by a very wealthy family to help their daughter with her law resume," he said. "But I never got to see much of Mexico City. They had this huge house with gates around it and servants. They were afraid I'd be kidnapped and held for ransom so each time I got out, their chauffer would take me some place in a car."

There was a different attitude in Brett's Paros assignment. For example, proving that knowledge can be found anywhere, even in a spud, tutor Brett and student Gabriel were laughing about one of their offbeat, impromptu projects created while studying physics: They built a potato gun.

"I wondered what we could use to propel the potato," said Brett. "So, we tried men's deodorant."

When they lit the propellant, Brett laughingly explained, "it turned out one shot of men's deodorant was enough and the thing took off."

"Can you imagine what's in that stuff?" Jane asked.

"I think I'll stop using it," I said, not wanting to set off an inadvertent explosion in my armpit.

The tutor's travel adventures confirmed my theory of the benefit of exploring other countries: It gives you a better perspective of your own country.

EXITING THE DARKNESS

This day, as the students came out of the cave, it was obvious they liked and admired Jane. When John led them back to Jane, they gathered around her as if she were a comfort after the darkness of the cave and, perhaps, a great dispenser of knowledge and wisdom.

One young woman said she'd been a little frightened going through a part of the cave where the height had diminished to about four feet. She managed to stoop, crawl, bend and make it through but admitted to being a bit panicked.

"Were you ever shut up in a box or anything like that?" Jane asked.

"Yes," she said. "My brother put me in a box on the porch."

"I was shut up in a suitcase by my brothers," said Jane. "The cave doesn't bother me but it seems to bring back memories we have – like being boxed in.

"I don't think it's natural to feel afraid in a cave unless you are reacting to something that was bad in your past. Since we're natural cave-dwellers we probably are not encoded to fear being in a cave."

Sandy asked one of the Greek-American students where her parents were from. "Different parts of the Peloponnese [the huge southern peninsula below mainland Greece]," she said. "My mother was from near Corinth and my father just outside Sparta. He says I'm Spartan! Yeah, I'm a Spartan woman!… Now we live in Los Angeles."

Greek-born Gabriel inspired youthful laughter with his light-hearted summary: "I'm an American living in Greece and you're a Greek living in America!"

As these incoming Aegean Center students gathered around John to discuss their cave experiences, it was obvious that they already looked up to him.

"I changed the application process five years ago," he later told me. "I've gotten more the kind of students I want. If I'm going to spend six months with people, I want it to be a group I like being with – like this one."

UNEXPECTED VOICES IN THE SILENCE

Imagine you are alone and still in an unfamiliar place such as the once-busy land near these ancient quarries. You are there with the remains of long-ago mineworkers' barracks, once-powerful and noisy machine shops and the warehouses that held the marble riches of the French company. You see corporate achievement-become-remnants on a piece of island land where the noise of commerce has been replaced by the sound of the everlasting wind conquering the silence.

In that moment, you find unequaled opportunities for your imagination to expand your thoughts and dreams.

I do not profess in any way to have any psychic powers but as a writer I have had some success, perhaps real or imagined amid endless failures, in trying to pick up vibes, however vague, from the near and distant past.

Near the three caverns of the ancient quarry, there was another road on the side of the hill and it can take you more directly to crumbling remains of the 19th century quarry installments.

Once, as I drove alone past the entrance on the narrow rock and dirt road that goes around a hill, I experienced a vivid shock-effect sensation. I had driven ever so slowly to squeeze past an oncoming car from the other side of the mountain, safely maneuvering with mere inches to spare.

As soon as I successfully negotiated this tight pass, a flock of pigeons camping on the road in front of me suddenly took off with an unsettling flapping of wings while, simultaneously at a nearby farmhouse, dogs inexplicably began barking and howling and roosters crowed.

Startled at all the sudden motion and racket, I sat straight up in the car seat and bumped my head on the roof. Then, I calmed down and drove in silence for a few minutes. Finally, I parked on the side of the road on the hill where huge and assorted sizes of pieces of white marble were scattered everywhere. It was beautiful.

I explored the area, finding the perfect vantage point. I found an old building and decided I could take pictures through the window of what had once been a chapel. The view from the old chapel's window perfectly framed another small, nearby church.

Then I walked around the area and found a resting place on stones in the ruins of a one-story building. I closed my eyes and, by meditating, tried to clear my mind, usually not much of a chore.

Suddenly I heard – or thought I heard – faint voices and felt briefly as if I might have drifted into a time warp. Then I opened my eyes, blinked the sun out of them and discovered that no one was around. Finally, I decided I must be hearing the sounds of people talking somewhere out of sight or perhaps, far away, their voices carrying in the stillness.

Paros has always been a place where voices carry beyond their intended destinations.

My thoughts moved away from what I believed I'd heard to what I hoped I might hear the next day. I was excited and hopeful. John Pack had invited me to meet him at the Aegean Center, and I was amazed by what he had accomplished in spite of temporary setbacks.

And it turned out that we even had something in common from our younger days – a brush with an American tradition. He handled it smartly, as you'll read, while I, on the other hand… well, read on about John, the Navajo Nation and our personal challenge.

CHAPTER 14
THE AEGEAN CENTER'S ENDURING LEGACY

"To thine own self be true."
— Polonius in Shakespeare's *Hamlet*.

"To marvel is the beginning of knowledge, and when we cease to marvel, we are in danger of ceasing to know."
— Ancient Greek quote favored by John Pack.

***

THE AEGEAN CENTER for the Fine Arts is headquartered in a coral-colored, neo-classical building dating back to 1850 which in Greece is "like new."

The two-story structure, its brilliant white trim contrasting with the beautiful – and as it turns out, "controversial" – coral, is just off Market Street in Paroikia. It has front balconies dating back to 1885, a courtyard and office and a lounge in back, and classrooms, an art studio and auditorium upstairs.

The front entrance has a tall window by the door and classic, timeless outside lanterns atop a curling metal base attached to the outside wall. The lanterns add quaintness to the building and so does the narrow, hewn-stone pathway intersecting the street where the Center is located.

The building stands there, a survivor in a struggle against strong odds. It and all it represents remain vibrant due to the determination of John Pack, director of the Aegean Center, and that of the dedicated faculty and the former students and supporters who appreciate the school's importance and managed, at a key point, to come up with what seemed an unreachable amount of money to buy the building.

FOR JOHN PACK, IT BECAME PERSONAL

So many people spend their lives out of place, compromising so much that they forever wonder what they really wanted to do.

After getting to know John, I would characterize him as someone *in place*. He is where he should be, doing what he wants to do – he lives a destiny that helps others achieve their own destinies.

John was a very successful photographer and spent seven years creating the acclaimed *Ganado Portfolio* from the 1970s, his photographic portraits of the people on the Ganado Reservation in Navajo country in northeastern Arizona. He also taught photography at the University of New Mexico's campus in Gallup on the legendary old American highway Route 66. This is in the northeastern corner of the American state of New Mexico, known as "The Land of Enchantment."

"The University was as mainstream as I could possibly handle," he told me. "I felt constricted by the stultifying academic environment. I was still searching for something that was right for me."

One day two of his students were talking just outside the photography lab at UNM. He joined them as they were discussing a Grecian island called Paros, a magnetic place that was inspirational and beautiful.

"John, you would love the place," one of the students told him.

John thought about what the student said and he looked into the possibility of the island. And he decided he would go to Paros. He made plans to spend only two years on Paros, then come back to the U.S. and get on with his life.

I suggested that he must have been a bit skeptical about going to a strange island without having any idea of what to do or expect both emotionally and professionally.

"Wasn't it dark out there?" I asked, and he agreed but smiled and replied, "The way it turned out, it was light out there."

He wasted no time becoming established on Paros in his first year, 1983. He contacted the Aegean Center for the Fine Arts and talked to Andy Whipple, who had taken over the directorship when the center's founder Brett Taylor died earlier in the year. (Whipple was a former editor of the *Berkeley Voice* and a writer and photographer.)

John was signed to a two-year contract to teach advanced photography, a formidable task considering the lack of equipment and facilities at hand. It did not deter John and he thrived and, the next year, he replaced Whipple as director of the Aegean Center when Whipple moved on to other challenges.

"Now I've been here 32 years (2007) and will be 58 (March 2007) and consider myself very lucky."

During our talk in 2007, John said, "In Greece, instead of saying you're 57, they would say I'd be 'going into my 57th year.' That sounds better."

It does. And John, going into his 57th year declared, "I don't want to do anything or live anywhere else. It's not only Greece and the Mediterranean but also life on Paros, the school and choices. I turned away from the commercial art world and gallery scene to continue my work for myself and teach."

***

The Center celebrated its 50th anniversary in 2016 with John still at the helm. He's still there in 2018 and the Center thrives under Brett Taylor's enduring guidance.

THE CHALLENGE: LEARNING WHILE BEING YOURSELF

More than 100 institutions of higher learning now accept credits from the Aegean Center, even though the teaching philosophy diverges from the traditional mainstream. The Center has its own mainstream.

Students come to the idyllic island of Paros from their homes around the world. They arrive not only from the Greek mainland and other islands, but also from Great Britain, Canada, Taiwan, Russia, Japan, Thailand and other places.

But mostly they are from the United States.

For years students lived with Paros families in order to experience daily life on the island. Now they are housed in studio apartments near the Aegean Center but, as the founder wisely wanted, the students still mingle with the locals.

Students are encouraged to discard contemporary and popular concepts – the academic climate of conventional studies – and choose their own projects, while defining their own goals and the manner of expressing themselves and being true to their inner selves.

"There's freedom instead of regimentation," said John Pack. "Being away on Paros enables them to find their worth, sometimes for the first time in their lives.

"You know, we all make choices. The bottom line of the thing is this: I tell my students about choices. We can't always make the right choices but we're still making choices. Don't be afraid. You're better off making choices, right or wrong, and assuming responsibility.

"Anything is possible if you're willing to take a deep breath to clear your mind. Learning your strength takes time. Some things we have to work our way through, especially from the culture in which we were raised."

John and his wife, Jane, who heads the studio arts department at the Aegean Center, and Jeffrey Carson and his wife, Elizabeth, are faculty members who are all accomplished professionals in their fields. They embraced this philosophy: They lead by example, providing an atmosphere of essential information and support in which students, as John hopes, "awaken aesthetic appetites while immersing themselves not only in their chosen studies but also in the beauty surrounding them on Paros."

Students are also encouraged to explore the island's culture and hopefully expand their Greek vocabulary.

Besides being director of the school, John also teaches advanced and digital photography and Jane, a noted artist, works with students in drawing, painting and printmaking. Jeffrey holds classes in Mediterranean art history, creative writing and literature while Liz, a professional photographer, teaches classes in her trade. Jun-Pierre Shiozawa, a student of Jane and Elizabeth, joined the faculty in 2008 to teach drawing and painting.

John had been thinking about adding music to the school. Then it became reality when he sought the help of John Munsey who established a department of singing. In turn, the Aegean Center Vocal Ensemble was created.

A CONDITION OF THE SPIRIT

Jane was a student at the Center in 1984 and John was so impressed with her expertise in art that he hired her to teach in 1986 and they married that same year. They spent their honeymoon in Kostas' House No. 5, the same wonderful villa that Sandy and I claim as "home" when we are on Paros.

Jane's students tend to remember a passage she often cites. It is from the noted French painter and graphic artist Andre' Dunoyer de Segonzac (1884-1974) and captures the spirit of art she hopes her students achieve. He wrote:

"For the creation of works of art there is a condition of the spirit that must be achieved and preserved at all costs. The condition can be compared to the religious term 'a state of grace.' It is a state of exaltation, of communion with life, nature and their fellow beings, which enables artists unconsciously to exalt, recreate and transcribe the world around them."

The atmosphere is also a plus for the students because professional artists are attracted to Paros, its people, the magic light and the beauty of the island. Among these artists was Dalhart Windberg, a Texan famous for his oil-on-canvas creations with vibrant light and vivid colors enhanced by his dramatic use of shadow.

A VANISHING CULTURE

John and I had a conversation years ago, before the arrival of smart phones and the invasion of apps and handheld tablets.

He said that when he came to Paros in 1984, it enjoyed a pure island culture with people sitting on their porches, talking to one another and walking along the seafront.

"Then television came along, destroying some of the valued culture," he said. "Now, everywhere you go you see that little light of televisions. I hate TV, the mindlessness. It wasn't so bad in the early years, not so sophisticated and more innocent. Now television uses psychology to establish what you think, what you eat and wear.

"Just getting away from television alone can be so beneficial. I think television was the worst thing ever perpetrated on the American people."

In a state of agreement (in the pre-handheld device era!), I said to him, "It's certainly detrimental to the imagination of young people.

When we were growing up, we listened to the radio and used our imaginations, picturing people and scenes in our mind's eye. Now many young people are glued to the TV set."

There were some elements of Paros, however, that were surviving, John said. "Although the tourist restaurants and motor scooter rental shops and things multiply and grow, the ancient still survives: the turquoise Aegean, the farmers hauling vegetables into town on donkeys, having an evil eye pinned to children's shirts to ward off evil, fishermen catching octopus just off the shoreline rocks – all much as it has been for thousands of years."

The past never fades like a dream as long as people keep remembering and talking about it. The past will survive as long as people remember to look up and see it while it is still there on beautiful Paros.

EXPANDING THE CENTER

John had a vision, a goal seemingly almost unreachable: to establish an Italian session of the Aegean Center. It came true in 1989, and from that time on The Center has been holding sessions in beautiful Tuscany at majestic Villa Rospigliosi, a 16th century estate in Pistoia. Each Aegean Center school has its own time and place: The Paros session is held in the spring through June and the Italian session takes place from September to late December. Some students attend both sessions.

Thus, he says, "I realized another dream of mine was to connect the Classical and Renaissance period in a single season."

Leaving a contemporary art instruction culture for the Center campuses in Greece and Italy relieves these artists of the burden of fitting into traditional thinking and allows them to concentrate, instead, on what moves their hearts.

"We also go out of our way in order for the students to acquire a better informed global understanding and comprehensive worldview.

Extensive time spent outside of one's own familiar place in order to experience and understand a strange environment, that is surely one of the best ways to acquire a new world perspective as well as a sense of self."

John calmly, confidently said, "We emphasize to our students they can make a difference. It can have a ripple effect. Even living here, by osmosis, they can recognize that they can live without commercialism."

AN UNEXPECTED COLOR AND ITS CONTROVERSY

Things are not always smooth.

Just when it seemed everything was in order at the Aegean Center, the school ended up without a home. For more than 30 years, from one century to the dawn of the next, The Aegean Center had been in a building near the main part of Paroikia. It might still be there had the owners not decided to reclaim the building as their residence.

So John began looking around and found a more spacious building to his liking, although he would learn there were possibly insurmountable problems attached, i.e., the price and finding the drachmas to pay for the place.

The building once housed Parostia, a popular garden restaurant that Sandy and I liked a lot. But it had been closed for years and the structure was vacant, so John assumed he could rent the place for the school. But he was told by the owners that renting would not be possible. They wanted to sell it – for an overwhelming price beyond the reach of the school and its accounts – millions of drachmas, i.e., a ton of U.S. dollars or euros. John was worried but undeterred. He put up his savings; former students and supporters of the school chipped in and the joint effort of lovers of this great Aegean Center not only raised the money to purchase the building in 2001 but also to transform it from a vacant restaurant into a vibrant school.

John Pack is a force of constantly moving energy who can tire you out just watching him. So naturally, he was gung-ho as he not only worked on but also supervised the renovation of the new quarters for the Aegean Center of the Fine Arts.

He painted the old building coral. And the coral color caused some controversy with the tradition-minded residents of Paroikia. They wanted the conventional white with blue trim, so prevalent on the island. Because of their feelings, the refurbishing effort was closely watched by the traditionalists.

"I'd like to see the whole street in our color!" said John, who stood his ground.

"I can't tell you how many times some people sent the police out here during the reconstruction of the building. People would complain about the color, and I tried to be above board about the whole situation. But it was distracting. I had to pay Social Security for all the workers and make sure they had proper papers because they were Albanians. It cost 20,000 euros just for Social Security."

In spite of the coral choice, locals respected him. However, he had been judged by some Parians to be something he was not. And it had nothing to do with the color of the building. They thought that surely he must be with the CIA and The New Aegean Center was his cover.

"It's a typical thing for the Balkans and Middle Easters," he explained. "They wonder why in God's name would an American want to be here. It's a historical belief. I must have been a front for a CIA operation.

"But there certainly have been American schools that turned out to be CIA operations so their thinking is not unfounded."

BEFORE PAROS, THE NAVAJO EXPERIENCE

John Pack was raised in the Brandywine River region of Delaware and Pennsylvania where he met noted artist Andrew Wyeth who also was a Pennsylvanian and had his studio at Chadds Ford.

After John graduated from high school in 1968, he moved to the Bay Area and attended the University of California at Berkeley, noted in those years as radical because of all the young people there who were revolting against the establishment.

"It was wonderful and wild and I wouldn't change that experience for anything," John told me.

He was fortunate to have had renowned photographer Ansel Adams as a mentor. Adams was a master of black and white photography and of capturing scenes in Yosemite Valley in Northern California.

Then John experienced something that left a lasting impression on his life.

"I was on the fringe and desperate for a change, instead of just falling into doing something… [I wanted] something that made sense to me," he said.

A friend of John's was a pediatrician who lent his services to the Native Americans living on the land in the sprawling portions of Utah, Arizona and New Mexico that were combined to be known as the Navajo Reservation from 1868 until 1969 when the name was changed to Navajo Nation. Through that friend John met people on the reservation and wanted to live there because, among the people, he could visualize an ancient culture that to him was new and alluring.

But there were rules against outsiders actually living on the reservation. So John came up with an idea, agreed to by the Navajo Nation Help Foundation, that would allow him to live on the reservation and use his visual arts talents to photograph life there.

"That was one of the most important transitions of my life," he said. "The Navajo were such a different culture, one that I liked. You learn to listen to nature, so many things.

"The spiritual and mystical things on the reservation are just matter of fact to them. They don't have distractions like we do. They're still in touch with the very subtle things that speak to us on a continual basis if we listen, really listen."

Through John I learned that the Navajo believe the God they receive is a Navajo and both Mother Earth and Father Sky. The four commandments from the Great Spirit are:

Respect Mother Earth;
Respect the Great Spirit;
Respect our fellow man and woman;
Respect individual freedom.

John told me the Navajo also surround themselves with truth, love and perseverance, extending the family and joining others in giving and believing we are all related.

"They believe everything is in God's hands," he said. "What is going to happen will happen. You are responsible for yourself. You have to be."

During the seven years in the 1970s he spent in the sprawling "Navajoland" in the southwest desert, he studied the ways and philosophy of the Indians. That was when he created the respected *Ganado Portfolio,* a photographic portrait of the people on the Ganado Reservation in Navajo country. His time on the reservation was life-changing.

John had talked about the Navajo people the first time we met in the mid-1990s. I felt somewhat envious for not having spent time with the Nation. And after reading a number of books about the plight of these Native Americans and how they got what might be called the "shaft," especially in early American days, I felt lousy for them.

There we were, two guys from the United States, sitting on an ancient island in the Greek Cyclades and discussing an ancient people in the land that had produced us, one a photographic artist and the other a writer.

What else might we discover? Oddly enough, we both were intrigued by something else from the Great Southwest: rodeo.

MAKING THE RIDE LAST

When we were talking about his stay on the reservation, John mentioned that he became intrigued with rodeo because it was popular in the Navajo Nation.

In area, the Nation is nearly as large as the state of West Virginia and that makes it larger than 10 U.S. states. The U.S. Census Bureau puts its population at under 300,000 people.

During our conversation, John happened to mention that he'd once met Larry Mahan when the superstar of professional rodeo visited the reservation.

I had become friends with Larry when I was working on my sociological study of the rodeo cowboy for my book *On Down the Road* in the mid-1970s. John and I sat there and exchanged stories, and I told him that when I got back home I'd send him my book on rodeo, which I did.

Mahan was aware that John had the perfect build for bull-riding, being small and compact with stout, long legs. Mahan had done shows on the reservation and noticing John's build told him, "You're a bull rider."

John said he thought, "Why not give it a try?"

But practicality raised its sensible head, something John listened to and I have a history of ignoring.

"I was on deck to ride the bull, which turned out to be a monster," John recalled. "Everybody was all excited, and I kept looking at that monster. Then I chickened out and got out of there."

Oddly enough, Mahan also had a hand with my bull-riding career. I got on a bull during an exhibition at the Mesquite Championship

Rodeo in a suburban Dallas town called, yes, Mesquite – named after a local creek that is lined by the skimpy desert tree.

Mahan and Walt Garrison, the Dallas Cowboys football star who also was a rodeo cowboy, teased me that I would never get on a bull. But with expert tutoring from my friend Don Gay, the multi-time professional bull-riding champion, I was confident enough to give it a try.

When I saw the bull I had second thoughts, but you never dare someone of Irish-Scottish ancestry. Besides, publicity had gotten out about my madness and that drew a crowd: Friends, neighbors and a photographer for *The Dallas Morning News* were there as was a cameraman from a local television station.

So John obviously had more common sense in the Navajo Nation than I did in a Dallas suburb. I stayed on the bull for 4.9 of the required eight seconds and when he threw me, I fortunately landed on my head or otherwise I might have been seriously hurt. A friend got a video off television and everybody loves to play it backwards with me leaping off my head to land atop the bull.

"I disgraced myself, my family and my country," I admitted to John.

THE AGE OF AMBITION

In Paroikia John is a recognizable figure, warmly greeted by the locals. People continually greet him when he's walking in the Market Street area. Once when John and I were leaving the Center, two women, one holding a baby, stopped and hugged him. Then one of them proudly announced, "You have become the baby's uncle." John smiled and said, "Yes, thank you, I will be."

One afternoon John and I were visiting when a few students with the bright enthusiasm of youth came back from lunch and paused to talk to him. Two of them were earning extra money by helping with the school's business office tasks.

But not all the students were "kids." Working on a computer near the back entrance of the school, was another student, a middle-aged woman. When we'd talked earlier, she'd said, "I bet you're surprised someone my age would come to the school with all these young people."

"No, not at all," I said. "I'm impressed and glad you're here, still interested in learning and having new experiences. Actually, I'm proud of you."

There's a Guest Book in which students express what the Aegean Center experience has meant to them. Reading through these comments, you discover that the goal – shared by founder Brett Taylor and determined director John Pack – has been to create a haven for free expression and personal education every semester. Some of the comments:

"I utter the complete truth in saying I learned more in three months than I learned in two years at the university. I learned not only about art but also relationships with others, relationship with myself and to appreciate whatever is thrown my way… The Aegean Center has been the best series of memories of my life." – Stephenie Taskey

"Our daughter left in September rather shy and reserved and came home an enthusiastic, outgoing confident young woman, prepared and ready to embrace the next stage of her life." – Margaret Taylor about her daughter, Arina.

"The Aegean Center remains the single most inspiring arts education I have ever had." – Julian, a university graduate with a BFA in painting.

John said students are my*steriously attracted to Paros*. "Some of them have told me that they had been to Santorini and other beautiful islands but that Paros feels best for them. This hunk of marble has an inherent magic. It's like they're lured back here."

Sandy and I could relate.

CHAPTER 15
'OXI!' — THE WORD OF LEGEND

What came to Paros before the Aegean Center and before Kostas built House No. 5? Long before Sandy and I claimed Paros as our tranquil home in the Aegean, there was a Paros that was a prize in a world war that brought agony and mayhem to an ordinarily peaceful place. That wartime history of Paros and the post-conflict Greek civil war have had an effect on the present and, probably, the future. But the island and its people are resilient and they prefer change that is for the better.

***

GREEK'S ANCIENT HISTORY is dramatically influential on its people and, now and then, the world. Its more recent history has had the same effect. And one particular moment in Greek history – before TV, before computers – continues to echo all the way to Washington.

In 1935 King George II, regarded as a figurehead, reclaimed the throne of Greece. Nine months later he named General Ioannis Metaxas as Prime Minister. They ruled together, with the king endorsing the general's ideas.

Then came a day that would be celebrated into the 21st Century on Paros and throughout Greece. On October 28, 1940, in response to Italian dictator Benito Mussolini's demand that Greece open itself to Fascist occupation, General Metaxas forcefully spoke a single word and achieved everlasting fame throughout Greece.

"*Oxi!*" he declared.

One word. "Oxi." "No" in Greek; "No" in Italian and English. And the Greeks were suddenly fighting the Greco-Italian War as World War II began to explode.

All these decades later, we can look to the 4th Century BC Greek philosopher Heraclitus for hope in such situations. He declared, "There is nothing permanent except change."

THINGS CHANGED FOR THE BETTER

On an *Oxi* Day in the mid-1990s, we saw massive crowds in Paroikia and glorious speeches given by dignitaries and members of the army marching and every time someone shouted *Oxi* the crowd went crazy with glee. I could not help getting excited and feeling proud for this nation that Sandy and I regarded as our adopted country.

There is concrete evidence that the Greeks' stalling of the Italians affected the outcome of World War II. German Field Marshall Wilhelm Keitel, Hitler's *Oberkommando der Wehrmacht* (Supreme Commander of the Armed Forces), said, "The unbelievably strong resistance of the Greeks delayed by two or more months the German attack against Russia. If we had not had this long delay, the outcome of the war would have been different."

This delay meant Germany attempted to conquer the Soviet Union in the horrific Russian winter in 1941. German forces, defeated by both winter and a Russian army fighting for its nation's life, pulled out, making the Third Reich vulnerable on multiple fronts and changing the course of history.

***

FYI: There is even a link to "Oxi" in the United States: The Washington Oxi Day Foundation is a non-profit that tells "American policymakers and the public about the profound role Greece played in bringing about the outcome of World War II." It also celebrates current heroes who "fight to preserve and promote freedom and democracy around the world." And, in a bit of irony, the Oxi Day Foundation also reminds us that Greece, the nation that created democracy, was instrumental in saving it.

PAROS AND MEMORIES

By late 1942 the horror of World War II was a global fact and vivid on Paros and Antiparos. Decades ago in time but perhaps only yesterday in some island memories.

My friend Kostas, like so many of the "Baby Boomers" and subsequent generations, learned of the war from stories heard growing up. The tales came from the "elderly" who had been there when the Germans and Italians occupied Paros and Antiparos.

"The Greeks didn't mind the Italians so much here," he said. "They were easy-going and even married Greek women and seemed to like it here."

But then the Germans came. Within a few days they established a brutal, iron-fisted occupation force, brushing aside the Italians and focusing on the residents of Paros. They made the sure people on Paros, Antiparos and nearby Naxos suffered from horrifying starvation and other indignities of war.

But to paraphrase Heraclitus, "Things change."

HISTORIC CURIOSITIES

Exploring Paros is a joy for people who are interested in ancient churches and ancient cave drawings and the "old ways." You may also encounter "forgotten" elements of the island's past.

Once when I was talking to restaurant owner Theo Maniatis of the Apollon Garden in Paroikia, I mentioned that I'd been told that during World War II the German forces had built an airport and I'd been led to believe it was where the present Paros airport was located. But Theo, who'd rather make meals than war, said he thought it was at Marmara, a quiet, quaint eastern village. To enter Marmara, you drive across a small bridge and right away you are in a small business area with a small store for groceries, a shoe shop and, just outside the main part of town, a very nice bakery.

Sandy and I took off walking east of Marmara – that is Greek for "marbles" but not an indicator of the terrain! – and we were passing beautiful gardens in front of houses and what Sandy called "the most glorious field of poppies I've ever seen." There was no sign of a German airfield.

When we came back into Marmara, a man showing his many years was moving slowly along and we apologized for interrupting his walk, but he said he didn't mind and I asked him where the old German airport had been. Sandy was speaking Greek but he couldn't understand her accent. It didn't help when I used my hand to demonstrate flight and made a noise like an airplane.

Then we encountered a passerby, a woman who turned out to be a teacher, and Sandy asked in Greek about the World War II German airport and told her we couldn't find it. The woman replied that we probably had not gone far enough on our path and just to keep walking and we should find the German airfield.

She was right. We found it below in a valley obviously long enough for Nazi planes to lift off on bombing missions to other islands, such as Crete with its stubborn resistance. Perhaps we were standing where Parians threw makeshift bombs, home-made grenades and fired down on the Germans and their planes.

That was where a young man named Nikolas Stellas, a hero of Lefkes village, attempted to sabotage the airport. Sadly, he was captured by the Germans and hanged May 14, 1944, but he is not forgotten. There is a bust of Stellas in the village of Marmara and each May 14 there is a memorial service and celebration honoring this hero.

THE WAR AFTER THE WAR

When the Germans withdrew from Greece in 1944, the British brought the Communist and loyalist guerrillas together in an uneasy coalition. But after the Big War, the Communist groups refused to disband and the Civil War broke out as the rival partisans turned their guns on each other.

In 1947 Secretary of State George Marshall enacted the Marshall Plan which was designed to diplomatically prevent Communism from taking a stronghold in war torn countries such as Greece.

That same year U.S. President Harry Truman strongly advocated that America provide money, military and economic aid to two struggling nations, Greece and Turkey. It would be called The Truman Doctrine and would allow the U.S. to take action and arm any country threatened by Communism.

Greece came under influence of the U.S. and joined NATO in 1951. And all of this help and respect is why there's a statue of Harry Truman in Athens – it's there in gratitude for helping rescue Greece from Communism and for the American Allies' efforts to block its expansion.

***

These wartime challenges and triumphs – they all affected an island where beauty and peace are appreciated and where art is treasured and people are endearing. Sacrifices and heroism and determination all combined decades earlier to give us House No. 5 on a peaceful island in the Cyclades.

CHAPTER 16

A NEW AND BETTER REALITY: BUILDING MODERN PAROS

After World War II, Parians suffered economic problems and, as older people clung to the past by making their living with such things as farming and fishing, the younger generation wanted more and began relocating to the mainland. They went not just to Athens but also to the United States and other countries where opportunity beckoned.

On Paros the exodus slowed to a degree when education, housing, communications and other services were progressively upgraded.

And for years practically the only outsiders who visited Paros were European travelers on holiday and especially wealthy Athenians seeking respite from the city.

Certainly there were exceptions, but generally, Americans in the 1950s and 1960s didn't seem to think that much about vacationing on the Greek islands, other than well-marketed and tourist-friendly Santorini and Mykonos. Americans were more drawn to spending their holidays on the U.S. coasts and nearby islands or, perhaps, taking a slow cruise to England, Italy, Spain, France and/or other countries far and wide. As the Jet Age evolved into a profitable reality in the late 1950s and as aircraft became bigger and faster, the world shrank and Europe became more accessible and, of course, marketable to a wider range of American travelers.

FICTION INSPIRES REAL TOURISM

The writings of Henry Miller (*The Colossus of Maroussi*) and Lawrence Durrell *(The Greek Islands)* certainly drew attention to Greece and Athens and, of course, the islands, including the Cyclades, and movies about Greece cultivated the interest of foreigners.

A popular hit that attracted a lot of attention in the U.S. was *Never on Sunday* (1960), directed by Connecticut-born American movie director Jules Dassin and starring the woman who would become his wife in 1964, the internationally adored Greek actress Melina Mercouri. She portrayed an entertaining, so to speak, and engaging prostitute who never practiced her trade on Sundays. Dassin not only directed, but had the male lead as the man determined to reform her.

The movie was filmed in Piraeus, and the English version became a success in America and was nominated for five Oscars, including Melina as best actress. She certainly captured the attention of American moviegoers with sexy displays that, today, would probably not even inspire a raised eyebrow. She made other successful movies and later became Greek's popular, successful Minister of Culture, and was honored and mourned when she died at 69 on March 6, 1994 in New York City. She received a state funeral in Athens four days later. Greece embraced Jules and he embraced Greece – he was 96 when he died on March 31, 2008, in Athens.

In 1964 Greece enjoyed another boost when Anthony Quinn captured imaginations as the fun-loving title character in the celebrated film *Zorba the Greek.* Many more films were shot in the Greek islands and distributed around the world, inspiring visitors from the

U.S. and other nations. Movies, yes, became travel commercials for these beautiful islands and their beautiful people.

Tourism increased on Mykonos when celebrities such as the actors Yul Brynner and Jean Seberg built houses there. Monaco's Prince Rainier and his wife, the beautiful former American actress Grace Kelly, frequented the island and they also visited Santorini, known for its volcanic beauty, the happy tourist-attracting remnant of a 16th century BC eruption. Some historians believe that cataclysm there was the inspiration for Plato's famous story of Atlantis.

THE TEXAN MEETS THE MAYOR OF PAROS – BUT, WHY?

More and more visitors came to Paros, and by word of mouth and limited publicity, the development of tourism began in earnest in the late 1970s, then received a huge boost in 1982 when the island's airport was completed near the coastal village of Alyki. Instead of the six-hour ferry trips from the mainland, visitors could fly from Athens to Paros in about 40 minutes or less on two-engine, propeller-driven planes of Olympic Airlines or take the more expensive hydrofoils that cut trips on the ferries in half. And Paroikia city officials also became more aggressive regarding tourism.

I was surprised one mid-October morning in 1998 when Kostas came by House No. 5 and told me the Mayor of Paroikia would like to see me at my convenience.

I assured him I would be flattered to meet Mayor Kostas Argouzis, although I couldn't imagine why he wanted to see me. Neither could my friend Kostas.

But I hopped onto the back of Kostas' motorbike and off we went to the mayor's office in Paroikia. Fortunately, Kostas was there to interpret because Mayor Argouzis did not speak English, and as usual I had trouble conversing in Greek, although I believed I was right on schedule after Sandy gave me in a book called *Learn Greek in 25 Years* by Brian Church. Sandy considered my abilities for a few seconds and said, "I think you're behind."

Mayor Argouzis was very cordial and interested in my ideas for attracting more tourists to Paros and perhaps paying travel journalists to write about the island. I made suggestions, and as we left, I still wondered how he knew about me.

Were the Famous Fates, once again, at work making connections?

A TEXAS CONNECTION

Chris Semos was one of the good guys in Texas politics, a longtime member of the Texas House of Representatives and also a Dallas County Commissioner and a tireless civic worker. As a youngster, he had helped his family establish the legend of the Torch Restaurant, a popular dining spot that his father Victor opened in 1948 after migrating to the United States from Greece. The Torch, operated by the family until the structure burned in 1970, might well have been the first Greek restaurant in Dallas, perhaps even among the first in the entire southern U.S.

When Chris retired from politics, he began taking groups of Texans on tours to his ancestral homeland of Greece. But he never led tours to Paros. I kept telling him what a wonderful place Paros was and how nice Parians, such as Kostas Akalestos, are, and that Sandy and I had first visited the island in 1992 and we'd kept returning ever since because it was so great.

So I convinced Chris to include a Paros tour on his itinerary. In the summer of 1998, he finally put together a group of 54 Texans who I hoped were NOT going to be the "wild and woolly" type. I wished we could have been on Paros when Chris and his group were there, but Sandy and I had already scheduled our trip to Paros for October that year.

I got a postcard dated June 23, 1998, from Chris who wrote: "The

54 Texans all fell in love with Paros! I saw Kostas Akalestos and his wife and daughter briefly tonight and told the mayor how much you have already written about Paros. They're all waiting for you in October."

The global reach of Texas, that was the answer to the mystery of how the mayor knew about me.

PAROS EVOLVES IN THE NEW CENTURY

So tourism increased even more on Paros in the 1990s, but that was nothing like the boom of the 2000s when the tourist season grew and stretched from mid-April to mid-October, when the weather was usually unpredictable. Tourism became the island's main source of income, and white with blue trim apartment complexes and villas and houses began to spring up everywhere. Fortunately, the ever-thickening layer of progress had not obscured the island's ancient history nor relegated the elderly to the shadows of the forgotten.

Most Parians agreed that the coming of more and more tourists brought inevitable change but also prosperity to the island. In a way, the locals began to live separate lifestyles, one when the tourists were on Paros and another after they left – yet both authentically warm, friendly and true to their Parian goodness.

Restaurateur Theo Maniatis of the Apollon Garden reminded me that the older, rural people did not change like residents in the larger cities. "They still work their farms and bring their goods – the olives, tomatoes, zucchini, the grapes, the onions — into town to sell what they have grown."

Then, with a twinkle, Theo added, "Of course, they are NOT opposed to *selling* their fruits and vegetables to *tourists*."

CHAPTER 17

TRYING TO REACH PAROS AFTER 9/11

There was a genuinely eerie feeling that afternoon of September 21, 2001, as Sandy and I arrived at Dallas-Fort Worth International Airport to catch our flight to New York City. The usual hubbub was missing because skycaps were scarce, there was a shortage of taxis and there were no large herds of people scrambling in and out of the terminal.

Ordinarily, the waiting area of the Delta Airlines gate would have been crowded yet there weren't enough passengers to fill half the plane. We were somewhat apprehensive to begin with but the situation would worsen.

This dramatic difference at one of the world's busiest airports was all due to the ever-present frightening and well-founded fear emanating from that bright, clear morning 10 days earlier, the horrifying events of September 11, 2001. Terrorists hijacked four commercial passenger jets, each filled with fuel that made them incendiary bombs. The terrorists crashed two of the planes into the Twin Towers of the World Trade Center in New York City. They crashed another one into the Pentagon, center of America's military organizations, in Arlington, Va., across the Potomac River from the nation's capital.

But the passengers on the fourth plane rose up and attacked the hijackers, resulting in the plane crashing into a field in Pennsylvania, far away from its intended target, possibly the U.S. Capitol in Washington, D.C.

No survivors.

Lingering, terrifying, surreal images flashed across television screens everywhere, first showing the North Tower with black smoke and fire rising upward and, as the cameras continued to roll, a second plane appeared and crashed into the South Tower, exploding in red and white clouds of debris. And there was pandemonium and people were trapped in the buildings. Some 200 jumped from upper windows or the roofs to their deaths and a couple, holding hands, leaped into space, and the towers shook and slowly crumbled in a kind of inanimate death rattle of debris. Fierce clouds of dust, spreading like wildfire, engulfed the area in waves as both towers collapsed within two hours. Other buildings in the area were destroyed. In all, from New York to Pennsylvania to the Pentagon, 2,977 people were killed. They were office workers, executives, first-responders and others who died as American heroes.

The suicide hijackers from Osama bin Laden's network of Al Qaeda terrorists had successfully accomplished what we could never have believed would happen. They struck our most prominent city, a global financial center and the hub of U.S. and world transportation, plus the symbol of our military power. All in one incident of terror. It became the strongest of messages that, in this 21st century, the American homeland was vulnerable.

IT'S ALL PERSONAL: THE ATTACK AND THE EMOTIONS

Sandy and I had planned our trip to Paros for months and made reservations with Delta Airlines well in advance to fly to New York City on September 16, change planes in Athens and then fly to Paros on an Olympic Airlines two-engine propeller plane. But after 9/11 the airline industry obviously was on alert and flights kept getting cancelled, so we had no idea when we might leave. Perhaps, we shouldn't go, we thought.

After all, the U.S. would certainly retaliate and war could be imminent. It was determined the hijackers had been trained in Al Qaeda camps in Afghanistan and our country might be attacked again. The situation could cause an upheaval in the Middle East. There were just so many dangerous possibilities.

Because America keeps moving, selected flights began to leave again. But our Delta flight was called off day after day. Maybe that was a sign we weren't supposed to go. After all, the world which was erupting in turmoil seemed pretty close to Greece.

Then we got a call from a Delta representative telling us that the airline's first flight to Greece since the terrorist attack was a "go" on September 21, five days after we were originally scheduled to depart. We weren't particularly happy about being on the first flight going through, but we'd already lost time on Paros and didn't much want to miss any more time there. And, frankly, I was also angry that a bunch of terrorists could change our lives. The Irish part of me wanted to challenge the rare possibility that a dangerous destiny awaited us whereas the Scottish part of me cautioned, "Let's think about this."

I thought perhaps I could go on to Athens, testing the waters so to speak, and if it turned out okay, Sandy could come later.

"I won't do that," she said. "If something happens I want us to be together."

"It just seems like a good idea that I go first," I said. "Nothing's going to happen. But if it did... I'm older and more expendable... and would be expendable even if I weren't older and...."

"No. We'll go together," she steadfastly declared. "It'll be an adventure."

"Okay, it'll be an adventure," I said. "We'll be on Delta's first flight to New York City, which has already been attacked, and then to Greece, a place much closer to the action than Texas."

"Right," she agreed, recalling some of my escapades. "Another adventure."

PARANOIA, WIRETAPS AND PEOPLE

The strangest thing had happened before we left our home in the beautiful forested area of Northeast Texas for DFW International Airport, about 120 miles west of our house and right smack between Dallas on the east and Fort Worth on the west.) I fought my way out of a nap and got up to answer the ringing telephone. There was silence on the line. The same thing had happened a number of times recently. The phone would ring, I'd answer and there would be nothing but silence on the other end before somebody broke the connection.

But this time as I started to hang up, a man's voice seemed to be asking somebody which of the last four digits on our two telephones were correct. I said, "Hello, who is this?" two or three times, my voice getting louder and louder. Still no answer. Keeping cool in my own inevitable way I screamed, "WHO THE HELL IS THIS?"

Silence. And then I heard a recording of my voice – the dialogue came from a telephone conversation I'd recently had with a friend.

And again, I asked, "Who the hell is this!" The connection was cut.

"I think our phone is tapped," I told Sandy, explaining what had happened.

It was a little disconcerting that the National Security Agency or some such might have secretly wire-tapped my phone in search of possible terrorists and that this clandestine group had let me hear one of its recordings. That was hardly skillful cloak-and-dagger stuff.

With the delayed flights and our concerns about the terror situation, I had contacted our friend Kostas on Paros by telephone and asked if he thought we might, as Americans, have problems in Athens with, say the Revolutionary Organization 17 November, a leftist anti-American, anti-Greek establishment, anti-Turkey, anti-NATO organization. He said he didn't think Athens would be a problem and knew Paros wouldn't.

So here I was talking over the telephone about war and politics while maintaining contact with somebody in a foreign country. Key words probably would alert the NSA if indeed it had been authorized to monitor and pry.

I called a friend who had some expertise on wiretapping and he was puzzled. He said my description of what happened did not indicate the government was tapping my line.

"But there are private detectives who illegally tap telephones," he cautioned.

I couldn't imagine why a private detective would tap my phone. Yet, here I was in a situation where there might have been a mistake (goodness knows there were a lot of them in those days and days to follow) and I might wake up one morning with a military tank drawing a bead on our house, the gun barrel reaching out between a couple of towering pine trees!

I called the local telephone company and nobody was sure what to do, other than monitor my incoming calls for a week or so. But we'd be leaving for Greece. Just for the record – in case anyone is listening – I am not a subversive nor have I ever been a subversive nor do I have friends or acquaintances that I know of who are subversives. And the last time I checked, we still enjoy freedom of speech in America, on or off the phone.

I doubt that some people I told about this episode believed my phone had been tapped – until it was disclosed some five years later that President Bush had authorized the NSA to gather information on telephone calls of Americans all along. It was called the "NSA's warrantless surveillance."

Phones aside, there was one more big worry about going to Greece. A State Department advisory cautioned, "U.S. citizens and interests abroad may be at increased risk of terrorist actions from extremist groups."

There was also a warning for American citizens to be careful in certain countries and cities such as Athens, where the 17 November group was known to operate.

Tourists were advised not to be conspicuous, to vary their routes to where they were staying, to be on the lookout for anybody following them and "to just be cautious."

I pointed out to Sandy that, being blonde and light complexioned she could pass for Swiss or Norwegian or German. "With your camera strapped around your shoulder and wearing a Texas Rangers gimme cap nobody would ever figure you were a conspicuous American," she said, smiling "Nordically."

Friends and family didn't want us to go. They kept reminding us of the possibilities, such as a Muslim population in Greece that might not like Americans or, perhaps, if there were indeed another terrorist attack or war in the Middle East, we might not be able to come back home indefinitely.

Our friend Anne Edwards took down an address where we might be reached on Paros so she could send a care package if we got stranded. My longtime pal Bob Williams pointed out with a straight face that if we were taken hostage he could probably raise thousands to get Sandy released but the top dollar he'd pay for my freedom would be about 20 bucks.

THE FLIGHT GETS THE GO-AHEAD

Someone from Delta called to say that our flight was finally, actually going to leave and, as we began packing and getting ready to drive to DFW, heavy rains fell on our house in the woods of Northeast Texas. I was rushing to do some last-minute work at my desk when water started falling on me. The damn roof was leaking. No telling how long it would take to get it fixed. If we left, we might come back to a sunken house.

"Maybe this is another sign we shouldn't go," said Sandy.

"I was just thinking the same thing."

"Well?"

"Well, I don't know."

I talked to friends who said not to worry because they'd get the roof patched to keep out the rain until we could return and have it fixed properly. Still, we worried about the house. If this was just another in a series of forewarnings, perhaps we shouldn't go to Greece, a country of magnificent beauty but legendary foreboding.

This was counteracted by a lingering feeling that this could be the sixth and last time we'd be able to go to Paros because not only was the future of travel iffy but the present was a bit shaky. So, aching to be on Paros, off we went toward Dallas and the airport.

Security really didn't seem that different but surely it was without our noticing. Our carry-on baggage went through the x-ray machine but I'd expected they'd be searched. I hoped everybody's luggage would be searched forever more.

And once we were settled in the waiting area at the departure gate, two young Arab men showed up, got their boarding passes and sat near us. I thought: *Oh great! That's all we need. Surely they've been thoroughly checked. Or have they? They were talking and then whispering to each other. What were they saying?*

I had on sunglasses and pretended to read a newspaper while watching them closely, their every move. The glasses were loose and kept slipping down my nose. Later I would imagine that I looked like Inspector Clouseau, the Peter Sellers *Pink Panther* movie character. But that was later. This was now and I was concerned.

Sandy stirred in her seat, nervously. She was watching and wondering about them, too. You hate to profile but it was impossible not to at that time. Terrorists notwithstanding, she'd already had a frightening year of flying.

She was an entertainer in those days and traveled a lot. When she flew in a small plane in a snowstorm in Wenatche, Washington, the pilot landed blindly in the blizzard, almost missing the field. Another time, the pilot of a commercial plane, flying low in a thunderstorm, mentioned that the flight might divert to Austin rather than landing at DFW because it was running low on fuel.

And once, she'd been aboard a commercial fight that was coming in for a landing when it suddenly pulled up because another plane was on the runway.

She thought maybe there was a message there for her to stop flying. Did she need one more flight to tempt The Fates? But, of course, the strongest message was the September 11 tragedy.

FEAR OF THINGS ONCE NORMAL

A couple with a small child sat near us in the waiting area. The kid was wearing them out, running here and there. At least his parents started getting him under control.

And then another man appearing to be from the Middle East got our attention. He was very stocky, dark, with a shaven head. He sat down and began reading.

"It's a copy of *Penthouse*," said Sandy.

"Do terrorists try to look very normal by reading *Penthouse*?" I asked, my mind racing.

Damn, he's making eye contact with one of the Arabs. Is he one of them? *He's pretty stocky. I might hold my own against the young Arabs but he could be a problem....*

"I'm not sure we should go," said Sandy, who had turned very pale.

"I don't know. I could go on and you could come later," I mentioned again. "Why don't we do that?"

"No," she said, getting up and walking toward the restroom. She returned in a little while, confessing that she was trying to get control of her nerves. I felt terrible, endangering her by not insisting we cancel our trip. We weren't the only worried people in the waiting area. Others kept looking at the Arabs. Was it just inevitable paranoia?

"This is too obvious," I said. "Surely, they'd never get through security."

"Security didn't seem that secure," Sandy replied.

ON THE PLANE WITH OUR 'BAGGAGE' OF CAUTION

The boarding call came and we filed into a short line with no turning back. So we would fly to New York and then board the first flight after 9/11 from there to Athens. I figured it would have been better taking a second or third flight. Anyway, we took our seats. The young Arabs sat two vacant rows behind us, speaking their language.

The plane took off. There was no way I wanted them behind us. There were empty seats across the aisle and back of them so I nudged Sandy and told her we were moving. We took the seats at the very back of the plane, well behind them but with them in sight, and behind a big guy who was wearing a robe, earrings and a neck chain. I couldn't find the guy with a *Penthouse*. Maybe he didn't get on the flight or was hiding in the restroom.

Nodding toward a husky, red-haired man talking to a stewardess in back of the plane, I said to Sandy, "I think that guy back there is an Air Marshall or maybe not. "

Now, years later, it seems like we were engaging in a bit of overreacting, but under the conditions of the time I'd been sizing up passengers who might help in an emergency. I watched the young Arabs, who could have been the nicest, most peaceful people on the plane. Nevertheless, I was actually planning what I'd do if they started toward the cockpit and I was hoping help would be on the way immediately. People talk about how they'd do this or that in life-threatening situations, but it's very difficult to step over the line when you're scared beyond reason.

Yet, after what the heroic passengers in the fourth hijacked plane did, I suspect you'd be much more likely to react, knowing you're probably going to die anyway.

I prepared for the worst without much to aid the preparation. I had a pair of writing pens in my shirt pocket and figured they would be hazardous to the health of eyes. And I was thinking that somehow I'd have to try to tackle one of the guys if they started to the cockpit, maybe knocking over another one in the process. I'm not a bad tackler… as long as I didn't stumble and knock myself out. Maybe nobody would help and I'd be bludgeoned to death by the terrorists.

Sandy had the encased camera out of the carry-on. "I know what you're thinking," she said. "You're going to use the pens as weapons. I'm going to swing the camera and bash one of them on the head."

"You'd probably miss and hit me in the head," I said. There have been times when she's accidentally injured me, an innocent bystander.

I told her I could see the headline: "Woman Kills Husband with Camera on Peaceful Flight." She laughed. I don't know why but even during periods of stress our conversation takes on a lighthearted aspect.

The tension had exhausted her. I knew that because she skipped eating lunch. And she wouldn't take her eyes off the Arab fellows.

I wouldn't, either. "Okay, try to sleep," I said. "I'll watch them. I promise. I'm not sleepy. Please."

She drifted off to sleep. When she woke up she was holding tightly to the camera. One of the young Arabs had moved across the aisle and was thanking a stewardess who had brought him a soft drink. The other one had sprawled out over two seats, apparently sleeping. The large man in the robe kept dozing off in the seat in front of us. He'd doze, then wake up and look back at us and around the plane.

The 3½-hour flight to John F. Kennedy International Airport in New York City was smooth and safe and, like other passengers, we looked out the windows but could not see the devastation, could not see where the Twin Towers once stood.

But there was a very uplifting feeling when, as we left the plane, the flight attendants, pilot and co-pilot thanked us for flying Delta. We thanked them and told them they were appreciated. After 9/11, you could imagine how they felt each time they flew.

Our carry-on baggage – and that of other passengers – didn't seem to be scrutinized as we went to the gate toward our Delta connection that would take us to Athens. I worried, briefly, then remembered that we'd been checked out in Dallas and thus were in a secure area and that anybody boarding in New York would also have already gone through inspection. We'd also expected a three-hour, maybe four-hour, delay in boarding and we were concerned that, perhaps, the flights would be cancelled and we would have to stay in New York.

Sure, we were anxious to get to Greece, but if it took a long delay or a cancellation for the Delta people to feel safe, that would be fine with us.

A TAXI DRIVER'S VIEW

The then-new Athens International Airport is at Spata, about 20 kilometers east of Athens in the Attica region. The airport opened in March of that year and was world class as opposed to the old Ellenikon Airport, a former U.S. Army and U.S. Air Force base. The new airport was named after Eleftherios Venizelos, known for modernizing the country in the 20th Century, and it would be ready for the 2004 Olympics in Athens. But, in spite of the official name, even the Greeks just called it, "The International Airport at Spata."

Our taxi driver was a pleasant guy who talked about how he hated the cowardly terrorists. He also told us about how much Athens had changed and that when he was a boy people actually lived in houses as opposed to apartment buildings near the main part of town.

"Sadly, my old neighborhood has changed," he said. "People they are rushing everywhere without taking the time to visit as the city continues to grow."

"When I go back to the old neighborhood today in Dallas, nobody is sitting outside at night and there are bars on the windows of their homes," I said. "Everybody used to sit on the porch and visit with neighbors at night."

"It was the same with me here in Athens," he said.

We were speaking in English, although I'd throw in a Greek word or two from my limited vocabulary, unlike Sandy who had not only learned the Greek alphabet but also how to pronounce the different sounds.

The driver continued to talk about how he loved America and proudly took us past a statue. "Yes, do you know who that is?" he asked.

Of course, I did: President Harry Truman.

"He did much for us after World War II and is a popular figure here," the driver said.

It was nice to hear him say that although I knew some locals would not especially agree about President Truman's benevolence because they believed he wasn't particularly thinking about helping Greece but was just trying to keep Communism from spreading around the globe.

The driver told us he had taken two women from the United States from the airport to the hotel on September 11. He said when they got into the taxi they began to cry.

"Madams, please, can I help with the sadness you have? What can be the matter?" he recalled asking them.

"They told me terrorists had crashed into the Twin Towers in New York and they had friends there. They told me they worked there and would have been victims had they not been on vacation.

"It was so sad and made me very angry," he said. "I had not known what had happened that day until they told me. I hate the terrorists and wish them terrible deaths."

A NIGHT AT THE HERA, A DIFFERENCE IN MOOD

We stayed overnight at the Hera Hotel in Athens and, as suggested by a friend, tried to check in with the American Embassy, letting them know our names, passport numbers, where we were going and how long we'd be there in case we would run into trouble. It was the weekend. The embassy offices were closed but a telephone message gave numbers to call in case of an emergency. So, we mailed the embassy copies of our itinerary and passports, wondering if we'd used enough stamps.

"I'm not sure we want to go to the embassy anyway," Sandy pointed out. "Protesters storm embassies. Embassies get blown up."

"In these times you never know," I said. "No, you never know."

We bought wine, cheese, crackers and the wonderful, addictive Swiss chocolate candy from a small store near the Hera and then ate on the balcony of our room with a view of the Acropolis and the well-lit Parthenon. We always enjoyed our picnics at the Hera and the room with the wonderful view. There had been times on our previous six visits that we'd take long walks to find a restaurant and then return late down dark streets. It seemed safe then. This time we weren't so sure.

The hotel provided a well-dressed man wearing a suit and driving a new automobile to take us from the Hera to the airport so we could catch a flight to Paros.

We had another nice discussion – well, actually the driver and Sandy did, with Sandy making her typical efforts at Greek. She had been trying to teach me various Greek words. I hadn't gotten that far in my efforts to learn the language. One word I had difficulty with was *iremo* – meaning "I am calm." I could never say it correctly for Sandy. I would get it wrong. This time when the driver mentioned that women were chatty, which Sandy was at the time, I said, "*Iremo*" perfectly and the driver started laughing like crazy.

"You get more mileage out of your one word than I do out of my sentences," she said. "That's the first time you got the word right."

When I told her I'd try to teach her the important words she gave me a dirty look.

Thanks to the well-dressed driver we arrived at the airport very early and were sitting in the lobby when three Arabs sat near us. They were looking around nervously and had carry-on baggage and boxes tied with strings. Had it not been for 9/11, I never would have noticed. Greek officers or soldiers were watching them and then came over and asked them questions. The next thing I knew they were taking off, moving on. I guess security had improved since we'd left DFW.

CHAPTER 18

AFTER 9/11 ON PAROS

We made it to Paros without any issues. And after Sandy and I settled into House No. 5 in the last week of September, I would drive the short distance to Paroikia to purchase the *International Herald Tribune* to keep track of the ticking clock on America's response to the 9/11 attack.

Then on the evening of Sunday, Oct. 7, 2001, about two weeks after we arrived on Paros, that response began.

We didn't really have to wait for the daily paper to get the news. The skies over Paros were soon the flight path of warplanes.

The U.S. and the British launched a fierce, devastating six-hour bombing attack in Afghanistan on military targets. The goal was to disrupt and/or kill the ruling Taliban and Osama bin Laden and his Al Qaeda associates. This was followed by ground forces of the Northern Alliance, joined by Afghan refugees from earlier battles with the Taliban, entering battle. As always in war, civilians became victims.

In addition to newspaper reports, there were physical reminders in the sunsets on the veranda as jets probably doing maneuvers flew over. Sure, there was beauty as always as the wonderful evening and twilight skies lit up with multitudes of stars. But there was also the distraction of planes flying high overhead and leaving lingering white contrails in their wake. The normally comforting and beautiful daytime skies also were changed by these planes on missions to who-knows-where. One night we counted 16 planes passing high above us. We weren't sure they were part of the war or just maneuvers or Greek aircraft challenging Turkish planes that were violating Greek airspace over the Aegean.

Planes, bombs, missiles were on our minds. So one morning we were into a discussion in the kitchen about war in Afghanistan and Iraq when there was this incredibly loud roar coming closer and closer and raging so loud that it became ear-shattering as it seemed to shake House No. 5 and the terrain around us.

We wondered: Rogue fighter plane, launching a missile coming right at us? Was it too late to run? In unison in our beloved, peaceful House No. 5 we ducked… DUCKED!

Then, we started laughing. Sure, all we had to do was duck and it would zoom through the kitchen right over our heads and come out the other side of the house! We hurried outside and saw a jet flying at very low level over the houses at *Agia Irini*, banking and climbing back up into the sky. I hoped everybody else ducked in time.

Who knew why? Not us.

SUDDENLY NOT LIKING THE AMERICANS

Sandy and I have always been treated wonderfully on visits to Greece and especially Paros. But during the American war in Iraq a woman at the camera and video store on the corner of a strip of stores near the main street of the *agora* didn't appear to like me because I was American.

I thought maybe she was just having a bad day or two or three. Each morning I went into the shop I'd smile and greet her with "*Kalimera*" and she would just stare at me.

One day I noticed the television was on, showing tragedies of the war, such as images of maimed children. The woman looked at the television and then at me with disapproval in her eyes. Although it was my time to be waited on, she ignored me and accommodated a customer in line behind me. Her treatment had surprised me because others in shops were nice as always.

I wanted to say, "Hey, I didn't do it. I've never maimed or killed anybody and was totally against the war in Iraq."

I struggled but forced myself to remain cool, and she finally waited on me. I thanked her, waved goodbye and walked out. Though I understood her perspective, I felt bad, sensing her disapproval.

There had been one other time I felt censure in the face of public tragedy. After President Kennedy was assassinated in Dallas, I was traveling in Mexico. Anytime I mentioned I was from Dallas, relationships and exchanges with some people would suddenly turn cold.

SMILES AND A HUG

In Paroikia, Sandy had a similar although more outspoken experience with a produce man in a grocery store where she often shopped. She would go in wearing her Greek fisherman's hat and the man would smile and greet her with, "Ahh, the *Capitan*."

Then one day during our final week on Paros, when the U. S. had intensified its attacks in Afghanistan, she was in the grocery store and the man, who had never asked her before, inquired, "Where is it you are from, *Capitan*?"

"The United States," she said.

"Ah, the war nation, the one who likes war."

"Not me. I don't like war."

"It is your government. Ah, what is it you think about what is happening?"

"I don't like war for us or any country."

"You have the nuclear weapons…"

"Hey, all I'm here for is to buy some celery," she added, knowing it wouldn't be prudent to get into a big scene. I thought she'd lost an admirer. But a couple of trips later to the store, all was forgotten and he smiled and was cordial again.

I often stopped to get gas for our rental car at a service station near the airport. This huge Greek man, with long hair sticking out from under his cap to his shoulders, filled the tank and was always very cordial as we conversed in his limited English and my very, very limited Greek. When he asked where I was from, I told him the U.S. and he said, "Oh yes. Have a good stay here!" I said, "*Efharisto*" (thank you) and "*Signomi*" (excuse me) for my problems in speaking Greek.

"That is nothing!" he said. "*Signomi* for my limited English," he said. We always visited whether he was busy or not.

Another day, after leaving the woman at the camera shop, I stopped to fill up with gas before going home. "You do not look happy," he said. "Why is this?"

I told him about my experience with the woman at the camera shop because I was American. I was standing outside the car and he started walking toward me.

I thought he'd suddenly changed his attitude and I didn't know whether to run or what as he grabbed me, hugged me tightly and practically lifted me off the ground and patted me on the back.

"It was not you but your government she was angry about," he said. "We love you, the person, as other Americans. We are the same, nice people. *Ne* (yes), it is our governments that do things that make people sad and angry. But you and myself are alike. It is not you, OK. It is your government. Like the Greek one we have, they are not so honest, I think."

He was smiling and waving at me when I drove off. On the following trips to Paros, I'd stop whether I needed gas or not and visit him and he always smiled and is ever so friendly like so many Greeks Sandy and I've met over the years.

BOOK III
WHAT THE FATES GAVE US

CHAPTER 19

ONE MAGIC MOMENT IN A BOOK STORE

WE MIGHT HAVE missed Paros altogether if Sandy hadn't stopped in an airport bookshop to kill some time between flights back when she was traveling as an entertainer.

As she browsed this particular store, she came across a book titled *The Harper Independent Traveler: Greek Islands* which happened to be on sale for $3. And knowing Sandy, if it hadn't been on sale, she probably would never have bought it.

So, when she returned, she showed me the book and we scanned it together. All possibilities were open to us. So many intriguing places. What would we choose to do?

"Look!" Sandy said, "Lord Byron loved Samos. Here's a quote from him, 'Dash down your cup of Samian wine!'"

The mention of wine perked me up. I took the book and read about Samos with its beaches and hills and history that seemed to include just about everyone from Athenians to Zeus.

Sandy grabbed the book back. She is a grabber by nature. Pages rustled as she quickly maneuvered here and there excitedly extolling one island only to replace it moments later with another. Her mind works that way. I once told her that she reminded me of what Walt Garrison, the Dallas Cowboys running back and occasional receiver, said of his scrambling quarterback, Roger Staubach: "I just stay put while he runs all over the place. I figure eventually he'll come back to me."

That is my way with Sandy. So, I sat quietly, marveled and listened.

"Oh, Bob!" Sandy gasped. "Listen to this! 'Serifos is a lazy person's island; there are so many good beaches within an easy walk of the port that hotels have been built nowhere else.'"

We joked off and on about the possibility of going to the lazy man's island.

But finally we read and reread what the book said about Paros. It sounded idyllic with its beautiful marble, its beaches and tranquil Butterfly Valley (Petaloudes Park) near Paroikia. And there was this significant element: *It is quiet and "escapes overcrowding."*

And the final point. It is centrally located with good ferry service so that if we wanted, we could always see Paros and easily travel to visit some other place. Later we would discover that once you find paradise you no longer need the guidebook to tell you about "some other place."

We sometimes wonder what might have happened if Sandy hadn't chosen that particular guidebook, but that book seemed to find us as much as Paros awaited us to become our destination and our destiny.

Because of that book, we found beauty, joy, the grace of living and friendships that can, at a moment's notice from our hearts, transport us around the world.

THE WAY WE MET: TV SIGNALS

In fact, I can never think about Paros without thinking about Sandy. If I had never met her, I would never have known Paros. I would never have known the beauty, the sunsets, the white on white, the bougainvillea vines framing the blue doors, Kostas, Theo and all the other warm people of Paros. Sandy. The love of my life. And to think it all started with the Miss America Pageant and continued into a full-blown relationship in a Mexican town just across the border.

One evening in 1971, I was watching the Miss America pageant on television, an event I'd not seen previously because, as a sportswriter, I was usually working nights and weekends. During the talent competition, there was a skit by Miss Kansas that got my attention. Miss Kansas pretended to be a grownup back in the room of her childhood, surrounded by the dolls she'd had. Miss Kansas was a ventriloquist and was carrying on a conversation with her doll, a delightful exchange of old memories.

I not only thought she was very attractive but that she had a nice smile and seemed like such a sweet person. She won the talent event and was a semi-finalist for Miss America. That's nice, I thought, and went on with my life. Later I would learn she used her Miss Kansas scholarship to attend the American Musical and Dramatic Academy in New York. She lived in Greenwich Village for a while, relocated to Houston and later, taking a girlfriend's advice, she moved to Dallas.

Many years later I was a Metro columnist for *The Dallas Morning News,* and a friend suggested that Sandy Rings might make be an interesting column subject. She had entertained all over the world on cruise ships, was also a former Miss Kansas, had the Miss America experience and had occasionally opened a show for singers such as Glen Campbell and Donna Fargo.

When we were introduced, you couldn't miss her contagious smile, among other things. I flipped. Blonde, tall, beautiful. Fun. I was ready for my big hustle! What would be my strategy?

I considered a story about actor Robert Shaw, a favorite of mine. He saw actress Mary Ure at a party, flipped out and told her something like, "I don't care whom you're with. Nobody can treat you as well as I will, so you'll be better off with me." It worked for Shaw. They married. And, I decided, that would be my approach. Perfect.

Sure, I was interviewing her so I could write a good column, but I really wanted a chance to visit with her. Fortunately, it turned out that she certainly had many interesting experiences and was legitimately a good column subject.

Finally, it dawned on me that she was the person I'd seen so long ago on the Miss America Pageant broadcast. I plotted. I invited her to a party I was giving. My Robert Shaw approach never got off the ground. I chickened out. I tried to act so nonchalant, even introducing her to another friend, who put on a big hustle to no avail.

Later I got up nerve enough to call and ask her out to dinner, using my usual overwhelming approach, "I guess you wouldn't want to go to dinner." She said, sure she would, but she was fasting. I took that as a polite excuse she didn't want to go but was trying not to hurt my feelings. So I wrote that one off and pretty much limited my social life to drinks in the dimly lit comfort of Joe Miller's Bar, a media hangout.

A year later she called me at the newspaper – that totally shocked me. She said, "You're really easy to get rid of." Thereafter I wasn't. Sparks flew and we later married – the adventure has been more than splendid.

It has transported us to many places, including a wonderful island that deserves at least four stars in the next edition of the enchanted guide, *The Harper Independent Traveler: Greek Islands*

THE SENSATIONAL SAMBA OF MATAMOROS

Sandy was in show business for years. She's a wonderful singer and a bit of a dancer and, as I'd seen all those years ago, a Miss America talent competition winning ventriloquist. She needed a dummy for that – I finally claimed that role in her routine. Happily.

As a sidelight, I believe our relationship began to take on a more serious aspect after a group of us went to South Padre Island on the lower coast of Texas. The whole bunch went across the border to eat in Matamoras at a popular place called The Drive-In, which was a misnomer because, while it had outstanding food, the waiters wore tuxedos and there was a band and dancing area. You didn't drive in.

We had martinis and the Spanish wine of Pedro Domecq, which I joked was powerful like *mescal* and was the only wine with a worm in it. That night all of us felt as if we were magic.

When you dance with Sandy, she can make a slow-foot look good. My friend and fellow newspaper columnist John Anders and I quickly agreed we were overmatched and established a tag-team system with her because she was wearing us both out on the dance floor.

Yet that particular night I walked a bit tipsy onto the floor with Sandy as the band played what turned out to be a *Samba*. Later I learned we were doing our own version of a *Samba* with all sorts of twists, turns and dips that probably aren't in the *Samba Handbook*.

In the haze of the night I remembered Sandy telling me what a wonderful dancer I was. She is an incredibly kind person. After all, no matter which side of the border we were on, I was the same person who had spent a lifetime failing to master the two-step, for goodness sake, the great tradition of Texas bars and dance halls.

The next morning, I was having much-needed coffee with Anders and he said, "You were great. I had no idea you knew how to do the samba."

"What are you talking about? I can't even two-step."

"Well, you were doing the samba last night and impressing everybody."

Puzzled, my memory hazy, the best I could manage to say was, "Oh, sure, now I remember."

Anyway, Sandy is still waiting for a repeat performance. There must have been something in the air the night of that samba in Matamoros.

Of course, if you want romance, we did dance on our first starlit night on Paros in that hotel room in the Apollon and we have enjoyed music together and when I look back at one night at The Drive-In in Matamoras, I realize we were rehearsing as partners not just across the border, but across the ocean for our dancing at House No. 5 on the beautiful island of Paros where wine, life and love are all sweet.

This adventure has been splendid. We've met wonderful people in wonderful places, seen the heart of Paros and felt the pulse of its Aegean neighbor Antiparos.

We've been to places together that we'd never have seen alone and, besides, our hearts weren't mean to travel apart. So, we didn't.

CHAPTER 20
VISITING THE NEIGHBORS

ONE MID-MORNING, SANDY and I decided to make the voyage across the strait between Paros and Antiparos, the much smaller island to the west.

We'd leave on a ferry from the traditional point of departure for Antiparos, the seaside village of Pounta on the southwestern side of Paros. In only minutes, we'd cross this strait and arrive on the island Antiparos at its coastal port of Antiparos. If there is New York, New York, why not Antiparos, Antiparos?

This decision to visit the "neighbors" introduced us to an entirely different vibe than we'd found on Paros. Two different islands, two enjoyable islands.

This day's adventure began with Sandy *somewhat* confident in my *somewhat* driving abilities as we proceeded from House No. 5 toward the ferry dock at Pounta. I think Sandy's concern, based on having experienced my driving, was whether I could safely ease the car onto the ferry without mishap. I did. And, at the end of the short voyage to Antiparos, when the craft turned around and backed up to the dock and when the cargo door dropped, I joined the other drivers in putting our cars into reverse and backing safely off the boat. I managed to execute this maneuver deftly, both keeping the car out of the water and not running over anybody's foot on dry land.

I parked the car nearby because we'd decided to make this a walking expedition. That had nothing to do with my driving. Honest. Antiparos is a walkable village.

The island's name means "Opposite Paros." Across from Paros – that is where you will find it.

There was in days gone by a custom at Pounta that seems so wonderfully, warmly Greek to me. If someone at Pounta left the door of the village chapel open, it was a signal across the strait for a boatman on Antiparos to cross the narrow channel and get that person or persons for a return trip to Antiparos. For the people of these islands, it was just another act of kindness that became a tradition.

Our voyage from Pounta to Antiparos was swift and pleasant. Visitors usually make this trip on smaller, sometimes funky ferries with just a handful of people aboard. You cross the mile-wide channel in only 10 or 15 minutes.

If we'd wanted a different, longer route, there is – during the summer tourism months – a larger ferry that makes the trip to Antiparos from Paros's main port, Paroikia. That boat takes a northern route, traveling nearly five miles in about 45 minutes.

THE WAY THINGS CHANGE

On our first visit to Antiparos in the early 1990s, the majority of the islanders lived in the village Antiparos. At the time, the island's population of about 500 was enhanced briefly each day by the smattering of tourists who took daytrips from Paros to shop and see ancient attractions, then return to the big island at night.

Things change. Inevitably. With the advent of easier transportation around the world, more tourists have been attracted by unpretentious Antiparos.

From the late 1990s into the 2000s, Antiparos began to draw more and more visitors. Some of these people decided to stay. The island population has continued to grow and now, nearly two decades into the 21st century there are more than 1,200 people living and working in the residences and small hotels and tavernas and cafes crowded near the waterfront.

The *village* Antiparos had space to grow on the *island* Antiparos, a small bit of the Cyclades (35 sq. km/13.5 sq. miles) with a coast that's 57 km (about 35 miles). This island has everything big islands want: golden beaches and hills, mountains and coves. Visitors, charmed by the beauty and isolation, began buying land for homes.

We began our portside exploration by walking through the inner village along narrow cobblestone streets past whitewashed houses and courtyards brightened by geraniums and bougainvillea. There were shops and popular tavernas with people sitting outside and enjoying conversation and laughter under the large trees and traditional table umbrellas. It is, after all, a traditionally friendly Greek island.

When the weather on Antiparos is pleasant, locals and visitors will gather at those taverna and café outdoor tables along the waterfront. Fishermen, their faces creased by the sun and windy sea, also enjoy their favorite social spots, maybe sipping strong black coffee or a beer or Ouzo. When the island's men gather at a table, it could be that they are discussing how life used to be on the island. Or, maybe, they'll be talking about how to gently change things.

On our initial visit to Antiparos, we watched the scenes being played out in this natural theater of life.

As we walked, we passed a fisherman who was rhythmically pounding octopus on the concrete surface by the dock. This "manual tenderizing for market" is a tradition among the fishermen. He looked up and smiled good-naturedly at us, and I thought he surely must be very proud that Antiparos has been known as the "Octopus Capital of Greece." A place could be called worse things.

At times on fading afternoons, women, some with children, will meet fishermen as they come home after a long day. We watched the homecoming ritual as this particular day was beginning to darken. Some greeted each other with an embrace and then began walking slowly together from the harbor up the incline of the only main street past houses made brilliantly white in the style so prevalent in the Cyclades.

That beautiful day, Sandy and I continued to walk around in the inner village of the municipality of Antiparos, along narrow streets – more like paths – past more houses, courtyards, taverns and shops.

Three middle-aged women, standing outside a shop on an almost vacant side street, were talking and laughing. Old friends meeting while shopping – that sort of thing. But as I approached, they became quiet and took on a serious look. I tried, honestly, I did, to be appropriately congenial. I said, "*Kalispera*" though what I was supposed to say was "*Kalimera*." Yes, they laughed at my "Good afternoon" greeting that morning. Not knowing what I'd done, I bowed and moved on, the poor Texas boy who couldn't quite handle the difference between "Good morning" and "Good afternoon." At least I think I knew not to say "*kali nichta*" – which I think is "good night" but I'm not sure when to use it. "Howdy" and "See ya later" have always worked no matter what time it was in Texas, y'all. I got better. Later.

On this same visit, I ran into a memorable islander, a little girl in a bakery. There she was, running the front counter, her head barely visible to customers. The owners, perhaps her parents, had put her "in charge" while they were busy with other chores. She looked very business-like at first, but happily smiled and waved when I took her picture. After all, she may be in charge, but she was still a little girl who liked having her picture taken.

THE SEARCH FOR THE HISTORIC CAVE

For many, many, many years the major attraction on the Island of Antiparos has been the Cave of Antiparos. We were drawn to it, too. And one day we made it our mission to visit this magnificent cave.

We rented a car and explored this beautiful island with its cliffs dropping into the blue sea and, in more gentle terrain, easing down to its many beaches. The interior island roads took us through magnificent fields of lavender blossoms and red poppies. In these isolated areas, we could stop for a while and take in the view and feel the soft island breeze on our faces. We enjoyed this feeling – as though we were the only people on the island.

As we embraced this isolation, our tranquility was suddenly destroyed by a noise that sounded like a loud lawnmower gone awry. We were about to see – there is no other way to express it – we were about to see *a sight*!

An elderly couple appeared in a dusty three-wheeled vehicle that operated without the benefit of the usual dashboard or side panels. They were squeezed into a seat that barely accommodated two people and they were riding behind a center-mounted steering column. The whole ensemble was connected to a small trailer. They stopped for a while and stared at us and we waved at them although they did not wave back. Perhaps they were wondering what these strangers were doing in "their spot" on their island. They left. Without waving. It wasn't something we'd said, I'm almost certain.

We'd gotten serious about visiting the Cave of Antiparos, so in our rented car – no three-wheeler for us! – we'd traveled away from the port village on impossibly rough and rocky roads out into the countryside through flatlands and hills looking for the turnoff to the Cave of Antiparos, also known in Greek as *Katafygi,* i.e., "The Shelter."

After we'd driven on a particularly difficult road for a while, and frustration had begun to take its toll on us, we saw a small, elderly gentleman with a weather-beaten face and a straw hat standing inside a rock fence and resting his arms atop the barrier.

We also heard him. He was yelling at us.

However loud he was yelling, we couldn't understand him when he shouted and pointed as we passed him. So I slowed, turned the car around and drove back to him. I got out of the car and walked over to him. He was a friendly guy with a delightful smile that was missing some front teeth. He'd been trying to help us, to tell us something important.

"*Kaave clo-sed*," he said over and over until we finally understood that the cave was closed that day.

It made him very happy that I finally understood what he was saying and Sandy got out of the car and took pictures of the two of us by the fence. We thanked him again and again as he pointed toward the turnoff in the road where we should have gone. We said our goodbyes and in the rearview mirror I could see him watching us drive away. I am almost certain I detected him shaking his head as he probably wondered if he'd have to soon call someone and tell them about the American who'd driven a rental car into the ocean.

Thanks to the old man at the fence, Sandy and I picked up another expression. "Kaave clo-sed" became part of our vocabulary and, outside of the man at the fence, nobody else would understand. Whenever we'd find a café or store closed or when we'd finish a task, one of us would announce, "Kaave clo-sed."

THE CHALLENGE OF THE CAVE

Thanks to the old fellow behind the fence and his pointing to the obvious turnoff to the cave, we were able to drive up the right road, little more than a single lane, to the top of the hill and the cave entrance. In the modern tourism era, you can buy a ticket in the village and go up the hill by bus or you can drive there yourself. But there was a time, not so many years ago, that guides led visitors on donkeys up to the cave.

The entrance of the famous cave, located under a massive horizontal layer of limestone, was indeed "Kaave clo-sed!" We shrugged, enjoyed the surrounding view and eventually went back to the car.

We'd left the car in a very small parking space dangerously close to a drop-off into the valley below. This was no easy-on, easy-off at the ferry landing.

Sandy, wisely, got out of the car, wished me luck and waited until I turned it around. It worked out all right, but a simple mistake while shifting gears forward or reverse could have meant the fastest of trips down the hill.

We made return trips to Antiparos several times, kind of winging it in hopes we'd find the cave open but it was always "Kaave clo-sed." Once we were driving back from the cave when we picked up an American couple walking down the hill because the cave was closed. They were tired, sunburned and didn't seem like they'd make it back to the coastal village on their own. Without sunscreen, the sun on the islands, unhindered by pollution, can burn you before you realize what has happened.

We took them back to a shaded taverna by the waterfront and they rested and drank a lot of water, thanked us, and as we departed, suggested we exchange addresses to send letters and get together again on Antiparos. Of course, polite people always mean to write but it doesn't always work out that way. So we're left with a nice memory not ruined by further conversation.

There was, finally, a successful visit. Once, at the cave, we joined a small group of people waiting to get into the famous cavern. It had been fenced off, but I led a daring group that decided to climb the rock fence at the entrance and go from there.

Unbeknownst to us there was a woman hiding, whom I now call "Watcher of the Cave." As I went over the fence shamelessly and was heading on into the cave, the Watcher popped up from nowhere and stopped us, which was probably good because there were certainly pitfalls inside the amazing cave. I tried to make amends by introducing myself as Saint John. After all the chapel *Agios Ioannis Spiliotis* (St. John of the Cave), built in 1774, is near the cave. Surely that carried some weight. I apologized, of course, but she just stared at me for a few seconds, then walked away, confident that Saint John and His Current Followers would not invade the attraction she was tasked with protecting from visiting nitwits.

INSIDE THE CAVE

There are different versions of the size in the cave but everybody agrees it is gigantic. When the electric lights are turned on, you go down 70 meters (229.60 feet) on 411 circular rock steps into the immense cavern with incredibly huge icicle-shaped stalactites hanging from the cave roof and massive cone-shaped stalagmites pointing up from the cave floor, sometimes as tall as five feet. Both are formed by a process that involves water, minerals and time. Lots of time. You can't stand there and watch them form, unless you have an eon to spare.

Years ago, before the 411 steps were installed, people who wanted to descend to the 100-meter depth did so by holding onto a rope and torch and easing down the, for lack of a better word, "path." They left by "reversing path." Down is surely easier than up.

Discoveries inside the darkness long ago confirmed that the cave was known in antiquity. There were items from the Stone Age and ancient pots and relics and a carved dedication to the goddess Artemis, who was worshiped by the people in the area ages ago.

Signs and carvings of names indicate that in the 4th Century BC, Macedonian generals, who failed in an attempt to assassinate Alexander the Great, feared his revenge and hid in the cave.

The cave's initial visitors also included the noted Paros poet

Archilochus (680 BC-645 BC). Much later Lord Byron (1788-1824 AD) left his name carved there, too. Of course, not everyone appreciates the "left-behind" notes and things that have marred the cave. And as my friend Jeffrey Carson (the writer and poet at the Paros Aegean Center) said of Lord Byron, "He should have known better."

On a huge stalagmite called the Altar Table there is an inscription dated 1673 by French Ambassador Marquis Nauntel, who had his priest celebrate mass there. He left another inscription in Latin: "Christ himself on His birthday came in the middle of the night to celebrate."

Another person who attended mass within the cave at this altar was Oliver Goldsmith. How would I know this? Because Sandy went into an antique store in Winnsboro, Texas.

This small antique store is where Sandy often rummages around trying to find pottery, vases, and such that she might use as subject matter for her still-life paintings. One particular day on such a venture she wandered to the rows of books instead of the usual shelves of knick-knacks. An old volume caught her eye. She reached up, pulled it down, and just happened to open to a page where Oliver Goldsmith told the story of attending mass at an altar in the cave on Antiparos. Ah, The Fates.

After the Greek War of Independence in 1832, France, Russia and the United Kingdom insisted that Greece become a monarchy and, at the London Conference that same year, named Bavarian Prince Othon to serve as King of Greece. In various guidebooks, he is also referred to as Otto and Otho and Othon, but he was indeed the first King of Greece during modern times. There are reminders that King Othon and Queen Amalia visited the cave. One inscription reads, "Othon 1, King of Greece, 27 September, 1840."

Photography and graffiti are forbidden inside the cave so, of course, the historical inscriptions are joined by modern graffiti inflicted by thoughtless visitors, preceded by officers of the Russian fleet who, during the war of 1700-1714, defaced the cave and made off with souvenirs. This practice was continued in the World War II occupation – first by the Italians and later the Germans. They took stalactites and also shot up the cave.

But years pass. Things outside the cave change. More and more tourists, many from nations once involved in a world war, arrive on Antiparos and mingle good-naturedly in the cave

As things changed so did the islanders, beginning to blend the past with the present, doing such things as replacing donkeys with buses to take visitors up the hill called *Agios Ioannis* (Saint John).

To the sane eye, it did not seem that there was room for the buses to park or turn around on the flat rock surface near the cave and the small chapel of *Agios Ioannis Spiliotis* (St. John of the Cave), built in 1774.

Their minds? "Kaave clo-sed."

***

A PERSONAL POSTSCRIPT: Agios is used with a revered name in Greece and it means "saint." It has been part of my name since birth. Back in the USA, some people I didn't know very well but who'd only seen "St." in a postal address, have called me "Bob Street John."

CHAPTER 21
FOREVER YOUNG: THE ONE AND ONLY GRANETTA

"You will always stay young like the Goddess Athena. The Goddess Athena never grew old."

– Kyriakos Skiadasto to his daughter Granetta.

ONE OF THE many side roads seldom traveled on Paros begins inconspicuously off the southern highway near the coastal village of Alyki and is little more than a wide, dirt path through native grass and weeds on mildly elevated terrain. It is easily missed, even when you know to be looking for it.

But Sandy has a knack for discovery and, this day, her purely-by-chance turn off the main road onto that particular dirt road in search of subjects to draw and/or paint became a most rewarding venture: At road's end was the home of the amazing, unforgettable Granetta Papadopoulou, nee Skiadasto.

Granetta lights up your life.

Now, there was no logic involved in this meeting, no logic at all in this discovery of this wonderful woman at the end of the road. Yet for artists and writers sometimes logic is no factor at all. What happens is the result of serendipitous winds. Thus, the spirit of happenstance, perhaps guided by the Famous Fates, once again favored us.

THE DAYS, THE CLOCK AND THE MIND

There is a psychological perception that either blesses or bedevils some of us: When we stay somewhere that we find ourselves enjoying for a long period, the days seem to go by more slowly at first and then as departure nears it feels as if they pass so suddenly. So a month's stay on Paros seemed to dwindle down to 4½ really quick days before we realized it was about time to return home.

I had been unsuccessful finding just the right elderly Greek lady to add perspective for a chapter in this book about the island. Then before I realized it, the tomorrows we anticipated became the today we faced. Time was running out on this trip.

I mentioned this to Sandy over coffee one morning, and she agreed it was a bit late to keep searching for the right, real character.

After all, she said with great practicality, we had to take care of odds and ends and say goodbye to our friends and face the dreaded, for me anyway, packing of clothes and tools of our trades. With Sandy's background in show business, she was quick, adept and knew how much time she'd need to "pack up and go."

Sandy figured she had time for another search for artistic subjects. She planned to head out on the winding highway south, one of her favorite routes.

"I just happened to notice a scene in the distance that I thought might be a good subject to paint, so I drove down this dirt road to get closer," Sandy told me when she got back. "I ended up stopping too close to this old house and didn't want to disturb anyone inside. So I turned the car around and I'd only driven a short distance when I saw this tiny white-haired woman standing by the glass door of the house and waving at me. I approached and with this buoyant merriment she invited me to come inside."

It turned out to be the 75-year-old house where the incomparable Granetta Papadopoulou lived with two cats, one named *Ela* (Come) as in "Come here." The other one wasn't, but came anyway.

The elderly lady – she was born at the dawn of the Roaring '20s – was indeed small, perhaps five feet tall, with somewhat sharp facial features and an endearing gaiety in her voice.

Granetta greeted Sandy like an old friend – their artistic spirits had quickly bonded. She showed Sandy around the house and they communicated in bits of German and Greek and, especially, gestures. In another example of fate's handiwork, Sandy had taken a German class in college and Granetta, who was born and lived on Paros most of her life, spent 20 years in Germany after she married. Sandy learned to speak and understand some Greek but her knowledge of German had faded a bit without use. Working together, they understood each other.

Sandy was beaming when she got back home and told me she found THE wonderful elderly woman for my book. That was an understatement. Granetta was not only delightful but extremely lively and amazingly active in many artistic endeavors and fueled with the energy of someone half her age.

Yes, Sandy had found a kindred spirit.

I AM VOV?

The next day we went back to see Granetta but we weren't sure she was home. However, there was a sign on the door in Greek: *Emai edo, Granetta* which Sandy was able to translate into English as "I am here, Granetta."

Then suddenly this diminutive woman was at the front door and clearly very excited as she invited us into her home. She had no problem with Sandy's name but was confused when, using my great linguistic skills, I introduced myself in Greek, "*Ime o Bob*" (I am the Bob).

Sandy thought perhaps she didn't understand my name because the second letter of the Greek alphabet is beta (β) which sounds like a *v*.

"Tell her your name is 'Vov,'" she suggested, which I did but still no sign of comprehension crossed Granetta's normally bright face.

Not to get too complicated but Sandy was wrong about "Vov." That's the price I pay for going along with my very intelligent, somewhat intuitive, and occasionally wrong wife. I once teased Sandy, "When you're wrong, you're not only wrong, you're adamantly wrong!" Anyway, I was probably the only person on Paros named Vov.

None of that mattered to Granetta who was happily bouncing around all over the place. She led us into the garden room where she kept easels and paints for her art projects. She invited us to sit, so we did and we began to drink in this bright, pleasant room with Granetta's paintings on the wall and cut flowers in vases and a window view of her flower garden and the distant blue ocean.

Paintings of her flowers were especially good and Granetta also was very proud of two paintings of landscapes, one with a boat in morning light and the other with a sailboat in moonlight. Granetta emphasized that she painted from nature, not photographs.

"I have been drawing and painting since I was little. I painted all the rooms of my grandmother's house and also drew flowers and little girls and lots of things to hang on her walls. It was natural for me to paint."

Granetta left for a moment, then returned with a box. She sat in her chair and took out red gloves generally used for sewing, and pieces of knitting and embroidery to demonstrate beautiful things she'd made: the homemade purse she artfully created from a skirt and scraps and a pretty scarf made from a discarded old blouse and pieces of material for chair cushions. She said she never threw scraps or materials away because she could always find uses for them.

Next, she showed us her creations in ceramics – swans and other figures – and then suddenly jumped up and left the room, then came right back with a jar containing two dead scorpions.

I'm almost certain neither of us expected that.

Granetta said the scorpions, which have poisonous stingers at the end of their tails, "bit" her twice but she killed them so they wouldn't bite any more.

As nearly as I could figure, Granetta the Scorpion Slayer also was a seamstress, a tailor, an artist, a writer of prose and poetry, a ceramist, a gardener and a worker in concrete.

Her writing table and chair were near the front door and family photos in black and white hung on the wall. When she wondered what my work might be, Sandy explained in bits of German and Greek that I was a writer. Granetta became very excited, smiled and announced, "I am also a writer!"

On her writing table were stacks of notebooks, written neatly in longhand, and when I motioned to them she said they were her books. "I write every day about things that I remember in my life," she said, asking what tool I used to write.

I told her I once wrote with a typewriter but had used a computer for many, many years. She immediately knew that word. "Computer! *Ne-ne-ne* (yes-yes-yes), my son works on computers in Germany," she said, proudly.

She brought out crossword puzzles, some partially finished, and said she worked them to keep her mind sharp and also wrote something else that, as she clearly saw, was a little confusing to us. So she got a piece of paper and pointed to the lines in Greek and said, "Da-da-da-da… da-da-da-da-da" so we understood the cadence of her poetry.

Granetta has the soul of a poet and finds inspiration in sunrises and sunsets. "The day before yesterday I saw the sun and it came to me immediately in a poem," she said. "Spontaneously, I saw the sun also today and my soul filled with joy."

After we had visited for a while Granetta asked how old we thought she was. I said, "You are 21!"

"Ah-ah-ah, *oxi-oxi-oxi* (no-no-no!)" she said, and so it would be clear wrote down her 87 on a piece of paper and that she was born in 1920. Granetta didn't seem anywhere near 87 because she obviously was forever young at heart.

The amazing Granetta seldom wore glasses, could hear very well without hearing aids and, although she had some problems with her knees, you would never know it by the way she was able to hurry around from one room to the other.

When we were getting ready to go, I kissed Granetta on both cheeks, a Greek tradition, and hugged her. She smiled and put her hand on her heart and said she preferred a big hug instead of the kissing since it was given from the heart. So Sandy and I gave her a big hug from our hearts.

As we were leaving, she followed us outside and pointed out a table and a concrete bench she had made by the porch and, in front of the house, stairs that could be easily climbed to see a nice view of the fields and the ocean.

She was obviously proud that she had built these things by herself and also pointed out a blue line drawn between the end of the old house her father built and the beginning of what she had added on. She was very happy that we admired what she had done and she was flattered that I climbed up the stairs to see the view before we left.

TRANSLATING GRANETTA

On our last visit with Granetta in 2007, we told her that if we came back again to Paros we would come to see her and she seemed delighted, then looked up to the heavens and said, "I will be here unless I go kaput."

Kaput became a common word of choice between the three of us and always drew laughter. At some point I referred to myself as "*Ime o kaput* (I am the kaput)." She laughed. I loved to see her laugh, which she did often.

And it was on our final visit with Granetta when our friend and my now-and-then translator, Lornie Caplan, an English woman who lived on Paros for years and was very fluent in Greek, came along. She would help me better understand what Granetta was saying in Greek and help Granetta understand what we were saying in English!

I worried that Granetta might be a bit shy or feel imposed upon if we suddenly showed up with an interpreter. So Sandy and I drove to Granetta's house to see if she would give her permission before Lornie came with us. Shy? Are you kidding? Granetta was all excited about Lornie coming. "*Ne-ne-ne!*" she said, smiling and I thought for a second she was going to clap her hands.

Granetta was all dressed up when we arrived with Lornie and they got along famously. Using Lornie as a translator was a wise decision. With Lornie interpreting my questions, Granetta not only answered but launched into a marvelous narrative during which she practically acted out the parts, her voice rising or becoming softer, depending on the situation. But more importantly Granetta was delightful telling her stories and enjoying it!

Lornie joined us in the garden room and Granetta held up some women's underwear she'd made. I quickly covered my face, feigning embarrassment, and Granetta laughed, as did everybody.

Granetta said, "I have always been that way – even as a child – laughing and joking because I was happy and could made people laugh."

Lornie told Granetta that I was working on a book about Paros and that I had written many books and thousands of columns for a newspaper, *The Dallas Morning News*. Granetta thought for a few seconds and said enthusiastically, "*Ne-ne-ne*, I wrote a newspaper column for *The Parian Voice*. For years I wrote critical columns about things that irritated me, something that needed to be improved, and I also continued to write about things that needed to be done when I lived in Germany."

She said that as she took walks in Germany she kept seeing where a bench should be placed so people could rest. "The show person on television said to write them if we see anything that bothers us. He said they couldn't be everywhere but would try to help. So I wrote to them about this place that needed a bench. When you are out walking the dog, or shopping, you need a bench to rest and relax!"

Time passed and one day she saw the bench in "a place where it should be." She laughed and said, "Ah, it was there and I sat down on it. Then I wrote the television station, thanking them very much. *Ne-ne-ne*, they agreed we needed a bench there."

She said she continued to write when she saw something wrong in Paros. There was a public *i tualeta*, (a toilet), that was only a hole in the ground. "Think about your grandmother who has to stoop down," she said and then demonstrated. She had written people at the local newspaper *Paros Life* that officials should put a regular sit-down toilet there.

"Days later I went to inspect and there it was, a sit-down toilet," she said. "They don't have to use the hole anymore."

FAMILY HISTORY ON THE WALL

Sandy asked Granetta who the people were in old photographs on the wall in the living room, one of which was of three very attractive young women smiling. Granetta gladly identified them as herself and her two younger sisters, Zafirenia and Lucia. There was also a photo of her mother and one of a young man in uniform that I thought might have been her husband. But she said it was the nephew of her mother. The photos reminded her of pleasant memories of her sisters and Kyriakos and Katina Skiadasto, her beloved parents who passed away so many years ago and would always be in her heart.

She recalled that when she was four years old, Zafirenia was two and Lucia was on the way.

Granetta told us that on a Saturday in 1928, she and her sister were buzzing with excitement because Katina's brother was getting married the following day at their grandmother's house. Katina had washed her two children and Granetta said excitedly that her mother, who was far along in her pregnancy, put lovely dresses on them.

"Nowadays people buy wedding gifts, but back then they would take useful things to weddings, like wine, a fresh loaf of bread," said Granetta. "So my mother had made bread and gathered some broad beans to take to the wedding. Bravo! We were on our way.

"We left for the wedding from this house right here and my mother was holding my hand as we walked along the road. Then she felt a pain in her stomach and squeezed my hand."

Granetta recalled the story vividly:

"Mama, Mama, what is the matter?" a frightened Granetta asked.

Her mother told her "Do not worry. It is all right. We will go on to Grandmother's house."

They walked a little farther and Katina began having pains again, worse than before, and said, "We will go back to our house! Hurry!"

"Why aren't we going to the wedding, Mama?" Granetta asked with an innocent child's disappointment.

"We aren't going there," her mother said.

Quickly they were home, Granetta said. "Then my mother went back outside. My mother started to shout and shout for Maria, her aunt who lived nearby.

"I shouted for Maria, too," said Granetta, raising her voice to scream "Maria! Maria!" for us.

"Aunt Maria was able to hear and told her 15-year old son, 'Go to see what that child wants.' He said to me, 'What do you want?'

And my mother told him to go to the village of Kamari, where the grandmother lived. 'Hurry! Hurry!'"

Granetta said many years later the young man told her, "I flew like a bird to get the midwife!"

Granetta's voice softened again as she explained, "The old woman had lots of children, twelve. So she knew exactly what to do. Opposite Kamari was a village where women acted as midwives. But everybody took Grandmother's advice."

The midwife soon arrived.

"In those days, they got two stools ready to deliver the baby," explained Granetta. "They put a sheepskin on each side of the stools and the middle. Then the woman sits on the stools to give birth."

" 'Come quick! Come quick!' my mother said.

"Grandmother was there and said, 'You have time yet.'

" 'I'm holding it in!' said my mother. 'I'm holding it in!'

"Then POP! The baby was born!" said Granetta.

Granetta and Zafirenia sat quietly on the bed to see what would happen next. "We were watching all the time to see what was going on," said Granetta. "The baby was all right. The people there lit a fire to warm the water and poured a lot of water to wash the baby. Everything was fine to that point."

"The midwife came back three to six days later," said Granetta, who was again watching what was going on with her sister. "The mid-wife gets hold of the baby on the back of her leg and makes little cuts with a razor! So the blood comes out! I could see this blood coming out of my sister!"

Granetta screamed and rushed out of the house and ran as fast as she could to find her father, who was hard at work creating a path to their well. Granetta was crying very hard with tears rolling down her face as she said to her father, "Papa, Papa, they are killing the baby!"

"Yes dear, yes dear, move to the side so I don't hit you with the shovel by mistake," Kyriakos answered calmly.

"I was in a terrible state, my heart was hurting, my soul was hurting," continued Granetta. "I was on my back with my legs kicking into the air and yelling that they are killing the baby! And my papa was not taking notice of me. Oh-oh-oh I was in so much pain.

"Then, even though I was only four years old, my father explained to me why they should be doing this to the baby… because it was a ritual back then and I was relieved. It had to happen. Baby Lucia was born and we all grew up and we were three sisters."

Granetta smiled when she finished the narrative and we applauded to her delight.

GRANETTA'S FATHER

Granetta's father Kyriakos was a special person in her life. He was well educated for his time. He was a metallurgist and in the early 1920s worked in the mines on Paros and Antiparos for a British company, making reliefs by carving and engraving the white marble slabs, and the company also mined for aluminum and iron and prepared them for use. Granetta said the boss of the English company was very proud of her father's work.

"My papa treated all of us (the girls) equally and was playful with us," she said. "And if there was something we didn't understand or know about we would go to him and he would explain it to us."

She said he always had time for his family and then, speaking softly, added, "My father loved his family very much and said to us that we must always be loving, too."

She laughed at a memory. "Once I was on his shoulders and we were walking down the road and he was explaining something to me."

They met a man passing by who teased her father by saying, "You've got the same head as she does, no more intelligent than a child."

This made her father laugh.

"The boss of the English company had a gold pen that he was very proud of," Granetta recalled. "He would take it out all the time and write things. One time the boss was on a boat with my grandfather and took the gold pen out to write.

" 'Come see my gold pen', he said to my grandfather. Then *oxi, oxi* (no, no)… he dropped it into the sea! My grandfather dived into the sea! When he surfaced and climbed back on the boat he proudly handed the gold pen to the boss."

" 'Ohhh, this guy is so honest,' the boss from England told everybody. 'So honest'." The Greek workers kept hearing the English word "honest" but when they repeated the word it sounded like they were saying 'honery.' Honery became my grandfather's nickname. To this day I am known as Honery's grandchild."

Later, her father went to work at a metal laboratory in Athens and also spent time in the mines from which the metals came. Once he was trapped by a cave-in for eight days. He lost time on the job and worked extra hard to earn money to feed his family and take care of their necessities.

SPENDING THE WAR IN ATHENS

During World War II, the family lived in Athens and Granetta went to college there. There were a lot of Greeks from Paros and other places who came to live in Athens during those days.

"There was a family living near us," said Granetta. "And every day those people would come by our house and ask for bread and my father would give it to them. One day my father said he had baked seven times in one day to supply them. He wasn't a baker but just wanted to help people. But they kept coming by saying, 'We're hungry, we're hungry!' And my father would go back and bake some more bread to feed them."

It was her father who told his daughters, "You must learn as much as you can for difficult times."

It was during these times that her mother taught them to be seamstresses, needle workers and tailors.

"You're going to turn us into seamstresses," the always outspoken Granetta told her father. "But all three of us learned as many things as possible. I learned to do needle work. I learned to paint pictures, to make crewel rugs, and embroideries."

A YOUNG WOMAN'S WORRY – LIFE'S CHALLENGES

As the years passed, Granetta said she worried about not being married. "I was 30 and still unmarried," said Granetta, frowning ever so briefly. "I was getting old, the years going by so quickly."

"Don't worry, my little daughter," her father told her. "You will always stay young like the Goddess Athena. The Goddess Athena never got old."

Many young men came to ask for her hand in marriage. But she had gone to a school of higher level in Athens, whereas her suitors attended lower degree schools.

Her father chased suitors away. "You wouldn't be able to get along with my daughter," he told them. "She thinks differently than you. She's educated."

"So the men would come to our house, turn around and leave," said Granetta. "But in the end the one I'd been waiting for came and we fell in love and married. I made sure he was tall. I am short and would have to look up to talk to our children."

In 1953 Granetta, at about five feet tall, married Konstantinos who was 6'1". "And now I'm getting shorter!" she good-naturedly told us before continuing her story.

"My husband was 25 and also a Paros native, and I was 33," she said, smiling as she paused and recalled the best memories of their marriage. Then she continued, "Ohhh, we were very happy for seven years. He would always pick me up to cuddle. We had lots of jokes and laughter in our marriage. We had two sons and Kostas (as Konstantinos was known) even called my parents 'Mom' and 'Dad' and they loved him so."

In 1958 they were living in Athens where her husband worked as a civil engineer. A German company was looking for professional people to relocate at a company office in Germany.

When Kostas learned about this job in Germany, he told Granetta that he must go there because he could make a lot of money. He did make a lot of money but – "Ah, but here comes the BUT," said Granetta. "In 1960 he went to Germany while I stayed in Athens for three years and would join him later. I lost him because he became involved with a German woman. He earned a lot of money… but lost it."

Kostas kept writing to Granetta, saying he couldn't stand being without her. "But he had a lot of friends in Germany and was going on about life without me," she said.

She went back to him in 1964 and lived some 20 years in Germany where she worked as a seamstress. "I could have stayed in Germany," she said. "But I had rather live in Paradise… Paros. So, it was in early 1985 that I came back here (Paros) while he stayed in Germany. My kids also stayed in Germany and married German women."

I wondered what happened to her husband and she said, "He died four years ago (2003)." And when I asked whether, after they separated, there were other men in her life, she said unequivocally "*Oxi-oxi-oxi!*" and added, "My father brought us up to be ethical, moral and honest."

One of Granetta's sisters lived in Athens and the other one in Germany after she married a traveling salesman from that country. Granetta was silent for a short time, then said, "We are three sisters in their 80s. My sons are in their 50s. I never thought I would live to see my children in their 50s!"

I told her she was forever young and, kidded her that if I had not been married to Sandy, I would ask her to marry me. "*Oxi, oxi, oxi,*" she said, turning me down. "You are too old!"

CHAPTER 22
SNAPSHOTS IN THE PARK

A SHORT DISTANCE from the landmark windmill and dock in Paroikia is a park bordered by the waterfront drive on one side and, on the other side, a strip of commercial endeavors.

The park is a personal refuge in the downtown area where people can sit on benches and watch the passing parade of locals and tourists young and old and meet friends or make friends or just sit and ponder.

In addition to the benches, the park has monuments, a small chapel, a building with restrooms and public telephones.

And to the delight of all visitors, the park is a place of abundant flowers that brighten the day and it is a place where crowds gather on holidays to mingle and listen to dignitaries giving speeches.

In the later years of our visits, I've gone there sometimes to observe the people in the park or the people going past and to try to figure out what they are about based on their mannerisms, the way they walk and their speech patterns, even though I barely understand the Greek language.

And I also try to get a feeling of the evolving times from when Sandy and I first came to Paros a quarter of a century ago in 1992.

On certain days, middle-aged and elderly men come to the park in their pickups and rickety vehicles and, on the path that goes behind the little chapel, they set up stands where they can sell their fruits and vegetables from boxes. People on this island have probably been doing this sort of thing since the first harvest.

On some of our visits, we encounter a cheerful old gentleman who seems so spry for his age and bounces around, hoping to attract customers with his good cheer, and he especially likes to see Sandy coming and might even do a little jig for her. She buys goods from him even if we don't need them because it makes him happy. I think it makes her happy, too.

THE PEOPLE IN THE PARK

My time in the park is one of observation and learning.

During one pensive visit:

Right there, sitting on one of the benches near "my" bench, are two elderly men, one holding the crown of his cane in front of him, the tip carefully secured to the earth. They are talking and watching.

The man with the cane dresses in a dapper manner, and as he appears to begin to rise, I fear he might stumble so I jump up and start to help him, but I have misjudged. As if I do not exist, he finishes rising without incident, says goodbye to his friend and walks away at an amazing pace while periodically tapping his cane – tap, tap, tap, tap – on the sidewalk.

Possibly, I would have misjudged him in any language. In any park.

It is a public park. The public comes to it. All ages. Young girls in school uniforms of blue and white walk and skip along, laughing and joking because school is out for the day. And in this kaleidoscope of humanity, the old fellow sitting near me and other Parians in the park get a firsthand look when young people, getting off the ferry or coming from where they stay in Paroikia, pass by in short shorts and hip-hugging jeans that clearly are on the brink of slipping down. No doubt the older men think them shameless – but we all stare at this generational parade.

There is a wooden kiosk on a corner across the street on the west side of the park. In late afternoon, a man is sitting inside the small wooden structure with his goods to sell – newspapers, magazines, paperback books, soft drinks and cookies and candy and so forth. He is waiting, undisturbed by shoppers. Suddenly, a tall gentleman with graying hair crosses the park to the kiosk. Soon the man in the kiosk and the tall gentleman are chatting and laughing, perhaps at one another's stories, and then they seem to get more serious, possibly discussing the changing times and how things used to be. During later visits to the park, I observe the tall gentleman with gray hair returning – about the same time in late afternoons – to the kiosk to talk with his friend. Perhaps I am witnessing a friendship that has been decades in the making.

Elsewhere, on a walkway in the park, a man who isn't Greek rudely passes an older couple causing them to move over, and another fellow, perhaps in his 80s, walks slightly bent over with his hands clasped behind him, and a priest in black wearing a *kalimavkion* – a sort of brimless stovepipe hat that adds about five inches of height to a figure – silently goes by without looking right or left. He speaks only when someone speaks to him.

Cleric or civilian, this park is a place where people can be alone in a crowd.

One hot mid-afternoon, Sandy and I walked across the park when it was nearly empty. We saw a poor woman on a bench near her four young kids, all wearing raggedy clothes and sitting on the ground under an unforgiving sun. We couldn't understand what she was saying but maybe she was waiting to meet someone.

At dusk, two young people walked ever so slowly across the street toward the windmill. They held hands and sometimes stopped to embrace. It was a sweet scene, played out as if they were the only people in the world, as if they were unaffected by changing times and intent only on making the memories that would, decades later, make them smile fondly at the passion of their youth.

BE DIFFERENT: SPRINT THROUGH TRAFFIC

When we first came to Paros, there were a few motorcycles and motorbikes, some tiny three-wheeled vehicles and maybe six or seven cars on the entire island. But during the early 2000s, automobiles multiplied like locusts on Paros, especially in Paroikia and, to a lesser degree, in Naousa, as people started making more money and buying cars or, if they already had one, joining the ever-increasing parade of two-car families. During busy times in Paroikia, such as a holiday or ferry arrival or a shopping day, drivers in the smaller cars claim the parking spaces while some other drivers become very creative and park in various angles in "open" spots.

Cars and pickups and vans and motorcycles whiz around a partially blind corner near the park and obviously you must look, then look again, before attempting to cross the street. Sandy is so careful when she crosses the street that I sometimes tease her as we wait for an opening during the busy hours.

This particular time, my left foot is sore from the previous day's jog up the hill near *Agia Irini*, so I'm limping a bit but I carefully look both ways and start walking merrily across the street anyway. The more cautious Sandy waits on the curb and, suddenly, as I approach the heart of the traffic, I hear her call, "Look out!" I smile because she's always so careful and, after all, I'm an adult and know what I'm doing and sure enough I'm in the middle of the street when this van comes barreling around the corner right at me and I take off sprinting, probably missing being struck only by inches, and I keep running into the park, jumping small hurdles such as plants. Then, of course, I brake to a halt as people stare at me, a crazy foreigner, and I try to act as if nothing happened and I try to whistle a happy tune but nothing comes out of my mouth but air.

Yes, it was a close call.

Sandy is very upset and when she safely arrives she asks me her usual question for which I consistently have no answer. "What in the world were you thinking?"

I shrug, shuffle my feet and am silent. Then she said, "You might have been killed!"

"I'm sorry," I said, then added with a smile, "But the point is that even with a sore left foot I probably sprinted faster than I ever have."

"WHAT?" she exclaims, then shakes her head in disbelief and repeats a recurring refrain: "You're different."

"Thanks," I answer proudly, as always taking that as a compliment, then I add, "I do not want to be like everybody else."

"You don't have to worry about that," she replies.

ESCALATING TOURISM AND THE ISLAND

Perhaps some tourists dash off the ferries with the idea that they have no time to stop and rest, they must keep going, they must press on to see things they don't want to miss. In reality, if they'd sit in this park and just observe, they'd see things they are glad they did not miss.

One person I'd interviewed about Paros told me he was worried that escalating tourism, commercialism, the faster pace of life and competition for money to be made might cause some of the people on Paros to lose the warmth, friendliness and sweet dispositions for which they have always been known.

I told him we'd been coming to Paros for many years and that everybody was always very friendly and courteous to us. Oh, sure, there were a few exceptions such as supermarket cashiers frazzled by the long lines at checkout, but that could happen anywhere. It was also a consideration that, perhaps, I sometimes stretched their patience when I bungled around trying to figure out the value of currency in an era when *drachma* evolved to the European Union's *euros* which went into circulation on Jan. 1, 2001 and immediately confused me. I'm a writer – money is always puzzling.

The two Paroikia supermarkets always seemed to be busy and some of the shops on and around Market Street did all right and others survived or changed hands but didn't seem to do much advertising at all.

But, our friend Theo Maniatis of the Apollon Garden Restaurant took publicity and advertising to a new dimension. There was a place for it and Theo filled it.

CHAPTER 23

THEO, THE APOLLON GARDEN AND THE WORLD

Theo Maniatis' popular Apollon Garden Restaurant is near the east end of Market Street, the main passage through the tangled web of shops on narrow stone walkways that form the *agora*, the major shopping center of Paroikia.

Paros had been an island of no traffic lights and only small, limited commercial placards identifying various businesses. That all changed when Theo came on the scene. He had lived in Canada and the United States and was aware of the value of promotion and advertising, especially in the form of signage.

His Apollon signs became legion. There were placards promoting his Apollon Garden Restaurant on mountainsides and on twisting, curving roads, vacant buildings and homes and if you were not careful he might hang one around your neck. When I went into the ancient Quarry of the Nymphs, I half expected to see one of Theo's posters welcoming visitors at the entrance.

The dining establishments of Paros are mentioned in travel guides and in the island's monthly magazine and on-line site *Paros Life & Naxos Life*. Praise for these restaurants spreads also by word-of-mouth. Most of the places serve good-to-wonderful meals, but I've often wondered if their owners and/or managers were a bit peeved by Theo's ubiquitous signs.

The sign war all started when a lady was opening an Italian restaurant next to Theo's place. She put up a sign to let people know her restaurant was there. Theo immediately replaced his placard with a sign larger than the one she had. When she responded with a bigger sign, Theo got an even larger one and on and on it went.

She eventually surrendered and moved elsewhere. I hoped one of Theo's signs wasn't waiting for her. But signs notwithstanding, the reputations of the Apollon and Theo not only bring in islanders but also tourists and celebrities.

Among the photos Theo proudly displayed near the entrance of the restaurant were pictures of himself with movie stars Sean Connery and Billy Zane and with Jeffrey Carson. There is also an autographed photo of Sweden's King Gustav who just happened to drop by for a meal one day.

Another celebrity in the photo display is Yiannis Parios, the popular Greek singer with an international following. Parians lovingly call him "Parosita," an enduring expression of affection from residents of Paros where he was born and raised. The local authorities even named the seafront road in his honor.

So you see, from royalty to stars, one never knows who is going to drop by the Apollon Garden Restaurant.

THE FRIENDSHIP BEGINS

Theo picked a distinct historical building near the end of Market Street for his restaurant. It came with remnants of old equipment from the era when donkeys were used to turn a presser to crush olives. Theo took this building and its history and converted it into a renowned restaurant.

History became an exhibit in the Apollon Garden. As you moved toward the three dining areas there were displays of the old equipment, including the presser, a rifle from the early 1900s and other objects from the past that Theo had collected and preserved.

That first time Sandy and I ate at the Apollon Garden, Theo treated us as if we were famous.

We dined in the main garden area in the courtyard adorned with orange and fig trees and eucalyptus and smaller plants that were all dwarfed by a towering palm that must have been four feet around at its base. After an excellent dinner, Theo insisted that we accept drinks on the house and also a sack of olives.

The next time we dined there, Theo gave us after-dinner drinks, a large jar of olives and dessert on the house. Another time he insisted that we accept two fine bottles of his wine.

I figured if we kept dining there we might end up getting a full meal with all the trimmings and eventually a table and chairs and perhaps the large palm tree, which kept catching my eye.

It was on that initial visit that we stayed long after closing in what would be the beginning of a friendship with Theo Maniatis.

OLIVES, TOURIST SEASON AND FRIENDSHIP

Early one afternoon, I joined Theo as he relaxed in the dining area after finishing his shopping for the restaurant's fresh vegetables. What an enjoyable conversationalist!

Theo is perhaps 5'7", with a burly upper body and he wears his hair down to his shoulders, *a la* "Greek cool," and has a round, pleasant face. His deep voice can be bellowing when he is joking around but becomes soft when he speaks of personal matters. He has a quick, playful wit and has never met a stranger and, if you are a stranger, you quickly get the feeling that you have known him for a long time.

As we were talking, a young Asian woman came in and looked around as if she could not decide whether to stay or move on.

It is typical of Theo that he would invite someone he'd never seen before to come in and have coffee even though the restaurant would not open for hours. I could not imagine this being commonplace in the United States – but, of course, this is Greece and hospitality is a national and personal trait.

"Please, you sit and I'll get you coffee," Theo said to the visitor. "Perhaps it would be tea you drink. But at this time, I am sorry, all that is ready is coffee."

She said coffee would be delightful, introduced herself as Vivian from Taiwan. Hearing this, Theo stood, pulled back his shirt collar to show the garment tag, and said with a smile, "Ahh, THIS is from Taiwan, too!" Vivian laughed and their friendship was launched.

In those days the assistant to the Apollon Garden's Chef Vassilis Zikos was Yannis Baios. He would sometimes join us when we were chatting with Theo. But mostly he would smile and listen and seldom say anything, yet when he was working he talked a lot, much of the time to himself and in English.

"Yannis, go make the salad!" he would tell himself or "Yannis, get yourself to work this second!" And then he'd answer himself, "Yes, I will do that soon!"

It was early October and the tourist season that began in May was coming to an end and Theo and his sister-in-law, Zoi, who helped him run the restaurant, would be leaving the island soon.

This is a common thing. Many others operating tavernas and restaurants and shops during the tourist season also leave the island when traffic diminishes.

Most are from Athens but for Theo, leaving after the tourist season meant returning to the place of his birth, the small village of Myrtia. That is near Lakonias in Sparta on the Peloponnese, a famous peninsula in southern Greece on the Gulf of Corinth.

For half of a year, Theo lives in Paros, where he has a house. The other half of the year is spent at his home in Myrtia.

It is there that he raises oranges and olives on his "thousands of trees" – he also grows some eggplant and green peppers. But mostly he is concerned with cultivating the Greek staple of olives, of which he speaks with great pride.

As he was saying that afternoon Vivian joined us, "This morning I watched the ferry come in from Athens. Two hundred people, they are leaving. Twenty are coming. Yes, it is time to close for the season.

"I'm a professional and love my work. Others get into this business for only the money. I make the money but get the pleasure out of it also. I love to meet the people coming from so many places."

Vivian was being very quiet so to break the silence I said, "You know, Sean Connery, famous for 'Bond, James Bond,' was here and his picture is on display over there at the entrance."

She brightened up immediately and said, "Really? Sean Connery?"

"Yes, he was here, but he's gone now," Theo told her and added hopefully, "Maybe he'll come back when we open again for the tourist season so you must come back and you might see him."

Vivian said she had to leave and Theo said he was disappointed that she was leaving. Then he told her the restaurant would be open for a few more days and to please come back to have dinner or perhaps another coffee or tea.

She said she had to leave to go wake her brother, who, no doubt, was still sleeping after they had gone to bars in Paros and had too much of a good time the previous night. She would tell her brother about Sean Connery – and about her new friend Theo, too.

THE STARS COME TO THE APOLLON GARDEN

On an earlier afternoon Theo and I sat alone at a table in the garden and I mentioned the photos at the entrance and he said, "It was a few months ago I get this call from Doli Goulandris and she asked me to make reservations for the night for fifteen. Okay, that's good. I will."

"Then they came in and I looked up and there is Sean Connery."

Connery and his wife, Micheline Roquebrune, were guests of Doli Goulandis, whose family has the charitable Goulandis Foundation and owns many things including the islet of Revmatonissi, between Paros and Antiparos.

Theo said, "I introduced myself and we are talking at their table and, oh no, the three tax men come in to check the restaurant for what we owe."

He apologized to Connery for embarrassing timing. So Connery got up and went over to the three men and said, "Lads, what are you doing here? This is a fine place and this man is a wonderful, honest owner and my friend. So why not let him be?"

The men were mesmerized by Connery or perhaps the James Bond movie character which made him famous – or both. But they quickly completed their business and left. Connery had mentioned to Theo that he really didn't want it known he was on Paros and this request was honored – at least it was honored by Theo.

"The tax men left and told everybody that Sean Connery was here and all hell broke loose when people found out he was here," Theo told me. "They came to look for him. Oh, yes, he was very nice to everybody. He said he loved Greece. His wife, Micheline, is an artist and had a showing in Athens and he went there with her and enjoyed it very much. Yes, he is a very nice person.

"Do you know of Billy Zane?" Theo asked, switching stars. "Did you see Billy Zane's picture there?"

I certainly knew Billy Zane had played a bad guy in *Titanic* and I had seen him in other movies but had not recognized him in the photo because he was surrounded by Theo and others. They were all smiles and obviously having a good time. I looked at the picture again and, sure enough, there was Billy Zane. But why would such a movie star as Billy Zane come to Paros rather than Santorini or Mykonos? I had missed the obvious.

"He said Paros is a quieter, more relaxing place," explained Theo. "He loves Paros and likes to be here and not at the more known islands for tourists. Here he can blend in with the rest of us.

"You know he is from Greece. His family moved to Chicago when he was young and then he went to California where he changed his name from William Zanetakos and became a star.

"And you never know who is going to walk through the door – like the King Gustav of Sweden. He was another nice man who seems very regular and likes this place."

THEO AND THOUGHTS

During another enjoyable evening at the Apollon Garden, we'd been talking with Theo when he excused himself and went over to visit a group from France. Soon they were all laughing and talking and having a good time with their new friend Theo. Noting his last name was Maniatis somebody mentioned a noted artist in their country by the same name.

"Of course," Theo said matter-of-factly. "He is my brother."

And they believed him – until he laughed.

I remembered once when Theo was talking about his family and he told me, "We are five brothers." So when he came back to our table that evening I said, "You are six brothers, counting Maniatis."

"Oh, yes, of course, we are six brothers!" he said, laughing.

I stopped by again to say goodbye just before he left to go back home. He was staring at the palm tree, not really seeing it but deep in thought.

And then he said, "Yes, I go back to Sparta now. Where I live in the village there are the mountains with a short walk to the sea. It is very beautiful there. You and Sandy must come to visit me there.

"The people in my village, the older ones especially, are kind and feel the pain of others. When President Kennedy was killed they rang the bell of the church as they do when somebody special dies. He was this man they liked, like a son, and it caused great grieving in my village."

Theo was quiet again for a short time, and then laughed and added, "Yes, I go to my village now and then travel to see more of this world. And I invite you again to my village in Sparta. You must know there is much history in Sparta."

THE WAR, AFTERMATH AND CANADA

Sparta is in a horseshoe of the Taygetos and Parnons mountain ranges on three sides and opens into the sea. There are remnants of ancient times and Byzantine ruins with modern olive groves and hyacinths blooming in the spring.

As most people know, the word "spartan" is derived from the Greek city-state Sparta whose fighting forces were renowned in ancient Greece for their toughness, tenacity and tendency to battle to the death. Some historians believe Sparta was the first totalitarian state. The men were raised from childhood to be soldiers and were legendary as the finest fighting force and once dominated the Greek world.

The 20th century was a different animal. I had been researching World War II in regard to Paros and Antiparos. You cannot tell the story of anywhere in Europe without examining the way war changed lives. Theo had a view of the aftermath.

"I was not born during the war but heard all the stories," Theo told me. "The Italians did not come to Sparta for the war. They came to Sparta with guitars and singing and some stayed and married with our women. The Germans came with guns and were mean and burned a village near ours two times. I believe the Germans thought the Greeks would be easy to conquer but they fought back and caused the Germans many problems.

"For so many years it seemed like this country of Greece was always in a war, that there was nothing but war.

"The Civil War (1946-1949) was the worst kind of war in Greece with brother fighting brother. There was a fascist in my village who killed for nothing. He remained living where we were and people kept trying to kill him for revenge but could not. They don't try now. He suffered the loss of two sons, one in an automobile wreck and the other in a helicopter crash."

Theo's father, Poulikos, had been a very strong and able man who farmed and took care of his family. Nobody in the village was wealthy. During World War II, Mr. Maniatis was in the Greek Army and fighting in Albania. He was driving a jeep on a road where troops were moving along on foot when an enemy plane, appearing first as little more than a dot, became bigger and bigger and was soon right on them and bombing the road. The jeep was hit and Theo's father survived but his leg was injured. It could not be treated at the time and the injury worsened.

"When I was growing up, all the time his leg was straight and would not bend," recalled Theo.

"He had spent much time in Albania fighting, then when he came home permanently injured, he could not do much work. So we became a poor family without much hope. My mother, she talked to her sister, who lived in Toronto. Her sister told her, 'Why don't the boys come to Canada and make a better future and help the others in the family?'

"Greek families are very close. They stick together and help each other," Theo said. "That time was difficult and we wanted to make a better future. So all there was to do was go to Canada in 1965."

Theo was 14 and his brother Dimitris was 15 when they departed for Toronto to try to make a better life for themselves and their family.

They left behind the only life they'd ever known. Things would never be the same.

"Yes, I would miss my family when I left the village, but I was so young and it was something that I must do," said Theo.

THE CANADIAN EXPERIENCE

It was strange and difficult in Toronto and the language was a terrible barrier. All the brothers could say in English was "yes" and "no" but they got jobs in hotel restaurants because Greeks owned restaurants, and once these businessmen had also been faced with a challenging language barrier.

"Always, the Greeks have restaurants," said Theo, shrugging.

In those days, Toronto had few minorities in a predominantly Anglo-Saxon population.

"The idea of many immigrants coming there didn't please them," said Theo. "And they did not like you to speak a different language. But, no, they did not mistreat us and would be helpful. So we would work, then go to school at night to learn English."

The brothers sent part of their earnings back home. Theo studied hotel management in school and soon Theo was managing a hotel. And Toronto was changing as other minorities began to arrive. Joining the postwar Greeks were Italians and Chinese. Theo and Dimitris learned the English language, which was very difficult for them. But the brothers were different. Theo was very friendly and outgoing and got along well with people, whereas Dimitris was quiet but very polite. They both did well.

Theo noticed that places featuring steak and seafood were popular but that people were also becoming more interested in Spanish dishes. So he opened a restaurant called El Conquistador.

When a Greek man came of age in that era, it was required that he must go into the army. However, if he was living in another country he could pay the government or army a fee and be excused from duty. This was what the brothers did, and when they were very successful they sent even more money back home and eventually paid for a younger brother to go to college and become a lawyer and another brother to study economics.

The clever and determined Theo now had money, which gave him the opportunity to see the world.

After managing El Conquistador for 10 years, he sold the restaurant and told his brother, "I'm not going back home but to travel." Theo was single but his brother was married with two small children and could not run around the world.

Theo never married, although there have always been women in his life. He once told me about one in particular. "I did not want to tell you about the sad things but perhaps you should know. I was with this woman for seven years in Toronto. She was very bright and happy. One day I decided maybe we should break up. A short time after that she was driving in Toronto and had a wreck with a truck. She was killed."

He paused, as if painful silence might somehow ease the painful memories, then he continued. "No, I think I will never marry. I am like family with my brothers and their wives and children. I do not think I should be tied down to the marriage."

He also will never forget another great sadness in his life. He became a close friend with a man in Toronto. They traveled together, played together and shared happiness and grief for some 20 years. His friend was on Korean Air Lines Flight 007, a passenger flight shot down by the Soviet Union on Sept. 1, 1983, because the Soviets thought it was on a military mission.

"It's a crazy world now… a crazy world," he said. "But you must go on with life and enjoy it as I do. Perhaps tomorrow you won't be here anymore."

THE WORLD TRAVELER

Theo had been in Toronto 25 years. He traveled around Greece, Europe and spent a lot of time in the United States, going to New York, Los Angeles, Pittsburgh, Detroit, Buffalo, cities in Arizona and to Hawaii.

He was in Waikiki, a beach and resort area in Honolulu, when he heard about a man who had a popular Greek restaurant and also performed an impossible feat for his customers. The man would place a small child in a chair on a table. He then would bend down and pick up the table and child with his teeth. After he stood up he began doing "the Zorba dance" from the famous movie.

"I knew I must see this and asked the concierge to please get me reservations for four," recalled Theo. "He told me it was impossible because there was a two-week waiting list. I slipped him $100 and he said, 'Okay, sir, I am glad to help you. How many people?' I said four. He said but you are only one. I told him that was no matter. Three women were staying on the same floor at the hotel. I brought them.

"We had a big meal and party and watched this fantastic performance. We had too much to drink and began, as Greeks do, to toss glasses and then dishes to shatter them on the floor. The man who had the place came over to me and we started talking. He said he had this belly dancer that would perform and she might get cut with the glass. So please stop throwing the dishes. I got us all to stop right away!"

After that Theo found out the man was from a village near his in Sparta. "And then it was like we were brothers," said Theo. "We laughed and drank but he said again, 'Don't throw the dishes to break on the floor.'

"Okay, we won't." Theo promised his new friend.

LIFE IS TO BE LIVED

As we sat in the garden dining area, Theo asked how we liked the olives and was told they were wonderful. Then as he talked about his travels he remembered going to a fortune teller in Toronto and asking what might be in store for him. The prediction? "You are a person who does not want to stay in one place."

He smiled and added, "If I can't stay in same place so much, how come I'm still in Paros for these many years?"

Theo first learned of Paros when he talked to a friend he had worked with in Toronto. "You should go to Paros," his friend told him. "Why? Because it is a beautiful place. There is the sea around the island and the women are beautiful."

"Okay," said Theo. "I go to Paros some time. And I did."

When he first came to Paros in the late 1980s, he fell in love with the island.

Then he made friends, liked the lifestyle, the weather and thought it would be a good idea to have a restaurant. His venture began as a coffee house called Café Apollon in 1990 and grew into the noted Apollon Garden Restaurant.

But Theo is one of those people who is able to balance the lure of wanderlust while maintaining a practical holding pattern that is the foundation of his work. Yes, he loves Paros, he loves Sparta, and he loves to travel. He said he just might come to Texas next.

"Life is too short," he said. "I am a person who enjoys today because who knows about tomorrow?" Then he grinned and added, "I am like Zorba."

CHAPTER 24

SANDY, THE FRENCHMAN & THE FRESCOES

Our first year on Paros, we stopped at the village of Marpissa, then spent most of our time checking out nearby beaches and taking side trips in our quest to fulfill our Paros fantasy and failed to really appreciate the village.

It would be some dozen years later, thanks to a chance meeting with debonair Frenchman Georges Clemenceau, that we'd have a renewed interest in Marpissa, especially arousing my curiosity about an elderly woman who painted frescoes on a wall in Marpissa.

On a September day in 2003, Sandy loaded up her palette and paints and art paraphernalia in the car and drove into Paroikia, parking near the waterfront.

She began walking with her gear along stone pathways past houses with geraniums planted in pots and in old, giant olive oil tins. Some residents along the way kept their doors open in the mild weather – the effect was to create a scene from cinema with the light household curtains moving in the breeze against an aural background of the sound of muffled radios. And, as usual, a cat or cats followed Sandy along her way.

She continued to climb to the top of a hill by a church and then negotiated the labyrinth of paths until she found the site she was looking for with scenery of sailboats. Surrounded by white buildings and two pristine chapels as the sun cast shadows on steeple arches, she had found just the right place to paint and sat down on the steps.

As if on cue, an elderly woman came out of a nearby apartment and brought Sandy a cushion to make the hard stones more comfortable as she was working.

"I continued to work and the nice woman returned to give me a delicate flower with a sweet fragrance," Sandy remembered.

The kindness and the flower made her smile and she put the blossom in her shirt pocket to take home.

When she put everything in place and started painting, she attracted the attention of passersby and tourists. Locals and visitors stopped to watch.

THE ARRIVAL OF GEORGES

Sandy was concentrating on her work when a gentleman who turned out to be Georges Clemenceau stopped to admire her work. Georges was a tall, slender man with a full head of white hair, the ruddy complexion of an outdoorsman and dazzling blue eyes. Unlike us, he loved staying in the downtown area of Paroikia and rented a room on the upper floor with a balcony and view for 15 Euro, about $17.50 a day at that time.

When he told Sandy that he'd first visited Paros in the mid-1960s, she told him that her husband was writing a book about the island and would be interested in talking to him. He said he'd be delighted and a couple of days later we met him at a taverna along the waterfront in Paroikia.

"It suits me well," he said of his quarters in downtown Paroikia. "The woman letting the room remembered me from when I was here six years ago. At that time, I had a place on the roof and a wonderful 360-degree view of the *agora*, the port and all around."

Georges had been a publisher, writer and artist who specialized in creating reliefs and photography. His interest in architecture and various civilizations has taken him and his camera around the world. Among the archeological sites he'd studied and photographed were those in Peru, Mexico and in Greece at Delphi, Crete, the Peloponnesian Peninsula and Milos.

One endeavor he found both amusing and profitable was publishing – that took him in an unexpected direction.

"I published brochures, things like that and also once decided to publish a newspaper in Japanese," he said. "There are 400,000 Japanese who visit France each year, so it seemed a good idea."

Many people with whom I've talked had the common experience of stumbling onto the existence of our favorite island of Paros. Georges was no exception. "It happened quite by accident," he said. "We were driving about Europe and just happened to come in contact with this Greek gentleman.

"He said, 'Why don't you go to Paros? It's a very beautiful place.' I thought, 'Well, why not?' That was 38 years ago… in 1965. It was a very beautiful place and the people were exceptionally nice. Back then, mules were still being used for travel. You could take one up a hill but mostly you just walked wherever you were going and now there are cars in abundance and shops where a large park in Paroikia once was."

His wife had traveled with him, Georges said, then a brief sadness crossed his face as he recalled her death six years earlier. Then, Georges found a reason to smile as he told us about his son, who worked for CNN in Athens, and how he would stop and see him on the way home. Since it takes us so long to get to Greece I sometimes forgot you could actually drive to the Greek inland from other European countries.

As we sat talking, I was elated as Georges began to tell us about his feelings for Paros. I wondered if they would match ours and those of all we'd met.

"I like Paros best among the Greek islands," he said.

We discussed various villages of Paros when he asked if we had spent much time in Marpissa. "Not really," Sandy said. "When we first came here we rented an apartment on the highway at the edge of the village. But we were there only a few days because we were looking for a place by the sea."

"I liked it very much there," he said, then told a story that rejuvenated my interest in Marpissa.

GEORGES FINDS A MYSTERY IN MARPISSA

Some seven years earlier Georges was having coffee in a small square inside the village of Marpissa and became enchanted by simple frescoes of Greek figures going about their daily lives. They were on walls on either side of a door inside the square. Curious as to who painted the frescoes, he went through the door and found himself in a small room with glittering stars suspended by invisible lines from the ceiling to the floor. A tiny woman clad in black and gray was inside what turned out to be a hat shop – a *chapelière* in French, Georges said. Her name was Maria Agourou and as they talked she laughingly said she was "only" 82 years of age.

He later wrote in a sketch, "Maria Agourou has a lively look and the happy face of those for whom age does not change the interior vision of youth."

She was born on Paros but at the age of 10 moved with her parents to Athens and later took up the profession of creating hats. But she'd always longed to return to Paros and set up a business. She did so at the age of 72 when her husband died. She had never tried painting before but suddenly picked up a brush when she was in her 80s and found that she could not stop.

She told Georges that her subjects were "everything that I saw around me." He was impressed that she was painting for herself and not tourists.

So they became acquaintances and he promised to visit her whenever he returned to Paros. "I've been back to see her again recently but she has vanished. Nobody seems to know what had happened to her although, perhaps, she may have gone to live in Athens. She had left a group of paintings that apparently had to be placed in storage. I could not find where and worried how they might be rotting away because they weren't taken care of properly. It would be such a shame if someone who stored them did not realize what they had."

We drank our *ouzo* and exchanged addresses – e-mail and street – and telephone numbers. Sandy and I had talked about going to Paris and especially wanted to visit the Louvre. And, of course, we wanted to see all the many, many other historic and artistic attractions.

When I was in high school, I made a failed attempt to become more cultured by buying art books with pictures, some from the Louvre. And as an artist Sandy was especially interested in a visit. She would love to see the Louvre. Georges told us it would take days to really absorb all its glory.

"Let me know when you're coming and I'll meet you and help you find other places of interest, too," he said. We said our goodbyes, promised to stay in touch and majestic Georges walked away and disappeared into the *agora*, like a key character vanishing from a novel.

Sandy and I couldn't get Marpissa off our minds, nor could we forget Georges' story of Maria Agourou.

SEARCHING FOR MARIA'S FRESCOES

The next day, Sandy and I went back to Marpissa to take a closer look at the village of sparkling white churches and homes – and to find Maria's frescoes. We turned off the highway and drove up a steep incline to the village, about 40 meters above sea level, and parked near three deserted windmills – "The Three Mills", where wheat was once ground. Apparently, residents had not allowed the sometimes-blind march of progress to cast them aside. They reigned over this once busy agricultural area.

Georges had given sketchy directions to the frescoes, so we just took off without much of a clue and climbed through twists and turns in a maze of narrow stone walkways, some no wider than a goat path. We went past doorways and balconies adorned wtih flowers, then upward toward the holy church of *Panagia tis Metamorphosis*. It is one of more than 400 churches on this island. We saw few people but the doors of some of the residences were open and, coming from the inside, you could hear conversation and, sometimes, laughter.

A woman appeared by a doorway, seemed surprised to see me on the walkway, but then smiled broadly and we decided to give each other a congenial greeting. Up another walkway, two young men were working on a motorcycle. They stopped to wave back after I waved hello, then they went back to working on the motorcycle.

Just as there were no signs of frescoes, there were no signs of tourists, although, to be fair, it was the off-season. Tourists ordinarily stay along the highway, nearer the water or in one of the coastal villages such as nearby Piso Livadi. I'm sure there were rooms and apartments to let but they weren't readily identifiable at this time in the season.

SOMETIMES YOU LOOK BACK AND SEE CLEARLY

We had become somewhat lost and decided to split up on our search for the frescoes. We'd meet back at the Three Mills. Inevitably, after a bit of solitary searching, we bumped into each other on one of the many paths and continued to climb upwards towards the church at the crest of the village.

"I'm not sure where we're going," I said. "The directions don't work and maybe the frescoes aren't here anymore."

"Let's just keep climbing and maybe we'll get lucky and find them," Sandy suggested. She stopped now and then to take pictures as I continued on with no success.

Then I stopped to turn and look back for Sandy and suddenly, as if waiting for the right moment, there they were – the frescoes! Just like that. Sudden and astounding! They were on two walls separated by doors in a small square with a tree and an empty table with two chairs. It was the place Georges had described, the place where he'd had coffee. Nobody was around, so it was deathly quiet that mid-afternoon. But, after all, it was a traditional time for *mesimeri*, the Greek "quiet time," akin to the "siesta" in Spain, Mexico, Texas, etc. The Greeks enjoy *mesimeri* before opening for business again near evening.

As I faced the walls, the first group of frescoes were almost childlike paintings in sequence with, first, a windmill and a sailor sitting at a table with a ship on the ocean in the background. The other group of "people" pictures was on the other side of the doorway on the wall of this crumbling structure.

Later I asked Barbara Gilis, an Englishwoman and evangelist who lives with her husband Peter in Logaras, if she knew anything about Maria. Barbara had lived in Marpissa when she first came to Paros.

"Yes, I knew her," she said. "She would be quite happy to tell you about her pictures. She was a soft, gentle lady who had a hat shop with the pictures and things. You would go into the shop and she would give you little things. Once she gave me this white stone with the blue sea painted on it. She was still living here, maybe four years ago, in 2001."

We were in a seaside taverna in Piso Livadi when we were talking about Maria, so Barbara said she could show me how to easily get to the frescos. We got into my rental car, parked by the Three Windmills and she showed me a shortcut directly to the square where some of

Maria's frescoes were visible. Paint was pealing off one of the walls yet you could still make out the figures. There was a room above the frescoes near where a shop had been and Barbara said that was where Maria had kept her paintings.

We went about a block down the street to the popular *Haroula* taverna. Barbara thought the people there would know what happened to Maria.

The doors were open and a radio was playing music so, I figured, someone had to be there. We went inside and five or six of Maria's paintings were hanging on walls in the taverna. One featured child-like pictures of a little boy and another showed a man playfully chasing a maiden beside a windmill.

But it was just us, the paintings and the radio. Nobody was there. We looked in back and found no one; we called out and got no answer. I marveled at how you could do this on Paros and not be robbed.

As we started back to the car an old woman walked out of a nearby apartment. Barbara, fluent in Greek, asked her about Maria. The woman said she had indeed gone back to Athens to live with relatives and that she was in her 90s but still alive.

Even if Maria had not been with us still, her wonderful pictures had survived to bring new life to our visit to Paros.

CHAPTER 25

FRANK AND GAIL, THE SUNSETS AND CHANGES

A FEW YEARS into our romance with Paros – in the mid-90s – I met Frank Saunders at one of the outdoor cafes separated from the main port in Paroikia by the landmark windmill.

Across this divide, you could see a ferry approaching the main docking area while, nearby, fishermen on the waterfront were unloading their catches and untangling nets, and in the distance a yacht, its sails hoisted, swept through the blue waters of the Aegean.

It seemed fitting to meet Frank there because it was from the deck of a yacht sailing nearby that he and his wife Gail first saw Paros. They got to the beautiful island long before Sandy and I found it.

In the mid-1980s the Saunders were searching for a new life and decided to leave the United States and devote their vacation time to a backpacking excursion abroad. Frank disliked his job as a corporate lawyer – a kind of hatchet man for his company, he said. And Gail felt out of place as a management consultant. Perhaps they might discover who they really wanted to be and find that perfect place to start a new life.

While visiting mainland Greece they came upon an easy-going

man who appeared to be a poor fisherman. They preferred talking to such regular people because, they told us, you could really learn true things about a country without brochures and sugarcoated marketing. This fisherman told them about things in his country. For example, he said, in Greece it is not how much money a person has that matters, but the wealth of their character.

He asked Frank and Gail if they'd like to go sailing around the central Greek islands on his yacht. Just like that. They were discovering the legendary hospitality of Greeks – buy you a meal, find you a place to stay or even take you sailing on a yacht, no strings attached.

They thought he must have been kidding because, after all, they were practically strangers. He was not kidding and was obviously wealthy to have such a yacht. And one day the man guided the yacht with them aboard into the harbor near the windmill in Paroikia, the port city of the island of Paros.

"We immediately felt the magic of Paros," Frank said. "There was something that just drew us there. We knew one day it would be our home."

Gail was smitten. "Let's come back here one day!" she said.

They returned to the United States where doing something like moving to a far-off Greek Island was one of those dreams that people have but never fulfill.

THE OPPORTUNITY ARRIVES

When Frank's company announced a severance program, he immediately accepted. Gail quit her job. They took their $35,000 in savings and each said, "Let's do it!" as they made preparations to go back to Paros and stay.

Family and friends kept reminding them of what they'd be giving up and telling them that they'd expect them back home in a few weeks at most. Specifically, what they had given up to become much poorer but much happier people was a four-bedroom dream house in New Jersey near New York City, two sports cars and enviable jobs with incomes in six figures. They'd had to move around a lot in their jobs, but even in a nomadic corporate life, they were on the inside, running on a treadmill, which was going faster and faster.

"For me, there was constant pressure to win cases," said Frank. "We might win a case for $300,000 but still lose because you were expected to get a judgment for a million."

So Frank and Gail Saunders, prototypes of the era's upper middle class with a good income, chucked it all to become the quintessential expatriates on a beautiful Greek island in the Cyclades.

The decision had not resulted in disappointment, Frank told me that day at the outdoor cafe by the windmill.

From where we were sitting, we could see people gathering at the harbor cafes after the ferry docked and see them met by friends and others from abroad. There were older people walking stiffly or with canes and middle-aged and young people backpacking around Europe and locals talking or reading newspapers or just sitting and watching time and people go past.

And there was Frank: Tall, lanky and light-skinned, he could have passed for a visitor, except, he wasn't visiting. He was already where he wanted to be.

THE SIMPLE CONCEPT OF CHANGING LIVES

Later Sandy and I would meet Frank and, for the first time, Gail, who had darker features than her husband, almost Greek-like. One of their friends, Marcia, who had married Yannis, a Paros resident, came with them for dinner at Frank and Gail's favorite place for fish on the waterfront.

Frank knew the owner, a man who enjoys pointing out the prime catches to his friends. So the owner picked the fish we would eat. I was glad because some of the different species of Aegean fish are as confusing to Americans as are the Greek names given them.

The couples were close friends and were making plans to start a kind of center that would bring in lecturers to Paros to discuss writing and art and, perhaps, music. And Marcia and Gail were also taking an art course together at the Aegean Center for the Fine Arts. Frank and Gail became close friends with John Pack, director of the school, and his wife, Jane, the artist.

Gail spoke of the courageous decision that changed their lives. "Frank and I could see our lives going in six-year cycles as we made more money and got more things. Then we realized we'd wake up one day and see that we'd missed a lot of things that are more important than money."

Frank and Gail appreciated all the things they had earned, but the price they'd paid in pressure and stress was too great. They spoke of what they had missed. "We asked ourselves what we'd miss most when we were 85 and we realized it would be never having lived in another country and learning about its culture," Frank said. "You can never really learn about a place unless you've been there for a while."

When we met that day, they had been living on Paros for a dozen years. They had a house on a hill by the village of Naousa and many Greek friends and part-time jobs that paid "enough." It didn't take much to live on the island. One year they made $5,000 and maybe $8,000 or $10,000 in other years.

They had become part of the culture and had the time to watch sunsets, which may be "alike" to casual observers but are always different to dreamers and thinkers.

A sunset is to be taken in at leisure and not given the passing glance that inspires someone to say, "Oh my, isn't that nice" as they move on to something far less beautiful.

For the Saunders, there was time to see the beauty. The corporate pressure was off. Gail, who became an artist, wasn't even wearing a wristwatch, and Frank said he only wore one when he knew he had to be somewhere at a certain time or when they took a trip back to the United States.

"Usually it doesn't matter what time it is here," he said, then added, "We're rich beyond measure."

At one point a dog entered the restaurant as if he had reserved a table. A cat was under our table. Nothing happened.

There were many animals on Paros that year and I was told that sometimes visitors bring pets and abandon them, leaving their fate to islanders.

"On Paros, animal control is in the hands of the individual," Marcia said. "There are just so many dogs and cats and, so, we are animal control."

MAYBE JUST A JACUZZI

When the Saunders settled on Paros, their newfound idyllic life could not have been more different that it was in the United States. They rented a tiny house with neither heat nor indoor toilet. Gail also had to learn to cook from scratch over a wooden fire.

Frank wasn't allowed to practice law in Greece, although he found part-time work assisting lawyers. It also took three years to get their own telephone but after a few years they moved to the house on the hill by Naousa. Their new home was twice as big as the tiny house, had indoor plumbing and all the basic necessities.

As was their goal, they got to know the Greeks of Paros.

"Greeks are friendly people, even when you first meet them, but after they get to know you better, they become as close to you as any friend you might have had for many years," said Frank. "Many people from the U.S. judge people from foreign countries because they might do this or that. You can get along better with them when they realize you are not judging them."

Gail said, "Your neighbors here don't care whether you drive a fine car or ride a donkey. They might show up at your house to give you a bottle of wine or a fish for no reason. And they are always ready for a party.

"You feel safe here too," she said. "I have no fear of going out at night and walking around by myself. I would in the States."

At the time we met, the Saunders were also conducting life-decision seminars in Greece and during their annual visits to the United States. The workshops were designed to help people who were feeling at a crossroads in their lives go ahead and make the changes – just as they had done.

"Some want to do it but don't know how," Gail said. "We tell them how. We offer them an alternate way of life and try to give them the tools they need to pursue it, to take chances that can bring more happiness. It has worked wonderfully well for us."

Then she laughed and added, "But I do wish we had a Jacuzzi."

"We stress that if people enjoy the lives they're living, if it gives them pleasure, then by all means don't change," said Frank. "But if they don't have that enjoyment from living, we can help them."

If you're a married couple, you must also be friends, not just lovers. Frank and Gail are both. "I never realized just what good friends we were until we went backpacking around the world," said Frank. "If you aren't friends in a situation like that, it would be miserable."

THE REBOUND

Gail's father had been in the United States Air Force and the family moved around a lot before settling in McKinney, a city north of Dallas. Frank had lived in the Dallas area and also Paris, Texas, where his father had a home.

The Saunders met when both were attending Tyler Junior

College, about 100 miles east of Dallas in Tyler, the town that is also known as "The Rose Capital of Texas."

They married in 1967. She attended North Texas State College (now the University of North Texas) and became a management consultant in communications, and Frank got his law degree from Southern Methodist University.

Those are the career choices that led to the stress and pressure that sent them to Paros in search of sunsets and dreams.

NTSU is in Denton, about 20 minutes north of Dallas if there's no traffic tie-up on Interstate 35, but, of course, there always is. SMU is in University Park, a small city surrounded on three sides by Dallas and, on the south side, adjacent to Highland Park. Both cities are surrounded by Dallas and are called "the Park Cities."

Just as Paros is an island surrounded by water, the Park Cities combine to become a political island of two municipalities surrounded by the sea of population that is Dallas. Politics from the Park Cities can affect Dallas; traffic from Dallas can affect the Park Cities. The traffic in Dallas and the constantly under-reconstruction highway from Dallas to Denton simply added to the pressure of daily travel.

Frank and Gail, typical young Americans at the time, thought they knew what they wanted to do and then realized they didn't.

A year after our great evening at the tavern, Frank called me at my newspaper office. He and Gail were working at a spa in Los Angeles, he said. They'd simply decided that they wanted to be back in the United States.

But they would never be cursed with the fearsome regret of never having lived in a foreign country and learning about its culture.

***

CHAPTER POSTSCRIPT: *In June 1999, John Pack of the Aegean Center, posted a note on the island's online magazine. "The saying goes that everything grows big in Texas.*

Frank Saunders was from Texas and indeed was a very big man himself. In fact, everything about Frank was big: his warmth, his generosity, his laugh, his smile. Frank and his wife, Gail, lived on Paros many years, and returned to the States three years ago. Frank passed away on May 4, 1999, a victim of cancer. He said to Gail as soon as he was diagnosed that if he was going to die he didn't want it to be a dirge. He remained true to this idea and kept his amazing positive spirit to the end. At his death, he wanted his friends in Greece and everywhere to have a party to celebrate his life and not mourn his passing. For those of us who know Frank, the best homage we can pay to his spirit is to smile... big."

Gail has since become an author who has written a book inspired by the death of Frank at 51. Released in 2015, It is called Resilient Heart: Transcending the Death of Your Loved One. *And online you'll find that "Gail now lives on the Greek island of Paros with her one-eyed cat Romeo, writing and coaching surrounded by orchids in her office by the sea."*

CHAPTER 26

MR. PATELIS' KAPELOS, BINKOS & BASKETBALL

THE SHOP RUN by Ioannis Patelis in the 21st century exists in a building that is 400 years old. It is among the structures that line Market Street, the major shopping center in Paroikia.

The area is a magnet for residents, tourists and other visitors to the island. The spine of all this commerce is the long cobblestone main street that intersects with a labyrinth of narrow side streets that have restaurants and a few shops here and there. Some of these stores have been in operation for more than a century, through trials, changes and challenges of commerce.

Merchants with all sorts of goods – jewelry, newspapers, magazines, dresses, etc. – set up sales outside if the weather is fair. But they seek indoor shelter when a cold front invades the island and brings bone-chilling, blustery winds.

Sandy and I, occasional visitors to Market Street, once stopped in at a shop – no signs on the door! – run by a smiling, friendly gentleman who was not pushy – that's always an attraction to me, a genuinely reluctant customer! Shopkeeper Ioannis Patelis became one of our good friends on Paros.

As Sandy looked at goods on a table outside and I pretended to be interested in them, the shopkeeper asked us to come inside where he had even more items – blankets, rugs, clothing for men and women.

The interior of this store was a well-kept, long, cavernous, dimly lit shopping area. It's not the design you'd find in a U.S. mall or an American "power center" full of storefronts, but was somehow more comfortable and welcoming.

Mr. Patelis suggested that Sandy might enjoy examining the various sizes and colors of attire and told her she was free to take her time. She almost immediately tried on a black *kapelo* – the famous wool fisherman's cap with a soft top and short bill.

"How do I look?" she asked, the hat perfectly askew.

"Wonderful, you really look good in that one," I said inadequately. Sandy always looks good. I wasn't just a husband trying to guess the right answer.

It was right there in front of me.

By this point in our day, however, I was worn out from her shopping – she'd spent a lot of time trying to make a choice while simultaneously checking out other items and buying some, i.e., slacks in the prevailing color of Grecian attire, black.

It was uplifting for me when she said those immortal words, "I'll take this one. Are you ready to go?"

She began to love *kapelos* the way a Francophile loves a beret. But she had an idea. "I can use it as my painting art hat when I go out looking for subjects," she said, proudly.

It became a ritual on Paros that each time we stopped by Mr. Patelis' store to visit and shop, Sandy would buy new *kapelos* for her mother, sister, more for herself and one for me.

As so many others have done always, Mr. Patelis warmed to Sandy. She's not only very attractive (an understatement!) but also has a sweet, pleasant countenance that unfailingly attracts people and makes me feel so very proud to be with her.

It was easy to see Mr. Patelis was charmed by her.

On visits to his store, he was very nice to me but obviously was always much happier to see Sandy. I couldn't blame him – and I'm accustomed to that reaction from others.

Mr. Patelis told us proudly that he did not close his shop as others did after the tourist season. He gestured toward his shelves and said he stayed open because, no matter what the season, he had "everything for everybody – the women's clothes, men's clothes, underwear, blankets and whatever you might want."

Many of the restaurants and shops in the main market area shut down after the tourist season when that first hint of winter begins to occupy the island.

Athenians, who operate most of the establishments, return home but as Mr. Patelis proudly said with a twinkle in his English, "The Paros people only close a little."

SEASONS CHANGE

One mid-morning in winter, the shops along Market Street were shutting down because weather had reduced the shopping crowd to just a smattering of people.

As usual, I was able to make a spectacle of myself without even trying when the wind blew my baseball-style cap off my head, sending it skipping up the street and, as I chased it, bending to reach for it, it eluded my grasp several times. Finally, I caught up with the darned cap and managed to trap it under my foot, almost falling in this nimble run-fast-stop-on-a-dime-without-wrecking-the-cap process. This time, instead of bill-front, I pulled the cap down snugly backwards on my head. With both hands still holding to it tightly, I fought the wind for possession of my own cap.

Because of this raging wind and the wretched cold, I didn't think Mr. Patelis, who was getting up in years, would be at his shop.

But Mr. Patelis was there! In fact, he was standing outside his shop and shivering and talking to a smaller, older man. When Mr. Patelis saw me, he smiled, greeted me kindly, as always, and shook my cold hand (I kept the other one on my cap!). I am almost certain he was disappointed that Sandy wasn't with me. It occurs to me that such disappointment from others is a consistent reaction when Sandy isn't with me.

I once asked Mr. Patelis for the name of his store, since there were no signs to identify it. "It is only called 'Patelis'," he said, then declared, "Patelis is here all time."

Mr. Patelis was an aging gentleman who seemed content to be the shopkeeper on Paros no matter what time of his life. Besides Greek, he spoke German and a bit of English. I could only mumble a bit of Greek but we somehow communicated with Sandy's linguistic help by smiling and pointing and shaking our heads "yes" or "no." He was certainly impressed with her attempts at Greek, which improved each year while mine took a snail's pace toward "understandable."

SEASONAL TRANSITIONS, BOOKS AND BEASTS

While "Patelis is here all the time" with its consistent inventory, only a handful of the other businesses could make that declaration. For example, not the newsstands. During tourist season, there were nice selections of books in the newsstands, but when the tourist season ended the inventory was mostly boxed up and sent back to Athens.

Fortunately, we made friends with Lornie Caplan, who managed the bookstore with ample books in various languages just across Market Street from Theo's Apollon Garden Restaurant. Unlike other merchants, Lornie didn't send her books back to Athens in the off-season. She knew people needed to read no matter what the season.

The seasonal tourism changes weren't limited to people, exactly. Once Sandy and I were driving from House No. 5 to Paroikia on the narrow, rocky road that runs beside a pasture usually populated by a couple of cows. This day the cattle weren't there and Sandy, nodding toward the empty field, cracked, "They've been sent back to Athens after the tourist season."

MR. PATELIS' PICTURES AND AN AMERICAN GAME

I was very interested in the old black and white photographs of Paros that Mr. Patelis collected and displayed outside his store. In a 1930 picture of the business area of Paroikia, there was only a hotel on the hill with three windmills, one of which would become that landmark at the ferry dock.

And, of course, there was a photograph of the immortal *Panagia Ekatontapyliani* (The Church of 100 Doors), with no other structure close by – it was a photo from a time before "progress."

In a 1947 photo, there were only fishermen and their boats along the dock and no tourists or yachts. Nothing like the busy attraction it has become.

From 1950, there was a photo of scattered buildings on the busy street along the harbor – not a car in sight. The method of transportation recorded in this frame was that of island tradition: men on donkeys.

Looking at the pictures, Mr. Patelis reminisced, "For me, it was better back in the old days."

THE SON ON THE WALL

My attention kept being drawn back to a photo on the wall inside the store. It showed a young man playing basketball. Mr. Patelis' eyes brightened as he said proudly, "That is my son. He lives in Athens for basketball."

I told him, "I am a basketball fan and someone who loves to play the game and would have liked to have met your son."

Mr. Patelis immediately picked up the telephone, said his son spoke excellent English, and called him in Athens where he was playing for a professional team in a European league. He talked to his son for a minute or so and then handed me the phone. Binkos Patelis and I talked basketball and I learned from him that he'd played against Roy Tarpley, a former Dallas Mavericks star whose drug and alcohol addictions had ruined his NBA career. Binkos said he admired Tarpley's talent but not his habits off the court. *(Tarpley died at the tragically young age of 50 on January 9, 2015, not in Greece, but in a hospital in Arlington, a suburb between Dallas on the east and Fort Worth on the west.)*

Why was Binkos in Athens? He told me he loved his home island of Paros, but at the moment, he loved basketball more.

"By the time I was 17, I was so crazy for basketball," Binkos recalled. "I would play every day. There were some basketball goals on Paros then but they were very primitive."

Athens was already a hotbed for basketball so he told his father, "I would like to leave to try basketball. Paros cannot provide that. At the beginning, my father did not like that idea."

Mr. Patelis had once lived in Athens and feared his son was too young to be in the big city atmosphere and would be challenged by the many bad temptations. On the other hand, Paros was peaceful, certainly a safe place for a young man to be. But Binkos was determined to have a professional basketball career and, finally, his father changed his mind because he wanted his son to follow his dream. So off Binkos went to Athens.

SUCCESSFUL ON THE COURT

At the time we talked on the telephone Binkos was 28 and had done quite well. He played three years of professional basketball in Spain, three in France, one in Iceland and then played professional basketball in Athens where he lived.

"The last 10 years (since 2001) I believe basketball has become the more popular sport in Greece," Binkos said.

When you think of sports in Greece or Europe, soccer is always first. Yet basketball was introduced to Greece in 1918 by Michael Stergiadis, a pupil of the inventor of the game, Dr. James Naismith, a Canadian immigrant to the U.S. who created basketball in 1891 with a peach basket and soccer ball in Springfield, Massachusetts.

Over the years, the popularity of the game magnified, Greece joined the International Basketball Federation (FIBA) and the nation became one of the international powers with the best players from the country's professional leagues. Wealthy owners bought all the most prominent teams and games were televised.

The Greek National Team proudly won the European championship in 1987 and 2005, but pride swelled even more when the Greeks beat the United States' all-star team made up of millionaire-athletes from the NBA – Greece won 101-95 in the 2006 FIBA World Championship semi-finals. Greece played a game of patience, passing and teamwork, whereas the Americans were typically run-and-shoot. I pulled for my country to win, but also wished I could have shared the pride with friends on Paros, such as Mr. Patelis. Unfortunately, Greece was supposed to beat Spain in the finals but lost. Perhaps they were still celebrating the victory over the United States.

Basketball courts have sprung up on Paros since Binkos was a child. You now see youngsters playing on a court near the high school in Paroikia. And basketball courts, along with tennis and water sports, are advertised by resorts, such as the Agnanti Hotel,

Anixis Studios and other venues in the village of Alyki on the southern tip of Paros.

Binkos also gave me some insight into his beloved home. He always returns to Paros, where he was born and raised. There have been changes, he said. Then Binkos laughed and told me that when he was growing up, "Paros was a place that was about to go to sleep. Now Paros has adjusted to tourism. Some of the people live for tourism. It is like that everywhere.

"Fifteen years ago, people were happy and less materialistic. Now they have to have things, want to buy a car, a house instead of enjoying the other simple conveniences of life and a slower, less hectic pace and more peace of mind."

He spoke of a period of slumping tourism and explained that tight money in Europe had been the cause. "But then some English people and Americans still travel here on vacation for the sunny beaches. They come back for three or four summers and like even more what they see, considering it is still the slower pace of life to them. Then they buy a house and live here forever. In the neighborhood of my parents, there are Americans living."

When his basketball career is over he expects that "I'll come back to Paros, the way that life is there, or a place like it. I love the sea all around me… where you can see it from everywhere. I love the freedom the sea gives me. Yes, my final destination will be Paros."

I was talking to Binkos, scribbling notes on the edge of a tablet filled with other things and having trouble keeping the small pad still. Mr. Patelis noticed this and began holding down my pad. That was very thoughtful and I stopped talking to Binkos to thank his father for the courtesy.

"Your son was very nice, very polite and I know he must be a fine person," I said, speaking very slowly. He understood the essence of what I was saying when he stood up straighter, smiled and thanked me with *"Efharisto."*

Each time we are in Paros, we stop by to greet Mr. Patelis. I also ask him how Binkos is doing, and he beams, pleased that I asked.

And, of course, Sandy buys another *kapelo*. Or two. Or three.

CHAPTER 27
ANIMAL HOUSE & THE PLUM SWEATER

In our early trips to Paros, My Wife The Animal Lover would sometimes turn our villa by the sea into a temporary refuge for stray dogs and cats.

Oh, I liked the animals okay – in their place, not mine. *My place* was on the veranda where I staked out space to read, relax, ponder whatever and doze off as waves rushed to shore down below.

Ah, the best-laid plans moved aside by a cute dog and beautiful, tender-hearted Sandy.

It is difficult to shun animals when they get this sad, mournful look, and even I couldn't turn them away though I am a poor substitute for Sandy's warm and embracing attitude toward them. Animals are smart so they obviously like Sandy better than me.

But I was not enthralled when a stray dog went to sleep on my foot on the veranda or when another one jumped up on my lap, spilling my drink and knocking a book out of my hand right into the puddle of beer or when a stray cat climbed up on my chair, went up my arm and nestled on top of my head.

"Isn't she cute!" declared an excited Sandy, laughing at the wonder of nature.

The Greeks we encountered generally like dogs and cats whereas Sandy *loves* dogs and *loves* cats. No matter where she happens to be, if she sees a cat or a dog, she'll stop and pet the animal – mangy or otherwise.

(This tenderness for mangy critters may indicate why she was kind enough to marry me.)

Shops on Paros have lovely postcards and calendars picturing arrogant cats sitting on balconies framed with flowers or cats staring out to sea or flopped over beside people dozing in chairs. They wouldn't be dozing if a cat suddenly sat on their heads!

As far as I know there were no postcards or calendars with lovely pictures of dogs, such as of the old, lazy, mangy overweight mutt that slept on the sidewalk in front of the taverna across from the ferry dock in Paroikia.

LOVING THE ISLAND ANIMALS

We're gone from our East Texas home too much to have pets, but for several years running Sandy adopted cats that found their way to House No. 5. I didn't want cats around since I was somewhat allergic to them, although, well... I did admire their athleticism. So all my life I did not have much to do with anything cat-like, such as bobcats, regular cats, baby panthers or whatever, unless you counted the time as a mere child when I fell in love with *Catwoman* in the DC Comic Books.

I knew there would be trouble when the little Tabby cat showed up on the veranda of House No. 5 one morning. Poor little thing had only one eye. You couldn't turn him away. Sandy called him "One-Eyed Jack." I later thought it was a setup. Why? The cat was checking out the place and shortly thereafter another little cat appeared. They looked like siblings, except the other one had both eyes. I couldn't turn away a sibling. Sandy named him just plain "Jack." When she went out to sketch and/or paint pictures she'd sometimes take them with her.

Okay, I admit I'd make sure they had plenty of water and something to eat. At first, they'd take off when I sneezed but later froze in their tracks and just glared at me.

Three cats appeared the next year but frankly I especially didn't like the black one. She was a loud mouth, always making noises and selfishly trying to brush the other ones away so she could eat all the cat food. Then at various times the Calico would join her in chasing the yellow cat away. The yellow Tabby would hide, then rush in to get a bite and take off again when challenged.

Food notwithstanding, the Calico cat was passive. Often when she would go to sleep, the black cat would creep over and wake her up. They were fun to watch and did have a pecking order concerning food so I became the referee to make sure they all got their fair cat share.

Sandy also loves dogs. In 1972, when she reigned as Miss Kansas, she was hosting an event in Belle Plaine, Kansas, and stayed with a couple she knew. They had a tiny poodle who could do tricks and the dog captured Sandy's heart. Her hostess would hold up a cookie and the sweet little thing would jump up and get it.

"Feed me a cookie and see what he does," said Sandy, playfully. The woman held up a cookie which Sandy put in her mouth about the same time the little guy went for it. Seconds later she was bleeding. The little guy had bitten her lip while going for the cookie! Everybody was in a panic… a lacerated-lipped Miss Kansas! This did not diminish Sandy's affection for the cookie-grabbing poodle!

Always a trooper, Sandy went about her Miss Kansas business with a puffed lip and wasn't permanently scarred. Later, Sandy would adopt dogs and cats of all sizes and shapes. Or did they adopt her? Now and then she shares a treat with an animal. Carefully, of course.

THE ABANDONED ADOPTABLES ON PAROS

On Paros, there were tourists that cruelly abandoned pets, leaving the animals to an uncertain fate while they hightailed it off the island. Others visitors fell in love with strays and adopted them to take home when they left the island. Some tourists in Kostas' houses would take care of strays while they were vacationing and then pass them on to new arrivals when vacation ended – a kind of "rent an animal, too" chain.

One day, the woman renting the house next door came over all out of breath and excitedly asked Sandy if she would do her a favor. This would eventually lead to a frightening experience.

"Would you feed the dogs?" asked the woman. "We're leaving to go back to Sweden for home and we fell in love with these two dogs. Would you please feed them for us? I've already bought all this canned dog food."

Sandy agreed to feed the dogs as the woman unloaded cans of dog food for what seemed to be a sweet female brown dog with white spots and a black male also with white spots.

"They're no trouble at all," the woman told Sandy just before she hurriedly drove off with a clear conscience, knowing the dogs would be getting the most loving care on the island, maybe even in the whole Cyclades chain!

It appeared the dogs had been passed down before, so instead of sadly watching the woman's departure or chasing after her as she drove away, they immediately took over our veranda and flopped down in the shade of the marble wall near the archway.

"Once they learned about the food, they took charge," said Sandy. "I didn't call when I was ready to feed them. It didn't matter since every morning at seven they'd start barking and scratching outside the door. The only way to stop them was to go to the refrigerator, take out the expensive canned food and let them have it."

That was Sandy's relationship with these two. As for me, they just stared at me when I issued commands for them to shake hands or roll over. Then I got the wise idea that they didn't understand English and started using Greek words such as *oxi, oxi* for no, no. They just kept staring. Sandy said it was because I had a poor Greek accent.

Later they would invite themselves to jump onto my lap, causing itchy problems if they stayed too long, so I would brush them off. They loved Sandy because they had her undivided attention whereas I mostly tried to ignore them.

Sandy was like a kid, hugging the dogs and romping all over the place with them, playing some version of tag that only she and the dogs understood. She named them "The Friend Dogs" and also took them with her on painting excursions. Once Sandy stumped her toe on the base of our bed and was hobbled for a week. Honest to goodness, the female brown dog also started limping right along behind her.

Guilt got to me and I began giving the dogs extra food and water and even discovered they were good listeners when I'd tell them my life story. Good dogs, good dogs.

When I'd jog or run along the rocky road for a mile or so and then climb a hill to a chapel overlooking a small inlet, the dogs would come along, especially if Sandy joined me. They'd suddenly dart in front of me, causing momentary loss of what I alone considered a professional, dignified gait, and compelling me to hop and jump and once even stumble and just about fall so I wouldn't step on one of them. I do not remember them crossing in front of Sandy.

"Be careful or you're going to hurt one of them," Sandy cautioned. She never cautioned the dogs about hurting the human.

THE BASKERVILLE ROUTE

The wear and tear of years on human bodies altered our jogging route, with the most frightening aspect being we had to pass a house with an adjoining taverna and three canine guardians. All were passive and friendly except the gigantic, mean one that I referred to as the "Hound of the Baskervilles" after the famous Sherlock Holmes story. I called him "HB" for short.

Whenever we'd near "his" tavern, HB would come flying toward us like a locomotive, barking and baring his teeth and scaring me sterile – I thought I was his primary target. The owner usually yelled at HB to stop and he'd trot back to the house like a normal dog. "But what if he didn't?" I always worried.

HB would usually stay in his territory if we detoured in a wide half-circle around his domain. So wider and wider detours took safe precedent over the preferred route. But we were constantly concerned that HB's lust for attacking might take over so I began carrying a big stick. When I went jogging alone, there were positive aspects: I didn't have to worry about Sandy or Friend Dogs and could trim a minute or so off my usual time by sprinting until HB was out of sight, albeit never out of mind.

HB stopped The Friend Dogs from jogging along with us. One charge by HB caused them to turn tail and take off. We could still hear them yelping after they were out of sight. I could understand that. And they hadn't seen the last of HB.

Sandy's Friend Dogs would play and snap at each other, and sometimes the black one would sneak up on the dozing brown one and bite her. She'd growl at him and sometimes jump up and chase him off. Brown Dog was usually nice and calm and loyal. She'd curl up on the porch and apparently have sweet dreams. But mischievous Black Dog had a roving eye and would disappear at night, showing up the next morning looking like he'd just dog-paddled across the nearby inlet of the Aegean Sea.

Then he'd recover from a wild night on the prowl in time to join his mate, barking and scratching on the door to let us know it was time for breakfast. I didn't know that much about the psychology of "Dog World." Maybe it was just part of the deal that Brown Dog accepted the fact that her partner was a no-good two-timer.

One stormy night we heard loud, awful bloodcurdling sounds outside the door and furious barking and yelping and howling on the veranda. Great, I thought, a pack of wild animals in a frenzy planning to attack us when we go outside. It didn't seem especially prudent to open the front door, but it had to be done in case something or somebody was getting murdered – even if I'd end up in the middle of a massacre.

I opened the door slowly and went outside – Sandy was right behind me. We immediately encountered the fearsome sight of the big, mean HB growling and showing his teeth while standing near an obviously wounded Black Dog, bleeding and whimpering on the porch. HB appeared ready to finish the job and then pounce on anybody who interfered.

"Damn," I said, getting a broom. "Now I'm going to get mauled trying to defend a dog I don't even like!"

I was a ridiculous, non-charging Don Quixote as I held up the broom, standing between HB and Sandy, taking a step or so and bracing for the attack. HB growled, bared his teeth anew and, I swear, his eyes were glaring red. Suddenly he turned and trotted away – to our great relief.

HB had almost finished Black Dog's nightly prowling forever. There was an open wound where HB had bitten a piece out of the inside of the dog's upper back leg. We doctored his wound as best we could, all the time listening for the locomotive sound of HB returning. But the night was quiet and still and Black Dog curled up in an uneasy sleep. Kostas came by the next morning and took Black Dog to the vet.

HB didn't come around again and we used an ever-widening jogging path to stay clear of him. All was calm and peaceful once more.

THEN THE STRANGEST THING...

A master thief with Robin Hood tendencies began terrorizing the *Agia Irini* area where Kostas had his houses, including our precious House No. 5.

The crimes weren't serious and one had to admit the daring culprit had an impressively mischievous flair. Some of the clothes that we washed inexplicably vanished. Socks, underwear, workout shorts, blouses and T-shirts left hanging on the clothesline on the slight rise back of the villa would disappear. It was as if a master criminal were playing jokes. We'd hang clothes in the afternoon or evening and the next day one sock would be missing from the line. When we'd leave tennis shoes on the veranda overnight only one shoe would remain the next morning.

Sandy and I didn't think much about it at first, and I liked to assume we were so preoccupied with the arts and such lofty things that we absent-mindedly forgot to hang out the missing items in the first place.

There was also the possibility that one of us could be playing tricks on the other, which we did now and then. Or the thief was a needy one-footed person looking for a specific sock or shoe. They could take all they wanted. Just leave an explanatory note, OK?

Sometimes I cannot let some things go without an explanation for the mystery. So I pondered. My study of criminology in my younger days led me to arrive at the worst scenario. If a thief were successful stealing small items, a pattern developed in which the crook became bolder, taking more chances, going after more valuable bounty. But there was yet another twist.

Various items also began *appearing* overnight on our veranda.

There was a little rubber ball, a short rope, a woman's shoe that didn't belong to Sandy, a battered book and more.

Ah, the Robin Hood syndrome.

You would have thought Sandy's Friend Dogs sleeping on the

veranda would have alerted us if a stranger in the night showed up. I assumed Brown Dog was sleeping on the porch while Black Dog had recovered without learning a valuable lesson and maintained his randy pattern of chasing mates for the night.

There was this defining moment late one afternoon as the case was accidentally solved because the rogue became brave and plied his illegal trade in daylight. I was walking down from the clothesline in back when I looked up in disbelief.

Before my very eyes, Sandy's Black Rental Dog was leaping into the air, trying to snag our fresh wash with his teeth. As I marveled, he succeeded in pulling one sock off the line. Encouraged, he then jumped up to catch one leg of my wet blue jeans. He couldn't bring the pants down but swung back and forth a few times and let go. The Great Theft Mystery of Paros was solved.

Earlier, I'd put on a pair of clean blue jeans that felt like one leg was longer. It couldn't be, I told myself. It had to be my imagination. No way one of my legs became shorter overnight. Ah, Black Dog, the Clothesline Tailor!

I admired his high-jumping ability but as I approached him, he took off, unwilling to risk apprehension or accept praise. I don't know what he thought I might do other than pet him.

A day and a half later he showed up, looking woefully at me as he scooted along with his chin on the ground while wagging with his tail. I patted him on the head, but then he suddenly left me and rushed to Sandy when she came through the door.

A REASON TO ADORE BLACK DOG

Black Dog was a sensible dog. A good dog. Ah, sweet silence.

On the porch of a house on a hill nearby we could hear a guy practicing on his drums every afternoon… Bang! bang! bang! the drum loudly. It became a distraction, wrecking our tranquility. But the guy had rented the house and there was nothing we could do about it.

Then one day the drums were silent. And a big drumstick had appeared overnight on our veranda. I immediately thought of my best friend Black Dog.

I began calling Black Dog "good boy" as he showed his teeth as if he were smiling and wagged his tail and climbed up my leg and I petted him on the head. Kostas happened to come by, saw the drumstick and exclaimed with a laugh, "Oh no!" He knew the drummer.

I would love to have been there when Kostas tried to keep from laughing as he explained to the guy about the missing stick and handed it back to him. "Why would a dog want a drummer's stick?" the guy might ask. Then Kostas would just shrug, apologize, smile and walk away.

Not long after I bungled onto identifying our rogue clothesline culprit, I renamed him "Good Boy" because he snatched the drumstick, and even though the guy got it back, my favorite dog silenced the banging of the drum.

THE THIEF, THE CHICKEN, THE SWEATER AND US

The timing was just right when our close friends John and Helen Bryant Anders, both, like me, columnists for *The Dallas Morning News*, were in London and decided to visit us before they went back to Texas. We'd told them how wonderful Paros is and they decided they didn't want to pass it up.

John is an experienced world traveler and, with Sandy's expert travel advice, he and Helen negotiated the madness of the dock at Piraeus on mainland Greece with all the masses of yachts and ships and ferries and people going every which way.

It was on Paros at the dock in Paroikia that I began to worry about them. I feared they may have missed the ferry or taken the wrong one. We were there to meet them but they were not immediately there to be met.

Practically all the passengers had left the ferry and the flurry of trucks, cars and motorcycles had vacated the belly of the ship. We were on the brink of giving up when, suddenly, here came John and Helen down the ramp.

Helen had slept most of the trip. Because she feared getting seasick, John had given her a Dramamine, the first she'd ever taken. She really conked out and missed the beautiful scenery through the Cyclades to Paros.

After they arrived at *Agia Irini*, I led the way over a slender trail along the hillside beside House No. 5 and started climbing up to what remained of the ancient old farm and the shepherd's house. Most of the roof was gone, the fireplace had no chimney and walls had either fallen or were in the process.

"Here's where you'll be staying," I said. "Sure, it's a little rough but you'll have a wonderful view and the place will grow on you."

"What?!" declared John in astonishment. Sandy turned away trying to hide her snickering and the charade lasted about five seconds before we all started laughing.

Actually, Kostas put them into one of his best villas, a short walk from House No. 5. We could get together and they also could have the privacy of their villa and enjoy the spectacular view of the hills behind them and the ocean below.

The weather had been wonderful, but as fate would have it, November took a cold turn with strong, constant winds. Fortunately, John and Helen were prepared. They had brought heavy coats and Helen also had a warm sweater.

It was a brand new sweater described by Helen as "a dark plum color that I especially liked."

The problem was, she explained on their first visit to House No. 5, "It picked up the odor of the diesel on the long ferry trip. So, I put it out on the porch to air it out. Then, when I came outside to get the sweater, it was gone!"

She assumed some quick-handed person had stolen her sweater. "I can't believe it happened. Just like that," she said. "Somebody made off with my sweater."

So John and Helen were on the lookout for someone wearing her sweater.

There was a moment of silence. Then Sandy and I explained the double life of Black Dog, purposely not calling him "Good Boy" under the circumstances. We had no doubt that he took her sweater.

"You mean now I'll be on the lookout for a dog wearing my sweater," Helen laughed.

"I bought a frozen chicken to fix Chicken Cacciatore for our dinner," said John, a noted gourmet among his friends and acquaintances. "I put the chicken out to thaw near Helen's sweater. The chicken was still there. You would think the dog would have taken my chicken."

He took a deep breath, apparently relieved that the dog chose the sweater instead of the chicken and added, "I guess it was too frozen."

Later, after a thorough search and investigation, we located the animal's cache up the incline behind our house. There were socks, underwear, unidentified objects but no sweater.

We had a great time as usual with the Anders as we got together that evening and sang our favorite songs.

"It was a great session," declared John after one song. He, Helen and Sandy all have excellent voices and as John explained to someone later, "We were singing four-part harmony… even Bob managed his part."

While John and Helen were there Sandy wrote a little ditty song – "On the isle of Paros, not Antiparos I will spend my tomorrows – keep your Key Largos." There was a bit in the middle of the song which went, "though perhaps a hound or setter may be wearing your new sweater…"

THE STORMY 'RAVEN'

One evening Sandy and I were in for a rare treat: listening to John and Helen recite Poe's *The Raven,* as winds rattled the wooden shutters on a cool night and we sat sipping ouzo.

What an unexpected surprise. After all, how many visitors could recite one of Poe's most famous poems? The one about a guy on a dark night with mournful memories of a lost love, Lenore, and a blackbird showing up gently tapping… rapping at his door… When the guy asked a question regarding Lenore, the Raven would answer, "Nevermore." Chilling.

What I loved about the recitation was that the full moon was casting its white, numinous light through the living room window and onto the floor and in a sort of ethereal glow.

Helen is a high soprano, and John a fine baritone, who incidentally does a good imitation of Orson Welles, and their voices resounded inside the marble and concrete walls of House No. 5.

Unfortunately for John and Helen, the tourist season was winding down and Paros's cafes, restaurants and tavernas were closing for the season. But we were fortunate that George Mavridis' restaurant, Levantis, was open in Paroikia one more night, although George, famous for his cooking delights, wasn't around. We were the only customers and the friendly woman who was closing down the place for the year was typical of Greek hospitality and made all sorts of dishes for us.

Two aging dogs joined us at our table and the largest one parked under John's legs. This wasn't unusual for open door or outside-eating establishments on Paros. John asked the friendly woman to shoo them away but she just shrugged. Didn't he know that dogs were fed scraps most everywhere on Paros? Then John began feeling bad about being an uptight American and actually befriended the largest dog, feeding him bits of dinner. Then the dog left.

Meanwhile, we admired a brightly lit, magical-looking tree

inside Levantis not far from our table. We agreed that it added to the charm and ambiance of the place. We just didn't know it served a key purpose. When the big dog came back to our table, John didn't feed it and we kept talking. Suddenly John started laughing. "Hey, look at the dog. He's showing how he feels about me!" We looked to see the dog relieving himself on the tree, dousing some of its magic for a moment.

As we were leaving after dinner, the dog attracted to John followed us to the car, wagging his tail slowly. He was too old to speed up and obviously wanted to go home with us.

"That dog loves you and you're turning your back on him," I said, shaking my head in disgust.

"Will you shut up? I feel bad enough as it is," said John.

JOHN, THE GRILL AND THE FISH

One evening John decided to cook on a grill on the patio in back of House No. 5. He and I drove some six miles along a road crossing over a hill to Naousa, hoping something along the waterfront with fresh fish would be open in spite of the tourist season being over.

We found a place where we could order fresh fish to dine there or take some back to the house to cook. John picked out some fine Red Snappers, not knowing they were the most expensive food on the island. There was a problem translating dollars to *drachma*. We figured later that the fish cost about $25 each in American money. John had admired the fish so he tipped the guy another $10.

The guy liked John's way of doing business a lot and shook his hand vigorously in everlasting friendship sealed by misjudged *drachmas*.

We even got lucky heading back home – we found a store just before it was closing on the outskirts of Naousa. We were able to buy lighter fluid to start what appeared to be ancient charcoal. No problem. My assignment was to handle the old outside grill – it hadn't been used in years. But John is happy as can be when he is the chef, and Sandy and Helen could relax and chat inside the house.

Naturally, while they were enjoying a good chat, John and I discovered a major problem with the grill, coals and lighter fluid. The charcoal would not light.

The women came out to check on us and suggested they were hungry so why didn't we come in the house and use the stove. No way. John stepped between the women and the grill, and I stood behind him as he held up his arms in a manner designed to demonstrate that they dare not come forward or even contemplate touching the fish.

"Get away! Get away!" he said. The women, familiar with the way both of us operate, laughed and went back inside. Sure, John and I were ridiculous but we were not quitters, by gosh. Finally, at least two hours later the fire started itself when we weren't looking. Naturally I take credit for the miracle of the fully lit charcoal. And John, indeed, prepared a magnificent meal.

We hated to see John and Helen go, but they'd only allowed for four days on Paros and were off to other destinations.

When it was time for us to go back to Texas after John and Helen's visit, Sandy was obviously sad to leave The Friend Dogs and, considering their habits, couldn't take them on a plane. Maybe new arrivals coming during the off-season would adopt them. I was also a bit sad because it was fun watching Sandy romp around with the dogs. It was as if she liked them as much as, well, the cats. Or maybe even as much as me.

After we were back home in Texas, I emailed Kostas and asked about the dogs. He said a nice family had adopted them.

Sandy had explained to John and Helen before they left for Athens that they should go to the street *outside* the Piraeus dock to get a taxi. We also suggested that they might enjoy staying at the Hera Hotel, which was modestly priced at that time and within walking distance of the Acropolis. It was a bit funky (that has changed with remodeling), but Sandy and I liked the place and had many good memories there, such as walking to see the Parthenon and watching the sun set over it one evening.

When we all got together back in Texas, John and Helen said everything was just as we said it would be and they found the Hera Hotel delightful and Helen reminded us that the next time we were on Paros we needed to be on the lookout for a dog wearing a dark plum sweater.

CHAPTER 28

PAROS – A PLACE FOR HEARTS

On one of her painting excursions on the island, Sandy found an old, deserted village on a hill where the tallest structure was an old windmill. No telling how long it had been there, but no crop or wildflowers were growing around it because the island was enduring a drought. No telling, also, how many other droughts the village had seen.

But, miraculously, in the brown landscape near a house on the hills, she found three red blooms on a vine that appeared barely alive. It was sitting in a bucket. There was no way it could be blooming there without water.

So Sandy, the good soul who takes in dogs and cats and one particular writer, came home to House No. 5, filled bottles with water and returned to the vine to give it water. She poured it onto the plant and, as she is prone to do, she also talked to the plant, like she does for all the flowers around our home in Northeast Texas. Who knows? Maybe they can hear her. This became another of her continuing island projects: Go back to the hill and water the plant.

She loves the beauty of Paros and will take the extra steps to try to help it survive.

THE BEAUTY ABOVE

The astounding constellations are so beautiful and brightly shining in the Aegean sky. And they are also so very recognizable. Sandy had taught me much about the constellations, about Orion the Hunter, Leo the Lion, Delphinus the Dolphin… And she taught me the alignment of stars that represented this or that. I love the skies, the formations, the beauty of looking at them on a good night and almost floating along with them.

But sometimes I'd question the naming of the alignments. Some of those names seemed to really be a stretch.

Once when she was pointing out yet another alignment I said, "Look, the one-legged dog, Puchie Pazza."

She laughed her wonderful laugh. "And what is the legend of Puchie Pizza?" she asked?

"Please be serious," I replied. "It's Pazza, not pizza"

"Forgive me, kind knowledgeable person," she laughed.

And I pointed toward the pertinent place in the night sky and began to explain in such a sincere voice, "The constellations are just something I've studied all my life and don't appreciate making fun of a new, important discovery in the sky. The legend of Puchie Pizza, uh, Pazza, the one-legged dog is that her son, Poopie Pazza, once became angry and bit off three of her legs. If you'll look over there, you'll see the wayward boy. See that line of stars. That's his body and the seven streaks are his four legs and her three. So Puchie Pazza is forever destined to search the skies for her son and lost legs. In fact, Puchie Pazza in *Cosovococo* means 'Searching for three legs'."

"That is soooo sad," Sandy said, and I'm not sure she meant the story of Puchie Pazza or the fact that I'd create it.

"Brings tears to your eyes," I said.

And Sandy rolled her eyes, shook her head and said, "Anyway, dear Orion will be rising early in the morning and..."

It was unlikely that I'd get up to greet Orion. But she would.

WHEN SANDY SMILES...

I sometimes keep Sandy from sleeping because, inexplicably, I'll suddenly be wide awake and, failing to go back to sleep, get up to read.

Occasionally, especially when I was under pressure as a columnist, I'd sometimes hold my breath while sleeping, then wake up gasping. I'd asked that when she caught me doing this, she'd wake me. So she periodically wakes me up whether I'm doing it or not.

On the flip side, she shakes the foundation of the house when she turns over in bed. It's like she launches herself into the air and slams down on her side. It's much like she's high jumping from a prone position. My guess is her record is three feet into the air before crashing down to bed. Subconsciously, when I feel her stirring I brace myself in bed so I won't be knocked to the floor.

Delightfully, she always wakes smiling while I wake frowning until I've had coffee. With all the old injuries to my body, I get out of bed looking like a pretzel whether on Paros in the Cyclades or in the Piney Woods of Northeast Texas. Geography makes no difference. Besides, I loosen up – given enough time.

I have tested Sandy's morning happiness many times by nudging her awake and she's always smiling.

I mentioned this to my friend, John Anders, although I'm not sure he believed me. We were both newspaper columnists – you have a natural tendency to doubt cheeriness.

Once, when the three of us were driving home from South Padre, Sandy was asleep in the back seat. "Watch this," I told him and then said, "Sandy!"

He watched in disbelief from the passenger's seat as she woke with a big smile on her face. The world needs more people like Sandy.

THE BEST SUNSET

Some mornings in Texas, I wake on Paros. It is there, always, in my heart, in my thoughts and I reach back to a moment in that beautiful place and it inspires me to reach forward to the next visit, the next arrival on the ferry at Paroikia, the next marveling at the vivid white structures and the blue shutters and the people we know and love.

Because of friendships, our hearts are on the island and the island is in our hearts.

I had to go through my journals to find this particular island moment. As a lifelong fan of the beauty of the earth, it seems appropriate that I write about this particular event. Please indulge me. Here's the way I recorded it:

"BEST SUNSET: On the 30th of March, 2006, we saw our best sunset, which is saying something because they are all beautiful. This one was dramatically, dazzlingly animated and colorful. A massive streak across the sky of orange and blue contrasts with gray clouds. Below, the clouds parted and the light made the whole scene look like a rising city in the distance – just for a precious moment and then it was gone.

"Then, above, it was suddenly rose-colored, then blue sky and gray clouds. Waters below were sparkling, yellowish and then evolving into a light purple. Water pale in front of us and purple farther out. And blue beyond.

"And, a little later, a gray sky with orange below the developing blackness. The hills were purple and, as minutes passed, the water became pale blue with a sudden sun-inspired jet redness.

"Then, peacefully, the sky became totally gray-blue to announce the arrival of the darkening of our part of the planet. The view from the patio at House No. 5 was so special that night."

HOUSE NO. 5 – THE HOME ON PAROS

As I read what I'd written years ago I realized that I'd described the view from House No. 5 as "so special that night." But, in reality, any view at any time from House No. 5 has been special from the moment we first saw the wonderful villa.

It is a house that belongs to our friend Kostas but he has helped us make it our home. On Paros such a thing is not a random act of kindness, but it is a way of life. It is the shared attitude of a good life being lived well on this beautiful island.

We have always tried to leave something good on Paros. Oh, not something that will become as ancient as the Cavern of the Nymphs or as important as the Aegean Center for the Fine Arts. But we hope to leave at the least a bit of a moment that someone else will remember: maybe a visit with the laughing couple from Texas or a happy commercial transaction or a conversation in a taverna with an American writer saddled with a great desire to speak Greek, but an ability to remember only a few words.

How fitting it is to end this book with a most heartfelt word, the first word I learned in Greek, which ever stays with me: *Efharistó*. That means, "Thank you."

Sincerely, dear Paros, *Efharistó*.

THE END

Efharistó, Vov!
(An epilogue)

THE AUTHOR BOB ST. JOHN

by Larry Powell

IN A DECADES-LONG career, Bob St. John wrote thousands of newspaper articles and columns, covering the Dallas Cowboys for *The Dallas Morning News,* then as its Metro page columnist. Along the way, he was winning prizes and readers, taking people to places they could not go on their own, frequently even into their own hearts.

He has written more than a dozen books on subjects ranging from life as a sportswriter to living and loving on the famous Padre Island in Texas [*South Padre: The Island and Its People*]. His acclaimed biographies include those of National Football League NFL Hall of Famers: Coach Tom Landry and President Tex Schramm of the Dallas Cowboys. His non-fiction work *On Down the Road,* about the life of a different kind of cowboy — a rodeo cowboy — was embraced by those both in the saddles and at desks.

But this Texan's heart embraces a place called Paros.

He had been working on this book about his adoration of the Greek island of Paros for several years when his "forever lingering" memories and the life he loved so deeply were disrupted. The depth of thought and appreciation for Paros has not faded, though it may have been misplaced now and then. His writer's gift protected those images and his personal drive to achieve created a deftly-assembled mosaic of a special place on the other side of the world from his beloved Texas.

This is a love story – a man in love with his destination and in love with his artistic muse, Sandy, his wife and companion on this journey.

In this book, we are given the opportunity to see a faraway island through the eyes of a writer whose heart was captured by its beauty and its people. This book is a labor of love and respect, a mission of saving a writer's reality from a disruption by fate.

Thank you, Bob St. John, for all the words and all the heart.

A Final Note about this Book
by Sandra St. John

Bob St. John did not live to see the completion of his Paros book. The pieces and parts had, for the most part, been written but had not yet been fully formed into a manuscript ready for publishing. There were so many documents and chapters from so many years, versions of the book from various times stretching across a decade.

Who could possibly pull it all together? Who could be funny and tender like Bob, and who had an affinity for Bob's writing style? Most of all, who would be willing to go through the many pages, folders and files, then digest, cull and coordinate them?

And then once more The Fates intervened. What about Larry Powell? Larry Powell had been one of Bob's editors at *The Dallas Morning News*. He was an admirer of Bob's writing. He understood his style, having had numerous editorial discussions with him as his editor. He understood what was important to Bob, how Bob fought to control his copy and how he gave way to changes only after a small skirmish was fought and won.

Larry was also a good writer, tender and sensitive at times but like Bob also able to write slapstick funny. Yes, I thought, Larry – who upon Bob's retirement gave him, rather than the usual bottle of scotch, a first aid kit – would be perfect! Larry was the one to approach to do the book.

He took on the behemoth task. It took time, probably more than he had expected, but he managed to artfully pull all the pieces into this book. When I read his result, I told him, "That's the best effort since Maxwell Perkins pulled Thomas Wolfe's formless mass of pages into the classic book *Look Homeward, Angel*."

So to Larry Powell I say thank you over and over, ever and ever.

Thanks go also to John Chapple for help with the spelling of Greek words and phrases and for his keen eye for history.

For Sheri Miller, and her son Kyle, who the luck of the Fates placed in my world.

And a big thank you to Lana Rings for her "eagle eye" and her helpful suggestions and corrections.

And finally, once again heartfelt thanks to Kostas Akalestos, our dear friend, whose kindness and generosity are unsurpassed. Because of you, our dream came true.

CPSIA information can be obtained
at www.ICGtesting.com
Printed in the USA
JSHW011510020919
1301JS00003B/5